Beauty
IS NEVER ENOUGH

Beauty
IS NEVER ENOUGH

Elizabeth B. Alton

South Jersey Culture & History Center
Stockton University
2021

Elizabeth B. Alton

Published by the South Jersey Culture & History Center at Stockton University

South Jersey Culture & History Center
Stockton University
101 Vera King Farris Drive
Galloway, New Jersey, 08205

Title: Beauty Is Never Enough

Author: Alton, Elizabeth B.

Copyright © 2021 Elizabeth B. Alton and Stockton University

ISBN: 978-1-947889-05-7

The South Jersey Culture & History Center received a project grant from the New Jersey Historical Commission, a division of the Department of State, which helped defray the costs of printing this title.

stockton.edu/sjchc/

Cover photographs: front: Elizabeth Alton presenting at New Jersey Realtor of the Year Awards at Hotel Traymore, Atlantic City, New Jersey, December 6, 1958; back: Diane Hugghins, Miss Texas, and Elizabeth Alton at the 1968 Miss America Pageant; Elizabeth Alton at the New Jersey State Federation of Women's Clubs annual convention at Chalfonte-Haddon Hall Hotel, May 1960.

Frontispiece: Elizabeth Alton at her installation as president of the New Jersey State Federation of Women's Clubs in 1959.

Whatever your hand finds to do, do it with
all your might.

Ecclesiastes 9:10

Elizabeth B. Alton

Foreword

Born at a time before women could vote nationally, Elizabeth Barstow Alton came of age during the Roaring Twenties, lived through the Great Depression, raised a family during World War II, and founded a college during the tumultuous 1960s. She was president of local and state women's organizations, an advisor to national and international committees, served on the boards of two New Jersey colleges, and ran two businesses. Yet, it was her affiliation with the Miss America Pageant which shaped her life. The Pageant is the lens through which she chose to frame her memoir.

As the archivist responsible for organizing her papers, I thought I knew Elizabeth Alton. I knew "Chairman Alton," Founding Mother of Richard Stockton State College (now Stockton University) and a chair of the board of trustees. Her speeches and letters campaigning for our four-year college in southern New Jersey showed her persuasive style and tenacity. Her book, *The Stockton Story*, also tells the history of this success. I saw evidence of "Mrs. John Alton," wife and mother, through photographs, cards, and letters pasted in the scrapbooks among her papers. These things that she passed on to the archives also showed that "Mrs. E. Alton" was proud of her work with the New Jersey State Federation of Women's Clubs and other volunteer organizations. Here and there, too, were scattered photographs of her with Miss Americas or other less fortunate Pageant contestants.

However, it wasn't until I read *Beauty is Never Enough* that I understood how deeply the Miss America Pageant shaped Elizabeth's perspective and life. When her granddaughter, Karen

Elizabeth Alton, handed us the box with the typewritten pages containing this manuscript, I could not put them down. As an Atlantic City historian, I knew all about the Miss America Pageant, its past and present, its scandals and triumphs, and its complicated relationship with the city it calls home. Reading about the Pageant from both the perspective of a spectator and an insider—as Elizabeth came to be—provided fresh insights into the history and culture of this century-old tradition.

The genesis of the Miss America Pageant was a 1920 parade in Atlantic City, New Jersey. Begun as a tourism promotion, a local businessman devised the event to attract tourists to town after Labor Day. As a participant in that first parade, young Elizabeth was enthralled by the sights and sounds and the contestants, who were not much older than she. The following year, the parade included a beauty contest in which young women would parade in swimsuits to compete for the title of Inner-City Beauty, later known as Miss America. The Pageant has evolved over the past 100 years, most recently reinventing itself as the Miss America Competition and eliminating swimsuits. This fulfilled a petition that longtime Pageant director Lenora Slaughter requested as early as the 1940s and which Elizabeth supported during her years of service as the chairman of the hostess committee and as the first female member of the board of directors.

An experienced leader, Elizabeth Alton championed the advancement of women in many ways. While many view pageants as a relic of a male-dominated society, Elizabeth emphasized the Miss America Pageant as a scholarship competition. She highlighted the many talented contestants and their successes after competing. She also reflected on the role of the Pageant in changing attitudes about societal ideas of dress and comportment. She lauded the organizational and executive skills of Lenora Slaughter and the legions of women who ran the Pageant as volunteers.

Elizabeth was involved in many women's organizations on the local and state level, as well as serving on national and international committees. College-educated, a graduate of Syracuse University, she pushed for the establishment of a college in southeastern New Jersey to encourage local youths' opportunities for higher education. She campaigned at the local and state levels tirelessly, speaking to gatherings in southern New Jersey and lobbying state legislators. A small business owner, she ran a yarn store, which also sold clothing made by local women. Later she earned her real estate license in order to take over her father's business.

Interwoven with detailed vignettes of local history and personalities, stories of Miss America contestants, and commentary on social issues of the times, Elizabeth Alton shared her views. Although she wrote from her privileged perspective as a white, upper-class woman in the late twentieth century—she completed the final form of the typescript memoir in late 1995—her commentary resonates with twenty-first-century readers. She noted the changes in the judging criteria of the Pageant, speaking out against the exploitation of the participants solely as objects of beauty. She advocated for women's rights, equal pay, and an end to gender discrimination. She remarked on the Pageant's slow acceptance of people of color and discrimination faced by Jewish contestants. Both through the scholarships earned by Pageant contestants and her own work with institutions of higher learning, Elizabeth's most significant achievement was her promotion of women to higher education and leadership. As Elizabeth reflected on her century of life, she imparted her experiences with hindsight and wisdom, and she advised all to consider that *Beauty Is Never Enough* by which to judge the worth of a woman when compared with other accomplishments.

Heather Perez,
Special Collections Librarian,
Stockton University

Elizabeth B. Alton

Chapter 1
In the Beginning

I was excited, there was going to be a big parade on the Boardwalk and I was going to be in it. I really didn't know much about the parade except that it was called an International Rolling Chair Parade. It featured beauties from other cities who would be attired and judged in bathing suits. I could not have guessed then, in fact I didn't realize until many years later, that I was a part of history in the making. I was an unimportant but willing participant in the beginning of what has become known internationally as the Miss America Scholarship Pageant, the largest scholarship foundation for women in the world. My childish mind could not begin to conceive the future possibilities of this forerunner of the pageant. It was enough for me to know that there was going to be a parade, and I was going to be in it.

I have never forgotten that September day in 1920. I lived with my family in the residentially developing Chelsea section of Atlantic City where I attended Brighton Avenue School, considered at the time one of the city's outstanding elementary schools. The board of education had chosen for its float in the parade six girls from the school whose families were well known in the community.

When parade time arrived, I remember riding in a jitney up Pacific Avenue to the Inlet, where I was to meet the float on Rhode Island Avenue. Jitneys today are small buses, but in those early days, jitneys were large, open, seven-passenger touring cars of a variety of makes. Most were pretty well mileage abused. Nine people generally filled the seven-passenger jitneys. Two passengers could ride up front with the driver, three could sit on the two fold-down jump seats, and three on the back seat. Maintaining a comfortable seat was difficult, and one could be squeezed almost breathless, if some of the passengers were excessively large or heavy, as was frequently the case. The bouncing and rattling of well-worn car springs, and the occasional small spring poking through from the seat cushions, made for a far from luxurious ride. Jitney fare was five cents—a nickel—which in the slang of the day was called a jitney.

When our jitney reached the business section of the city near the Inlet, I could see that, all the way to the Boardwalk, the long side streets were jammed with such a variety of floats of every description that each street seemed to contain a miniature parade by itself. As I rode by I twisted around uncomfortably, trying to see as many floats as possible on each street. At almost every corner, police stopped the jitneys along with traffic to allow steady streams of people to hurry across Pacific Avenue headed for the Boardwalk. By the time I got off the jitney and had finally found the board of education float, I was more excited than ever. This was going to be a huge parade, I thought, much bigger and better than I had expected. I was almost dancing with joy at the thought of being a part of it.

Our float was eventually positioned in the line of march on the Boardwalk near the head of the parade at Garden Pier. I had an excellent view of parade officials running around, shouting final instructions as they tried to bring organized order in the midst of what looked like a sea of humanity milling around a traffic jam of floats. Meanwhile, police made an effort to clear a path for the floats down the center of the walk. Even to my inexperienced eyes, the International Rolling Chair Parade was a colorful procession when, at last, it started to roll down the Boardwalk in tune with the loud music of many bands.

Interspersed at appropriate intervals between floats and bands, each inter-city beauty rode in a rolling chair artistically decorated with garlands of fresh flowers and greens. They wore bathing suits which revealed enough of their physical attributes to prompt whistles and other forms of enthusiastic approval from the huge crowd of spectators, and silent disapproval from the more prudently conservative.

I could feel the rhythmic beat of marching bands playing feet-tapping music, see the hotel guests packing balconies of public rooms overlooking the Boardwalk, young people climbing up available billboards and light poles seeking better vantage points, and everywhere people caught up in the enthusiasm of the moment.

In celebration of this special event, I was dressed carefully in my best outfit. The sleeveless white georgette dress, accordion pleats from neck to handkerchief hem—simple but elegant—was far too pretty to be subjected to the afternoon sun which broiled us as we walked facing the blinding glare of the sun's rays on the Boardwalk. I should accent the word *walked*, for we walked, and stopped, and stood and waited, walked and stopped, stood and waited, walked and stopped, until my feet began sending urgent messages of pain. No one had told me not to wear my best new shoes, or my best new dress either. As my feet expanded in the hottest hours of a scorching day, I suffered the agonies that childish pride had caused me, while I gamely waved back at the people cheering every float and every beauty in the passing parade. I never wore those shoes or dress again.

The Atlantic City Board of Education float was built over a rolling chair as were most of the other floats. It was impossible for six girls to ride on the float. I was positioned at the front of the float on the hotel side of the Boardwalk where I had an excellent opportunity to watch the parade activity ahead of us. We were following a rolling chair carrying a particularly popular beauty. I could see her in her long, woolen bathing suit all the way down to her knees, her legs covered with black non-transparent stockings. Her long, honey-blonde hair bounced in the breeze as she energetically turned from side to side, blowing kisses and waving vigorously to her admirers in enthusiastic response to

13

the tumultuous welcome she was receiving. Since the Boardwalk was unevenly rough in those days, it was difficult for her to stand up without losing her balance while the chair was starting and stopping. She kept a firm grip on the front of the chair.

At thirteen years of age, I was not old enough to appreciate fully the handsome young lifeguard pushing the rolling chair ahead of us. The fact that the lifeguards had been carefully chosen by the beach captain for their attractive appearances and muscular physique did not occur to me. His bathing suit consisted of a red woolen shirt top, conservatively cut out at the neck and armholes so as to cover most, or nearly all, of his upper torso. It was against the law for any man to appear anywhere in the city with his upper body exposed.

Prominently placed on the front of his shirt were the letters A.C.B.P. in navy wool to identify him as a member of the Atlantic City Beach Patrol. His loose-fitting navy blue wool bathing trunks, secured by a white canvas belt around his waist, reached to a point midway between his hips and knees. His close-cropped hair, bleached nearly colorless by sun and saltwater, made an interesting contrast to the rest of his body. His skin had been burned almost copper by constant exposure to the summer sun and generous applications of vinegar, the natural tanning agent commonly used on the beach during those pre-sunburn lotion days. As I marched along, I remembered lifeguards bathing themselves frequently from the vinegar bottle during the early summer days. It was an effective protection from the sun's rays, producing a deep tan without too much burn. It was also smelly. I giggled at the thought that anyone being rescued from the ocean might faint from the fumes. Such childish thoughts were quickly swept away, though, by the excitement of the parade. It was an exhilarating experience in my young life.

After we had walked down the Boardwalk, past most of the city's finest hotels, the parade left the Boardwalk at Missouri Avenue, proceeded past Pacific Avenue to Atlantic Avenue, where we reversed our march, heading back toward our starting point.

In those days, parades were often held on Atlantic Avenue without too much interruption of traffic, which proceeded much as usual without stopping or being stopped too often by the parade. Large trucks made deliveries to merchants along the route. Trolley cars traveled up and down the center of the street, clanging their bells as warnings of their approach. The parade intermingled with traffic until it disbanded at Massachusetts Avenue.

My lingering recollection of that first historic parade, after all these years, is one of painfully sore feet and physical fatigue. Perhaps the heat of the day, the unusual excitement, the stirring music of the marching bands and the noise of shouting and cheering crowds, had created a kind of stress I was unaccustomed to experiencing. I just know that at the end of that long parade, I was really tired, even though I was physically strong for a youngster and athletically active in several sports. My feet were absolutely numb from my tight new shoes. My pretty dress was no longer new and fresh. My face and arms, in spite of a summer's tan on the beach, were newly sunburned, bringing out many more unwelcome freckles. I couldn't wait to spend my nickel on a trolley ride home. When the open-air trolley came along at last, sitting down and relieving the pressure on my feet was exquisite pleasure.

I was able to see much of the parade as we rode downtown through the remainder of the parade, but my heart wasn't in it anymore. It had been a great event, bringing the city a tremendous amount of publicity. The *Atlantic City Press-Union* later reported that 100,000 people had watched a three-hour parade with nearly 500 floats. It had been a big, important day in my young life and I had loved it. Even so, it was a long, long time before I realized that. For the Miss America Pageant-to-be, it was also a historic occasion of considerable importance.

The written records of these first pageant years were lost in 1933. Lenora S. Slaughter, executive director of the pageant, in later years recreated the history of the 1920s by securing information from some of the civic leaders who had been instrumental in planning the early contest. Some of them continued to serve for a number of years on the board of directors of the Miss America Pageant. I was privileged to be associated with several. Their personal experiences and recollections had particular historical importance. Most memorable were the recollections of Louis St. John, an advertising executive who eventually became president of the Chamber of Commerce. Also important were the remembrances of Harry Godshall, owner of a prominent insurance firm, who often enjoyed calling himself "The Last of the Mohicans," for he lived to be the final survivor of the founding fathers. He was still on the board of directors a number of years after I was elected to the board. With a dry wit and abundant good humor, he frequently entertained the board with his humorous, often hilarious stories of those early years.

The first Pageant was a week-long series of events designed to encourage tourists and visitors to spend additional days in Atlantic City after Labor Day, the end of the summer tourist season. It used to be said that after that day we closed up the city and threw away the key. I remember in my early childhood that the lights on the Boardwalk in our Chelsea area, and the down beach communities of Ventnor, Margate and Longport, were turned off at night during the winter.

Unfortunately, the summer season was only three months long. When Labor Day came, tourist dollars disappeared, seriously affecting the economy and local businesses. It had been commonly recognized for some time that some means should be devised to extend the season, if only for a short time, to bring much needed additional revenue to the city.

Chapter 2

It all began in 1920 when A. Conrad Ekholm, owner of the Monticello Hotel on South Kentucky Avenue near the Boardwalk, proposed a week-long series of events called Fall Frolic, to be held after Labor Day to attract visitors to the resort. The Business Men's League agreed to sponsor the Frolic as a promotion for the city. There were several days of varied activities planned. One of the main events was the International Rolling Chair Parade down Atlantic Avenue from the Inlet to the residential area of Chelsea on September 25, 1920.

A beautiful statuesque woman named Miss Ernestine Cremona, dressed in flowing white robes to represent "peace," led the parade on a handsomely decorated float. The parade had been officially promoted to celebrate the paving of Atlantic Avenue that year. Formerly it had been a rutty, gravelly street. I remember how rough it was when I rode my bicycle to school.

Although not much of a financial success, the Fall Frolic's International Rolling Chair Parade earned the approval of the business community. Mayor Edward L. Bader called it "a pleasant surprise." The publicity produced in the news media, and the sizable crowds that had viewed the parade, suggested to some business leaders that another similar event might be promoted in 1921.

There were differences of opinion on who first proposed the idea of a beauty pageant. It became a matter of controversy and confusion in later years in the community. No one individual has officially been given that credit. My father was one of the city leaders who believed that Ekholm's idea for a Fall Frolic in 1920 had sparked the decision that led to the beginning of the

Pageant in 1921. The Ekholms were family friends. Their daughter Frances was one of my classmates. There were others who thought differently. According to the history Lenora Slaughter compiled from papers and memories of the founding fathers, it began this way.

During the early winter of 1921, Harry Finley, an Atlantic City newspaperman, attended a meeting of newspaper circulation managers who were seeking ways to increase the circulation of their respective papers. The group decided to run a popularity contest in each of their various cities to select the most popular young lady. Readers would be asked to send in photographs of pretty girls from which the prettiest would be selected. The winner of the contest in each city would be given a wardrobe by that city's newspaper. The idea was presented to Samuel P. Leeds, president of the Atlantic City Chamber of Commerce and co-owner of the Chalfonte-Haddon Hall Hotel, one of the city's finest Boardwalk hotels. The Hotelmen's Association agreed to entertain the young women for a week, provide them with transportation to and from the resort, and fund the various prizes to be awarded.

Leeds appointed a committee to conduct the Atlantic City Pageant, which included some of the city's most prominent and reputable business and civic leaders. Herb Test, a local reporter selected as publicity agent by the committee, dreamed up the idea of having a national beauty contest. He added the term International Beauties and suggested that the winner of the Bathing Revue Contest in 1921 be named Miss America. Harry Godshall, known as the Big Gun in insurance, who was appointed chairman of Inter-City Beauties, often recalled with much humor that he had selected the cities and the newspapers where contests would be held "off the top of his head." The beauties in that first contest could scarcely be called international. They came from Pittsburgh, Washington, Camden, New York, Ocean City, Harrisburg, Philadelphia and Newark.

Leeds appointed the following committee: Thomas P. Endicott, director general, owner of a dry cleaning business; Harry Latz, vice-director general, in charge of bathers review, owner of the

Almac Hotel; Samuel P. Leeds, finance, Haddon Hall Hotel; William Eldredge, rolling chair parade, owner of a storage company; William Fennell, night carnival on Steeplechase Pier, pier manager; David Braunstein, fashion display, owner of a fashion shop; A. J. Purinton, electric display, head of the trolley company; Albert J. Feyl, judges, editor of the *Atlantic City Press-Union*; Louis St. John, prizes, advertising executive; Harry Godshall, inter-city beauties, insurance; Linton B. Arnold, decorations, hotelman; William Emley, grand stands, realtor; Fred Packer, arrival of King Neptune, novelty store owner.

The committee planned a series of events for the week during the contest. One was a night carnival held in the Ballroom of the Steeplechase Pier, which extended quite a distance out into the ocean. Decimated by hurricanes and northeast storms driving huge waves into its structure over the years, and a nearly disastrous fire as well, the pier today bears little resemblance to the imposing structure it once was. I remember rushing to the Boardwalk with my parents to watch the spectacular fire in 1931. It was an amusement pier with many of the slides, rides, and amusement features owned by the George C. Tilyou family, which also owned the famous Coney Island amusement Park.

One optional entrance into the pier was through a large revolving barrel where keeping one's balance was a necessity. Those who couldn't had to be helped by attendants. Women unsuspectingly walked over blowholes in the floor, activated by an unseen operator who chose his victims to the delight of spectators. Often skirts rose higher than the women could quickly control.

I liked best the two slides that reached up to an extra high ceiling. One was narrow, just large enough for one person, with a long, steep descent into a deep round bowl where one slid around until stopping. Climbing out necessitated using the aid of a rope. The other slide was also ceiling high but wide enough for several people to slide down together. Old burlap feed bags were available to use as a cushion, if desired. The wavy configuration of the slide often caused people to slide down sideways or even backwards.

There were also a couple of fast revolving turntables, one flat, one cone shaped, which tossed riders off quickly and easily, and also a turkey trot where one gripped the rails while being bounced in the air as the floor jerkily rose and fell unevenly. It was a fun pier that we children, and people young at heart, loved. The Ballroom featured nationally known bands for dancing.

One of the most popular committee events planned was the Bathing Revue Contest held as part of the National Beauty Tournament. The parade route was on the wide beach between the Garden Pier and the Steel Pier, a distance of six city blocks. A wide path had been roped off near the ocean. Police were stationed in close proximity to each other to protect the bathing beauties as they walked along the center of the path. They also controlled the many enthusiastic spectators viewing such an unusual spectacle both from the Boardwalk and the beach.

Bathing suits worn in that decade were far different in intent and purpose from the overly revealing suits of today. The name explains the style. Women dressed to go bathing in the ocean. Today, women undress for the same purpose. Victorian modesty was still prevalent. The general style consisted of loose black suits made of wool, alpaca or similar material, high necks, skirts falling to or below the knees or, for the more daring, even slightly above the knee. A wide belt or sash sometimes held the suit in place. Bloomers were attached to the skirts. Black cotton or lisle stockings concealed the legs while rubber slippers were worn on the feet as protection from crabs and shells.

I never really understood why the bathing suits of the beauties were considered daring by some and shockingly so by the more conservative woman. My school friends and I wore similar suits on the beach as did many women. However, several contestants wore suits that rose to unmentionable heights by being well above the knee, definitely not "nice" by some standards. All but three beauties wore stockings that disappeared under their suits as the law required, but those three, including Miss America-to-be, had rolled their stockings down below the knees exposing bare skin!

That's what caused the scandalous controversy. Heavens to Betsy, look! She's showing bare knees! And look at that skirt!

I well remember the legal problems of exposing bare knees to public view. In that period, my friends and I always rolled our stockings down below the knee on our bathing beach. Lifeguards were required to enforce the law to keep the beach "decent." Whenever I was challenged I used to chuckle to myself as I answered that I was not yet eighteen. That always satisfied the letter of the law which lifeguards found difficult to enforce. Not many men can accurately judge the age of a woman.

It is also interesting to note that the police had apparently received instructions not to arrest any bathing beauty who violated the law with her revealing attire. Women had customarily been arrested for revealing much less.

During this period a woman visitor from Los Angeles named Louise Rosine was ordered by the police to roll up her stockings. Louise refused. In the argument that followed, she hauled off and struck the policeman breaking his glasses in the process. From her jail cell she issued a statement that she had a constitutional right to "bare feminine knees" and she intended to take the matter to the Supreme Court, if necessary. No legal issue ensued, but the law was changed a year or two later following a period of much discussion by the city commissioners.

In 1924, Atlantic City officials announced that women could now legally go without stockings and could wear one-piece suits made famous by Annette Kellermann, who had designed the new form-fitting style. Men, however, still had to wear shirts over their bathing trunks. The Mackintosh Law, requiring everyone, male or female, to wear an outer wrap or jacket on the streets, was not repealed.

Chapter 3

The history of what to wear on the beaches along our coastal area in the early 1800s has always fascinated me. There were not many ocean resorts in that era. No laws existed concerning bathing attire. It was most common for men and women to go to separate, secluded areas to undress and swim. Women selected old clothes, but the men wore nothing at all. Privacy was usually available by the existence of plentiful cedar trees, swamp grass, and separation of the sexes by beaches.

Ocean City passed a law in 1881 that stated:

> That Sea or Bay bathing in the NUDE state is strictly prohibited between the hours of five a.m. and eleven p.m. and at no time shall it be allowed north of Tenth Street.

The first law had as its goal separating the sexes rather than restricting fashion. Cape May used flags in the 1830s to ensure that men and women did not go in the water together. A white flag permitted women to go bathing. Men had to wait for a red flag.

By the late 1800s bathing suits had become mostly dark blue or black woolen styles. Around 1880, newspapers in southern New Jersey and Philadelphia began complaining about the habits of dress at the shore. One writer stated, "people would behave in a moral manner at home, but lose all shame abroad and improperly expose their persons without a blush." A Weymouth man was quoted as saying that "if women in Ocean City came to

Weymouth dressed as they dressed in Ocean City, there would be war." Even the Ocean City paper protested that the bathing suits were causing problems in the resort.

In 1907, bloomers attached to suits became popular but some women started rolling their stockings down below the knee. For decades law officials carried tape measures and arrest warrants to make sure that modesty prevailed.

Where bathing suits could be worn was another part of the controversy. In the early 1900s, it was only legal to wear bathing suits on the beach. Many public bathhouses were available on our Boardwalk. Individual bathhouses, not much larger than for use by one person, were on the beach in many locations. In later years, if one walked from one's home on the street to the beach, the law required that mackintoshes be worn concealing the bathing suit. I remember how uncomfortably hot they were. The law was enforced up to the 1930s on some beaches. Women eventually got around the Mackintosh Law by wearing playsuits. They revealed as much as bathing suits, but could not be banned under the law since they were not bathing suits. Bikinis came into fashion in the 1940s after test atomic explosions at the Bikini Atoll.

During these decades, men's bathing fashions had remained relatively unchanged. In the 1930s, men began abandoning their shirts and baring their naked chests. An Atlantic City law stated, "Stockings for women are not necessary, but men must have their tops to their suits under penalty of $1.00 fine." Men began ignoring this law. Those exposing their chests on the beach gained a reputation as "beach nudists."

In 1938, Atlantic City police arrested twenty-five "semi-nude" men for being shirtless; they were taken to City Hall in a patrol wagon. Bail was set at five dollars. As a result, a campaign was undertaken to repeal the law. In July 1939, a local head-line read, "Shirtless Bathing Ban Hurts Shore Trade." A week later the headline read, "Hotelmen Join Fight Against Ban on Tarzans." When the City Commission voted on the matter, the law remained unchanged. In 1940, although the City Commissioners still refused to change the law, one commissioner bathed topless on an Atlantic City beach, but the police did not arrest him. In 1941, city officials surrendered at last and topless bathing suits became legal. Soon other resorts followed and naked chests appeared all up and down the Jersey Shore.

❧

Atlantic City is built on one of the barrier islands found all along the east coastline of our country. According to publications of Rutgers University, the Atlantic Ocean in ages long past once covered much of the east coast. Our area was covered by ocean up to fifteen miles inland. As the ocean receded, the sandy island known today as Absecon Island came into being, separated from the mainland by five miles of wetland meadows. On Absecon Island, where Absegami Indians once roamed, lie the communities of Atlantic City, Ventnor, Margate and Longport, covering ten miles of sandy shore.

In the early years, whalemen, smugglers, and pirates visited the barrier island on which Atlantic City now rests, and from their activities arose many stories of buried treasure that no one has ever found on our island nor nearby islands. My father's family used to tell about a small inlet, or thoroughfare, in the middle of the island, which divided it in half. Historical records place the inlet at Jackson Avenue, the dividing line between Atlantic City and Ventnor, where crossing the inlet required a small boat.

According to early state records, Thomas Budd, a land speculator from Burlington, was the first owner of the island then known on shipping charts as "Further Island" and "Far Island." Budd was forced to close a deal which required him to accept title to 440 acres of the island in order for him to be able to purchase more valuable land he wanted farther inland. He finally settled on a price of four cents an acre compared against forty cents an acre for mainland property.

Jeremiah Leeds, born in Leeds Point on March 4, 1754, made his first purchase of land in what is now Atlantic City on January 7, 1804. By 1816, he is said to have owned most of the land in Atlantic City, a large part of which he sold to the Camden and Atlantic Railroad.

Dr. Jonathan Pitney, whose house still stands on Shore Road in Absecon, is often called the father of Atlantic City. He was the first to see its potential as a summer resort and devoted most of his time to promoting the idea. Dr. Pitney arrived in Absecon from Morris County and set up his medical practice in 1819. He was a friend of the Leeds family and discussed his "dream" at length with them.

Transportation to and from early Atlantic City was by stage-coach. Every Tuesday, Thursday, and Friday morning at 4 a.m., a stagecoach would leave Philadelphia, roll onto a ferry for a trip across the Delaware River to Camden, then East. The coach, drawn by four horses, would make its way along sandy roadways as it cut through vast pine and cedar forests. The coach would pass through small towns and villages as the sun rose. At inns along the way, the coach would stop, drop off mail, and allow the passengers to get out to stretch. With luck the coach might race along at ten miles an hour. If it had rained, the speed dropped considerably.

After stops at Long-a-Coming, Blue Anchor, the Winslow Glass Works and the Weymouth Iron Works, the coach would arrive at Mays Landing, in Atlantic County.

Sparsely populated, Atlantic County had been created in 1837 by lopping off the eastern half of Gloucester County, which originally stretched from the Delaware River to the Atlantic Ocean. At that date, the new county consisted of 18 villages with slightly more than 8,700 people.

Thomas F. Gordon's *History of New Jersey*, published in 1834, just three years before Atlantic County was formed, provides a brief description of the existing towns. Of Atlantic City it says,

ABSECON BEACH—on the Atlantic Ocean, extends eastward from Great Egg Harbor Inlet about nine miles to Absecon Inlet; broken, however, by a narrow inlet (Jackson Avenue) between its extremities.

No houses or people were mentioned. Stagecoaches eventually reached Port Republic, Leeds Point, Smithville and Absecon. Realizing that a railroad was needed, Dr. Pitney and Samuel Richards, proprietor of the Weymouth Iron Works, who also wanted better transportation in South Jersey for his bog iron empire, attempted to obtain a charter from the state legislature in 1851. They were initially turned down, but the following year they convinced the legislature of the need. Believing the road would never be built, the petition was granted March 9, 1852, amid many jokes about the "road to nowhere."

Pitney was not to be stopped. He founded the Camden and Atlantic Railroad Company June 24, 1852, and started work on a single track from Camden to Absecon. It was completed to Hammonton, about half way, in 1853. In July 1854, the first train arrived in Atlantic City. The railroad ran on Atlantic Avenue until 1876 with trains stopping every fourth street. Two hotels had opened by the time the first train had arrived.

Atlantic City received its name from railroad engineer Richard B. Osborne, the engineer who had originally surveyed the route of the iron horse through the forests of Camden and Atlantic counties.

Chalkley Leeds, son of Jeremiah, became the first mayor of Atlantic City on May 1, 1854. City Council first met at the United States Hotel. Our former City Hall stands on land once used as a stockyard where soldiers unloaded horses and military equipment in a railroad freight yard.

The first hotel was the Old Leeds Home at Massachusetts and Baltic Avenues. After Jeremiah's death in 1833, his widow, Millicent Leeds, conducted a "guest" business. The Leeds Home became known as the Atlantic House.

Spurred by the success of the "road to nowhere," a group of investors built a second road, the Narrow Gauge Road, from Camden to Atlantic City in 1877. The Philadelphia and Reading Railroad took control of the Camden and Atlantic Railroad. In my family's historical records, I have a railroad pass from the Camden and Atlantic Railroad issued to my grandfather, Joseph A. Barstow, when he was a city Councilman.

I remember that for many years, long after trolley cars had become the means of transportation on Atlantic Avenue, the Pennsylvania Railroad ran a "Milk Train" down the trolley tracks in the middle of the night to maintain its franchise on the tracks. The name "Milk Train" arose because dairy companies delivered milk to houses in the early hours before dawn. The train consisted of an engine and a caboose. It ran down the island to Douglas and Atlantic Avenues in Margate where there was a turn-around called "the loop." I was often awakened as a small child when the train sounded its whistle in the wee hours as it crossed side avenues, always a mournful sound. By 1925, there were 99 daily trains running to and from the resort in summer; 65 in winter. The two railroad companies consolidated on June 25, 1933, forming the Pennsylvania Reading Seashore Lines.

Chapter 4

When Father and Mother were married in 1902, Dad bought a brand new, modern house paid in full with cash. The house had three bedrooms on the second floor and two on the third. Our modern bath had indoor plumbing although cesspools were still in use in the city. Our toilet had a large wooden box located at the ceiling with a long chain that we pulled to flush the toilet. Long after modern-day toilets came into vogue, parents used to tell children to "pull the chain" instead of "flush the toilet."

We had a large living room and dining room with a Tiffany lamp over the table. Our kitchen was sizable by today's standards. A new-style enameled white sink contained two drain boards. The gas stove was a tall one with the oven reaching close to six feet high. A coal stove along one wall provided hot water and could also be used to cook or warm food. Before refrigerators were invented, we had what was called an icebox. It was about three feet tall and four feet wide with a top lid for entrance. Our iceman came every day and left ice in our box. We children in the neighborhood loved it when the ice truck arrived. As the iceman chopped kitchen-size pieces from large cakes of ice, we could cool off in summer with the clumps of ice that fell in the truck.

We had no electricity yet, although the city approved its use in 1882 and my Grandfather Barstow had been president of the utility created by ordinance, the Atlantic City Gas and Water Company. Small gas lamps swung out from the wall when lighted. Every evening when the sun set, a street lighter would walk down our street with a long pole, reach up and turn on the street light outside our house. I loved watching him.

Our basement was on the street level. The large furnace sat in the middle of the open space with huge pipes near the ceiling about a foot in diameter, extending to the four corners of the basement. The heating system was hot air, while the fuel was coal. A large coal bin occupied one corner by a window overlooking the side yard through which a ton of coal was delivered at a time. An enclosed toilet area was in an opposite corner. In a third corner was a double agate tub for laundry. The washer lady came every Monday morning, heated water in a small copper tub, did the wash on a scrubbing board and hung it out on the lines in a large yard. She was paid the prevailing $3.00 a day. She ironed in the afternoon by heating the irons on the gas stove. In the back of the house was a door leading to a closed-in area where two people could change their bathing suits privately. The backyard had a fine lawn, rose bushes, and colorful flowers along fences that enclosed the property.

There was a large porch in front, which wrapped around one side of the house. Mother kept it attractively decorated in summer with tall rocking chairs covered in colorful cretonne material and plants on tables. Striped awnings kept the porch comfortable. A good-size porch was available in the back of the house overlooking the yard where there was a wooden swing large enough for four people.

There was only one commercial block on Atlantic Avenue near our street: it had Brigadell's Drug Store on one corner, Jeffries' Paint Store, Blakemore's Grocery Store, McElroy's Garage and a candy store near the other corner. I could buy several pieces of candy there for a penny. Once I won a pound jar of loose tobacco from a punch card for a penny. That wasn't the prize I had wanted. My parents mailed it to my uncle in Boston who smoked a pipe.

George D. Blakemore, owner of the grocery store, had two daughters: Ruth, who was older than I, and Sarah, who became a long-time friend. He used to come to our home every morning and take Mother's grocery order, delivering it shortly afterward. We had hucksters in those days during the summer months, farmers who drove their fresh produce down the streets in horse-drawn wagons. Women on our street always gathered around, buying the locally raised vegetables and fruit, and chit-chatting in the process.

The bread man and the milkman made deliveries house-to-house. Milk was always on our back porch long before we got up in the early morning. Mother placed a note in an empty glass bottle each night for the next day's order. Our milk was not processed as it is today. Cream rose at the top of the bottle and could be poured off into a pitcher. I remember in the coldest days of winter the cream always froze and pushed the paper cap an inch or more higher than the glass bottle. I loved lifting the soft cream out of the bottle and eating it like ice cream. I shudder today at the thought of ingesting all that fat.

As many children do today, I learned a little about sex long before I reached my teens. An older sister of one of my friends took it upon herself to educate a couple of us girls in the intricacies of sex. She described in detail what I was not really interested in knowing. Even telling where she and several girls and boys went after school. It didn't sound that interesting or appealing to me, but it did sound shocking. After that, I tended to avoid contact with her as much as possible.

My home area was always a gathering place for neighborhood children. My father had been an athlete at prep school and college and still had all the equipment young boys loved: baseballs and bats, footballs, basketballs, hockey sticks and tennis rackets. Boys were often found playing on the gravel street outside our house with Dad's stuff. My girlfriends and I once made fudge in our kitchen. Instead of vanilla, by mistake I poured in some castoria, an old-time physic. We promptly fed it to all the boys outside, with many giggles.

I had one experience as a first grader I'll never forget. We had a granddaddy of a blizzard. Snow was piled high in the city, but the beach was a sea of beauty. Snow covered the sands to the water's edge, piled four, five and six feet high in what my childish eyes

31

saw as icebergs. Freezing temperatures had packed the snow solid enough that we children could climb up on top of it and play.

This afternoon after school we had spent a long time playing on our iceberg. Then we went to our schoolyard, which was solidly covered with ice, and spent some time sliding from one end of the yard to the other. I didn't really notice when my school friends left because it had been dark for some time. I was having fun.

When at last I headed home, it was approaching eight o'clock. Outside my home were a number of neighbors. A full-scale city search was on for me, since my friends had last reported me on our iceberg. The city had even turned on the Boardwalk lights. I was scared silly at the trouble I'd caused. Time had meant nothing to me. My parents were so glad to see me that I wasn't even scolded.

A few years later, Dad was popular with the neighborhood children for another reason. He had bought a two-seated Harley-Davidson motorcycle to run around town. In warmer weather he would take my friends for short rides from our house for several blocks on Pacific Avenue to the Knife and Fork Inn, around onto Atlantic Avenue, and back. The kids loved it. The Inn is still in business today, a fine restaurant.

Dad took me on one motorcycle ride that I remember. We rode down Atlantic Avenue to Longport, which in those days had only a few houses. On the boundary line between Margate and Longport a policeman was stationed. Dad was prevented from entering Longport because there was a measles "epidemic" there. While houses usually were quarantined when someone had measles or infectious diseases, this is the only time I remember a city—no it was only a borough—being quarantined.

Chapter 5

The 1920s were some of the most colorful, unforgettable years in Atlantic City history. Our Boardwalk, with its elegant hotels and many fine shops, was famous worldwide. Our new, recently opened ten-million-dollar Convention Hall was attracting large conventions, developing our city into one of the top convention centers in the country. The trains at our two railroad stations made frequent trips into town bringing hundreds of visitors each trip. Our bathing beaches were filled with visitors enjoying life in the sun and excellent bathing in an ocean well protected by the finest lifeguard system on the Jersey Shore.

Most memorable for us were the many theatres where Broadway producers brought their plays and musical comedies for try-outs before opening in New York. Top stars, some of whose names are legend, performed here: Flo Ziegfeld's Follies, Earl Carroll's Vanities, Eugene O'Neill's plays, George White's Scandals, vaudeville stars Will Rogers, Al Jolson and Eddie Cantor, songs by Irving Berlin, Jerome Kern, Victor Herbert, George Gershwin and Cole Porter. I remember especially the Apollo Theatre on the Boardwalk where students like me, along with the general public, could sit in the top balcony, familiarly called Peanut Heaven, for fifty cents a matinee.

It was the flapper era when girls began cutting their long hair short, straight across just below their ears, in what was called a bob. My good friend Ruth, several years ahead of me in school and a high school junior, had her hair bobbed without telling her parents. I was shocked to learn that, old as she was, her father had spanked her.

Women of all ages had begun claiming a more active role in society, particularly in the business world. During the First World War, America had sent overseas a huge army. Women had been called upon to fill the jobs left vacant in fields of employment not previously available to them. Many women were faced with the responsibility of providing for their families as head of the household. Their lives underwent surprising changes.

When the Pageant was first held in 1921, the flapper era had been developing as a result of newfound freedoms which women had obtained during those war years. If the contestants appeared daring or shocking to the more conservative of that decade, perhaps it was because they had different views of their roles in society. It was a changing world. Many women were no longer buying that old canard, "keep 'em pregnant, barefoot and in the kitchen." They wanted employment worthy of their talents and capabilities. "Women's place is in the home" was giving place to "women's place is everywhere." Fashions in those war years had changed to keep step with the progress of women. The longer the war lasted, the shorter the skirts became, forerunner of the miniskirt of today. I have in my attic a hand-crocheted dress that my mother bought for a reasonably expensive 25 dollars in 1918. I've worn the dress occasionally in plays for women's clubs with hilarious results. The dress had been crocheted in a fancy rose pattern with gold silken thread, its open work revealing under-garments. It was so short, the dress barely reached my fingertips. The bottom of the dress contained golden fringe twelve or more inches long, cut in uneven lengths handkerchief style, falling almost near the knees.

The war effort had been universal. The sale of war bonds and saving stamps was heavily promoted. In our schools, children were urged to bring one dollar to buy a savings stamp, which was pasted in a folder. Five stamps could buy a five-dollar stamp. I still have ones I never cashed in. Each room in my school competed with other rooms to have the highest number of purchases each day. I remember that my teacher once sent me home during school hours to get another dollar to bring back to class so that our room would have the highest total in the school.

My class also used school time to knit woolen caps for children in Belgium suffering from disastrous battles of the war. The caps were knit simply in a square, folded over and stitched in shape. I didn't know how to knit in the fourth grade, but knitting had become a patriotic pastime for the war effort, so my father, who had been convalescing from an illness, decided to teach me. He didn't know how to knit either, but figured out a simple method not commonly used today. On large celluloid knitting needles, size fifteen, he taught me so that I was able to do my share in making caps for those poor Belgian children. I still have those large old needles. We call them jiffy needles today. I didn't know that one day I would own a busy yarn shop providing hand-knit jiffy sweaters for the wholesale market in New York.

The 1920s had been an interesting decade, influenced some-what by the aftermath of the First World War as well as the prohibition era and the newfound freedoms women were exhib-iting in their lives. As a lively, jumping seashore resort, Atlantic City was a wide open town. It was the prohibition era, a country made dry by the Volstead Act. Speakeasies opened all over town, named so because to be admitted one had to speak the code name quietly or in a whisper. Rum running became a popular, busy and lucrative occupation, almost a form of sport. Speedboats, able to outrun most of the Coast Guard boats, made frequent trips out to mother ships, landing their cargo on our beach, under our piers, in the back bay, and almost anywhere. My boyfriend, John, was approached to join the crew of one of our city's most reputable businessmen. He declined, but we often used to laugh about it. Some of our city's most prominent citizens who owned boats were known to engage in rum running.

Gambling was a popular pastime. Back rooms of cabarets and taverns contained all kinds of gambling equipment. The well-known 500 Club, Babbette's, and others all had their tucked away "room." One of my good friends, a society matron of excellent reputation, was escorted by police out the door of the top floor, down a back fire escape of the 500 Club, just as other police entered the front door to raid it. Many important entertainment celebrities made their debut in that club.

Prostitution was everywhere. There were known streets in town. I occasionally drove up a street in the heart of town well-known for its "houses." There women would stand on their front porches, often scantily clad, and shout their wares to the passing vehicles. Political protection made it possible for the town to cater to the pleasures of men. Enoch Johnson, the political boss, in later years was convicted of income tax evasion and sent to jail for a few years.

I remember a gambling place opened in one of the stores my father owned on Atlantic Avenue. Either the store renter had not greased the right palms or the gambling place had been established in a store in such close proximity to the Guarantee Bank and Trust Building that it was an embarrassment to the city fathers. It had to close before it officially opened. My father took me to see the layout. I found it amazing. Another store that father rented to a man for many years was a cigar/candy store located in the same row of stores. After my father died, I discovered another form of gambling, card games, had existed quietly in a back room for decades.

One of the most popular forms of recreation in the city was dancing, often to name bands. Many local and fraternal organizations, civic and social clubs, as well as high school sororities and fraternities, held public dances regularly in the beachfront hotels and largest side avenue hotels. The latest jazz music was played by such famous bands of that era as Paul Whiteman, Benny Goodman, Glenn Miller, Harry James, Sammy Kaye, Cab Calloway, and Rudy Vallée. Social dances in hotels were always formal, evening gowns and tuxedos, the requirement. The popular dance craze was the Charleston, which I could dance with some of the best. Babe Ruth was the New York Yankees' home run king; Jack Dempsey, the boxing champion.

It was the era of gangsters. Al Capone and a number of other gangster personalities were frequent visitors here. Chicago, New York, and most large cities were more or less overrun by gangsters. I became indirectly involved with a criminal several years later. Alvin Karpis, a leader of the Barker-Karpis gang, had sneaked into town. I had decided one night to drive to New York early the next morning on unexpected business. I needed a little more cash than I had. Before the banks opened, I went to Hill and Farrell, a popular men's clothing store on Atlantic Avenue across from City Hall. Ed Hill was a family friend. My check was cashed and I went on my way.

When I returned, the FBI was waiting for me. It seemed Karpis, number one on the FBI's wanted list, had purchased a new wardrobe in the store. The money he had paid in cash was "hot money" and I had had 50 dollars of it. What the FBI wanted to know, after they exchanged funds, was where I had spent money. They had been tracing Karpis through the stolen money he had spent. It was not long afterward that the FBI caught him.

The prohibition era had come into existence with the ratification of the Eighteenth Amendment to the Constitution in 1919. The result had been immeasurable graft, murders for power over territories, and illegal controls over some governments. Al Capone had an interesting comment on the morals of the time. He had said, "I make my money by supplying a popular demand. If I break the law, my customers, who number hundreds of the best people in Chicago, are as guilty as I am. The only difference between us is that I sell and they buy. I call myself a businessman. When I sell liquor it's bootlegging. When my patrons serve it on a silver tray on Lake Shore Drive, it's hospitality."

Atlantic City in the 1920s truly lived up to its advertised name: The Playground of the World. The crowds of people who used to vacation here could find any kind of recreation they desired, along with the relaxation afforded by our seashore environment. There was so much to offer our families and friends.

A write-up in the local paper about old-timers in Atlantic City describes an interview with a long-time taxi driver. He described from memory how things were in those "good old days." He said everyone was on the make. The politicians, the police, and the racketeers shared in the profits. The town had illegal gambling, pornography, prostitution, opium dens, and smuggled bottled whiskey from Canada. He sold from his cab liquor of any brand desired. He simply put labels on the whiskey in his trunk to suit the sale. Marijuana was available. He sold it for five cents a cigarette. He described Enoch Johnson, the political boss, as riding around town in two limousines, one for him and one to carry his money. The taxi driver claimed Johnson carried a million dollars in cash. No wonder he was known as such a great tipper. Yes, Atlantic City had everything in those days.

I graduated from Atlantic City High School in 1925. John Alton (my future husband), his brother Clay, and I had been active in athletics. John became a varsity star in baseball, our high school team winning the state championship for the first time, a record unmatched for years. Clay became a basketball star, later becoming an All-American in basketball, lacrosse, and hockey and competing in gymnastics and track as well. I played basketball, gymnastics and track.

Aside from our scholastic activities in high school, we had an active social life. It was an era when sororities and fraternities flourished, their dances and parties popular when radio and television were not yet fully developed. John and Clay belonged to Bones fraternity, then known as Sigma Beta Phi, and I belonged to Gamma Sigma, both highly regarded.

It was customary for several fraternities to select a ticket for election of officers for the senior class. I was thrilled when John told me that Bones fraternity wanted to nominate me for secretary of the class, a position to which I was elected.

Many parties centered around our graduation festivities. My parents consented to my inviting ten girls to enjoy special seats for the latest musical comedy at the Apollo Theatre. My friend Ruth Babcock invited us to dinner before theatre time at Haddon Hall Hotel and Olive Filer entertained us at a post-theatre food party.

When I began college that fall in 1925, I had a small identity problem for a while. There are many nicknames for Elizabeth: Betty, Bess, Lib, Libby, Liz and Lizzie, among them. My parents had never allowed my brothers to call me Lizzie. Usually I was addressed by my full name. That changed in college. New friends began calling me Betty. Not used to hearing that name, I seldom responded, leaving the well-deserved impression that I was "stuck up." That soon changed.

❧

I have many happy memories of the years preceding 1920. Not yet a teenager, I looked upon my mother's youngest sister as a role model for what my immature years hoped and dreamed my life could be when I reached that wonderful time when I would be "grown up." Violet was only seven years older than I. She lived with her parents in Chester, Pennsylvania, but she used to spend her summers and some special holidays with us. She was almost a sister to me.

Violet was tall and slender, beautiful in my eyes and highly popular with a number of friends in Atlantic City. Her crowning glory was her red hair, straight and long, falling below her hips when not fastened fashionably upon her head. In her late teens, she had the warm, outgoing personality that made her most attractive to the young men of our neighborhood who were frequent callers. I was entranced with Violet's social activities, especially when I was allowed to sit in when her girlfriends talked about their clothes and their dates. It was a world foreign to my childish mind, one that I couldn't wait to hopefully experience as a teenager.

Before 1920, there were no movies, no radio, no television, no cars of any number, and no telephones in most houses. In addition to social events and parties in our family and friends' homes, entertainment outside the home consisted of visiting the live theatre where opera stars and great actors and actresses performed, visiting the famous Boardwalk hotels and piers, and attending dances and socials given by local organizations.

I remember crying as though my heart would break as a small child when my mother refused to let me go out with her one night. The occasion was the appearance of the great actress Sarah Bernhardt at a Boardwalk theatre. I knew nothing about the actress, but Mother and Aunt Nellie were dressed magnificently in long gowns with fur wraps. Before the age of automobiles, they had called a horse and carriage taxi for transportation. I longed to be a part of this great event. One day, I hoped, one day.

Before the days when women first cut their long hair in short bobs, Violet and her friends would preen before our floor-length mirrors, rearranging their hair in various styles, trying on the many hats women wore and occasionally changing their personal outfits. They experimented with face powder and lipstick. Face powders were mostly white or pale pink in color without the variety of tints and shades available today.

Once when I was sick with an upset tummy, Violet gave me a glass powder jar with some powder inside. A printed note in the jar said: "A little bit of powder, a little bit of paint, will make the mighty freckle look as though it ain't." Strange that I've remembered it all these years.

Women didn't smoke in those days. It was considered immoral by Victorian standards. Those who did were considered "no better than those in our local houses." Young women of Violet's era were trying cigarettes anyway. I knew when Violet and her close friends tried, although it was not repeated to any extent. Intrigued by this forbidden custom, I decided to try a cigarette when I was about ten. I went up to our third floor bedrooms, opened a window to blow the smoke out, and lit a cigarette. Almost the first intake of smoke went down my throat, strangling me so that I couldn't breathe. For a few seconds I struggled, absolutely scared silly. When I recovered, the cigarette went out the window and I've never touched one since.

When Mother and Dad went to visit my grandparents for a few days in Chester, Violet had a special beau who used to come see her almost every night. A medical intern in the hospital there, I thought he was handsome as well as nice to me. He used to give me a silver dollar when he arrived and directed me to walk a block away to a drug store where I bought a box of Whitman's chocolates for them. I never saw the box again and certainly didn't share any of it, but it seemed glamorous to me. A real live beau!

I also remember wearing my very first pair of silk stockings there. Just beginning to appear in department stores, how I envied the adult women of my family who wore them. I coaxed and coaxed my mother until she bought me a pair of white silk stockings. She warned me to be very careful with them for they would tear into holes and run. Unfortunately, I was still a young child. My greatest pleasure there was climbing up the wide stone fence along the terraced steps to the house. Stone and silk don't rub together very well. It was only a few minutes before my whole knees were visible through the holes. That was the end of my silk luxury. Back to lisle stockings for me.

Mine was a musical family in those years. We had a box-style Victor Victrola with a large horn on top for amplification. Mother played the piano every night after dinner. Dad played his cornet, occasionally a clarinet, filling the house with popular tunes of the day. Sometimes they sang. I remember that a postage stamp for a letter was two cents, a postcard a penny. Mailmen rode the trolley cars free from the post office to deliver the mail morning and afternoon, and policemen did the same to walk their assigned street.

My first experience with death in the family came when I was twelve. Violet became seriously ill and came to Dad for her care. He had studied for a year or two at Jefferson Medical College in

Philadelphia. Dad put her in our Atlantic City Hospital, where she died. I was devastated at her loss. So young, so beautiful, so full of life and energy, so loving and only nineteen. I mourned her loss for a long time.

Families and family life were predominant in those times, our parents the exercisers of fairly strict discipline and the teachers of good manners. Among the neighbors or parents of my friends, none of the women worked, with the rare exception of where there had been a death, divorce, or some other necessity. Women were more or less subservient to their husbands and children were taught to obey or be punished.

Women have come a long way in their progress from the turn of the century to today. In my personal experiences with the infinite variety of women, from those days to modern times, my first memories are of the majority of women who chose to be homemakers first, everything else second. They came in all sizes and shapes, personality and wit. Some were dominant or domineering; others withdrew meekly into themselves. They were women who also struggled to improve conditions in their homes and communities while they sought to secure for themselves the rights and privileges long denied them in a male-dominated society.

Chapter 6
The Pageant of the Twenties

The first time a pageant of any kind was undertaken in Atlantic City—the forerunner of the Miss America Pageant—it was planned and orchestrated by local businessmen of particular stature and prestige in the community. The Pageant itself was designed with as many public events as could be crammed into the days of the week. Economic largesse was carefully spread around the city, benefiting as many local businesses, large and small, as possible.

The commodity being sold to the public as "the attraction" was not only feminine beauty, but a taste of naughty feminine attributes revealed in somewhat shocking bathing suits, according to the strict, conservative standards of that day. It was all the more interesting since some of the main sponsors were Quakers, members of the thriving Friends Church here.

Public events were held at the many piers and hotels, on the Boardwalk and beach, and at marina areas with sailing events, swimming races, and events at country clubs and large restaurants. The format continued until World War II changed our lives.

The first Miss America was petite, blue-eyed Margaret Gorman of Washington, D.C., who wore a loose full-skirted black bathing suit with a colorful sash around the waist. Attached bloomers were revealed briefly below the skirt. Her blonde curls, Mary Pickford style, were held in place by a brightly colored bandanna. Her prize was a loving cup. Her story has been told many times.

John L. Boucher, an *Atlantic City Press* feature writer and one of the city's most reputable reporters for many years, described his first meeting with Margaret Gorman, who came from a respected family. Boucher was a young reporter on the staff of the *Washington Herald* when he was sent with another reporter to inform Margaret that their newspaper had selected her to compete in Atlantic City as Miss Washington, D.C. She was not home when Boucher and his associate arrived. Her mother directed them to a nearby park where they found her down on the knees playing marbles, one of the joys of her childhood days. Only fifteen when chosen, she had become sixteen just a week before she won the first Miss America title. In later years she claimed she never knew who sent her picture to the newspaper.

That the first Miss America was judged primarily on beauty is evident from the judges selected for the contest. They included John Drew, a famous actor and matinee idol, and Howard Chandler Christy, the artist most renowned for his pictures of beautiful women.

Judging had taken place on the Garden Pier, which was a much longer, more elaborate structure than it is today. The end of the pier has long since been washed away by destructive storms. Once it contained the beautiful Keith's Theatre where musical comedies and Broadway plays were performed. I've always remembered the beautiful, melodious *Student Prince* among others. There were other buildings with interesting exhibits. Among them was the famous Underwood typewriter, advertised as the largest in the world. I remember it was almost as high as the ceiling and nearly covered one wall of the room in width. There was also a basketball court on the pier where I used to attend Atlantic City High School games. The court was separated from spectators by a cage. Today the pier is a prominent art center.

I've often wondered what qualities Margaret Gorman possessed to earn her title. Having just reached her sixteenth birthday, she was still more child than adult. One of the two smallest winners in the Pageant's history at five foot one, weighing 108 pounds with unimpressive measurements of 30–25–32, she was not endowed with the physical maturity of her immediate successors. Her charm had to be in her pixie personality, her warm smile and her blondish curls. She resembled in a general way Mary Pickford, the famous movie star, who for many years was often called "America's Sweetheart."

Mary Pickford was not only the biggest star in the silent movies of the early movie industry, she was *the* star. Everyone loved her and her pictures. She married Douglas Fairbanks, one of the most popular male stars, idolized by many for his swashbuckling, athletic roles. In that era his trusty sword work and leaps from buildings were breathtaking. Both had a profound impact on the movie industry, even to founding one of the major movie companies, United Artists.

My father used to take me to the Colonial Theatre to see their pictures. We rode in the trolley car to the theatre between New York and Kentucky Avenues on Atlantic. The Colonial was a beautiful, large theatre. A full-size orchestra played popular music for half an hour or so before the show began, one show a night at eight o'clock. When it was time for the movie and Pathé News, a local pianist began playing an organ. With no sound from the screen, the pianist played according to the action, softly during love scenes, pounding the keys during exciting action. It was great fun.

After the show, regardless of the weather, we got off the trolley near Bettel's Ice Cream Store and took home to Mother, who had a really sweet tooth, some of her favorite ice cream—Mother stayed home with my small brothers. She trusted no babysitter for her precious children.

Since our home was only a few blocks from the store and their wonderful assortments of baked goodies, we walked home with our ice cream. I remember how cold and freezing I used to be after our walk in the middle of winter. I would race upstairs to get undressed, put on my long-sleeved flannel nightie, pull half a dozen woolen blankets up over me and shiver and shake as I ate my ice cream so I could shiver and shake some more. Life was simple and sweet then.

I don't know if Margaret Gorman's faint resemblance to Mary Pickford was an important or a subconscious factor in her selection, but it certainly didn't hurt. The first pageant had been a kind of haphazard affair that had just happened without too much organization, but it had been a definite success. The hotelmen, Chamber of Commerce, and important business interests of the community recognized that the lure of beautiful young women in attractive settings and in bathing suits was a strong stimulant in bringing tourist dollars to the city after Labor Day.

The many events planned for Pageant week had been organized for the entertainment of tourists and people visiting or living in the city. This was a practice that was to continue through the twenties and thirties. There were different places to go, different events to see and, essentially, three different beauty contests in one: an amateur bathing beauty contest, a professional bathing suit contest, and the Inter-City bathing contest from which Miss America was chosen.

The dominant industry in the city was the hotel industry, both the famous beachfront hotels and the large number of side avenue hotels, many of them excellent high-rise buildings, as well as countless rooming houses. Famous people from all walks of life often could be seen in the resort.

When I was a small child, my family used to dress up and walk the "Boards" on summer evenings. I was always fascinated watching the people sitting in rolling chairs lined up against the railing on the ocean side of the Boardwalk near the hotels. Rolling chairs contained the most elegantly dressed men and women, usually in evening attire, the women with luxurious furs and bejeweled with diamonds and precious stones. The chairs didn't move, they were just a place to sit and, I suppose, a place to be seen.

Our governing body was a five-member City Commission composed of businessmen of substantial financial stature who were also civic leaders beyond their governmental responsibilities. Atlantic City was a fine seashore resort with attractions suitable for everyone.

I didn't realize then how important women, in general, were considered outside the home. Women had been struggling for years to win the right to vote, to have a voice heard on public issues of importance. The year 1920 became a historic one when the Nineteenth Amendment to the U.S. Constitution was finally ratified on August 18, providing suffrage for women.

I wasn't old enough to vote until 1928. A senior at Syracuse University, in reality I could have voted legally twice on the same day in both New York and New Jersey. I didn't, but it happened this way.

Franklin Delano Roosevelt was running for governor of New York State against Albert Ottinger. Al Smith, the current New York governor who was immensely popular with his theme song, "Happy Days Are Here Again," was running for president against Herbert Hoover. Roosevelt had raised the issue of allowing college and university students to register and vote in New York State. Along with other Syracuse students, I registered to vote.

Meanwhile I decided to drive home for a couple of days and vote where I had lived all my life, in the Chelsea area. With my parents, I went to vote early in the morning so I could make the long drive back to Syracuse. We were registered Republicans, the prevailing political party for years in Atlantic City.

Our neighbor, who had lived directly across the street from us as long as I could remember, was a Democrat. When he saw me arrive to vote he decided that I was no longer a resident and challenged me at the polls as a precinct worker. Politicians, however, do what they do well on Election Day. Joseph Altman, who later became mayor of Atlantic City for a number of years, was city prosecutor at the time. He had a judge clear me for voting in short order.

I left for Syracuse immediately after voting, arriving shortly before the polls closed. I had time to cast a second ballot, but in good conscience I did not. My first day at the polls had been excitement enough anyway.

❧

The Boardwalk has always been the main attraction, synonymous with the name Atlantic City. While the soft, sandy beach and the excellent ocean bathing gave relaxation and enjoyment, the Boardwalk was where the action was. There were famous hotels containing shops to suit the tastes of the rich and famous and also the average citizen, excellent dining rooms with elegant cuisines, and ball rooms where the great dance bands of the era played. Five piers extended far out into the ocean with different types of fun and famous entertainers who drew large crowds during the summer season. Walking on the Boardwalk has always been a favorite pastime.

The Boardwalk is also associated with salt water taffy as an important treat to enjoy or give as a gift. Most visitors to our resort return home with salt water taffy as a souvenir of that trip to our city.

Joseph Fralinger was in the confectionery business in Philadelphia in the early 1880s. He originated a chewy candy he called "taffy." Its ingredients a closely guarded secret, he spent hours every day pulling his taffy by hand and cutting it into oblong pieces.

In 1885, Fralinger moved to Atlantic City and opened a small shop on what is now the Boardwalk. At the time, the Boardwalk was quite narrow and laid directly on the sand. People used to watch him pull and cut his taffy. One day, a storm pushed the ocean up over the Boardwalk into his candy shop completely soaking his taffy. When he was trying to overcome the damage, a customer casually remarked, "That's salt water taffy now." That's the story of how salt water taffy got its name. Fralinger's Salt Water Taffy is still sold on our Boardwalk today along with other well-known brands.

In my early childhood, Mother used to take me for an afternoon on the 'Walk. There were stores that used to sell fresh violets arranged in a small hand bouquet that Mother used to pin on my coat as a corsage. Thus beautifully adorned, I especially loved riding in a rolling chair for an hour or so on the "Wooden Way." The chairs were made of wicker with seats for two or three people.

Some chairs had solid tops to shield the eyes from the sun or protect from rain. The tops could be removed if desired. In case of stormy or windy weather, isinglass covers would close in the chair for protection. Blankets were available to cover the knees and legs in cool or cold weather. Rolling chairs were pushed by hand until later years when a small motor generated enough power for a riding operator in the rear of some of the chairs.

In the early years a smooth wooden lane for the chairs did not exist. They bounced along over the somewhat rough boards, hypnotic after a while, but a pleasant experience overall. One could watch all the beauties of the ocean, its waves, its ships, and varied activities on the beach according to the season. One could observe people "walking the boards" in their best finery and delight in the lavish displays in shop windows.

In the no-bathing months of the year, I enjoyed watching the horseback riders along the water's edge and the stands where horses were kept on the beach near the Boardwalk. I loved best of all the pony cart, which could seat four to six children or adults, with its horse trotting briskly up the beach in front of the cart. Sometimes Mother would take me for a pony cart ride. What childish ecstasy! The mothers of some of my friends would occasionally celebrate a birthday party by renting several for the occasion.

A good portion of my life I have spent on the beach during the summer months. Rolling chairs are still pushed manually along the 'Walk. For a time, they were replaced mostly by motorized trams, reminiscent in a way of the open-air trolleys that were the summer form of transportation on Atlantic Avenue. The silks and satins, furs and jewels that used to adorn people on the Board-walk have long since been replaced by blue jeans, T-shirts and occasional bikini-style outfits. The architecturally superb hotels, with their attractive Boardwalk stores containing magnificent merchandise, have been for the most part torn down or converted into casino hotels, their stores no longer on the 'Walk, but inside the hotels. The glamour of the old days has been replaced by the glitter and airy decor of the new. The grandeur of the twenties is but a memory. It is called progress, aimed at rebuilding Atlantic City into an era representative of its former glory. In these past few years, the lifestyle of our city has changed drastically from a family resort to a place where casinos are the main attraction.

Chapter 7

B y the time of the 1922 Pageant, careful planning had taken place. The Pageant began ceremonially with the arrival of King Neptune from the ocean on a handsomely decorated barge pulled by a boat carefully disguised as a dolphin. He was accompanied by a group of lovely mermaids posed amid the seashells and marine-life decor of the barge. When his barge arrived at the Atlantic City Yacht Club on Massachusetts Avenue, King Neptune, colorfully attired and draped with seaweed, descended onto shore at the dock while his mermaids showered him with fragrance-free fresh flowers. Hudson Maxim, in his role as King Neptune, was well known to be unable to stand any fragrance of flowers or powder; he was, after all, the inventor of smokeless gunpowder. He has been quoted many times in the news media as saying that, "If I were placed next to someone smelling to high heaven with perfume, I'd collapse and fall in a faint." The dock of the Yacht Club was decorated with poles and ropes of green foliage with flowers overhead. In later years, he arrived right on the beach.

Accompanying King Neptune was Margaret Gorman, Miss America 1921, who wore a large crown of pearls similar to the Statue of Liberty and a red and white striped cape attached to her arms, which she held open like bat wings. A dozen charming youngsters greeted her, dancing about her and laying floral offerings at her feet.

In the excitement of the moment, City Commissioner William S. Cuthbert, there to greet these distinguished arrivals from the sea, stepped off the dock and fell into the water between the barge and the dock, narrowly escaping being crushed to death before he was rescued.

The mermaids, who comprised the Court of King Neptune, consisted of twelve of the area's most prominent, social young women. One of them was Marie F. "Honey" Feyl, daughter of the editor of the *Atlantic City Press-Union*, who later became the wife of our late Senator Frank S. Farley.

In the Boardwalk parade later in the day, King Neptune and Miss America, accompanied by their beautiful mermaids, rode on a float lavishly decorated with a giant seashell and marine life symbolic of the ocean. King Neptune was a picture to behold in all his oceanic glory. He wore upon his head a golden crown shaped with three, sharp golden triangles like serpent's teeth, the center triangle larger than the other two. He carried his trident, symbol of authority, upright in his right hand. Rich, royal robes adorned his powerfully built body as far as his ankles, and sandals on his bare feet completed the picture. As I watched his long, naturally white hair and his lengthy, bushy snow-white beard blowing in the ocean breeze, I had the impression of seeing before my eyes a mythological figure come to life.

The mermaids all wore the official Atlantic City bathing suit of light blue wool with a wide white belt and a narrow white strap rising from the right side of the belt to the left shoulder.

Generally called His Oceanic Majesty or Monarch of the Sea during his official appearance, King Neptune was an imposing and magnetic figure as he ruled over his mythical kingdom. It was sometimes heard around town that the only reason Hudson Maxim had been chosen to be King Neptune was because of his long, flowing white hair and his extra thick, handsome white beard.

There was an elaborate baby parade of flower-decorated rolling chairs on the second day of the Pageant. On the third day the huge Boardwalk parade was held with fifteen divisions of rolling chairs decorated with real flowers and foliage. Not only were the contestants viewed in bathing suits, but everyone in the parade was required to wear a bathing suit. The police were outfitted in blue and white suits, the city colors. Firemen wore red suits, symbolic of their occupation. The mayor and city officials, members of civic and service clubs, and other organizations were all attired in bathing suits.

Prizes were awarded to the winners in eight divisions. The contestants appeared in the three main divisions of the competition: the amateur bathing beauty contest, the professional bathing suit contest, and the Inter-City bathing contest from which Miss America was chosen.

The winner's trophy was a golden mermaid, especially designed, consisting of a black teakwood base with a series of golden seashells around a golden mermaid lying on a piece of real granite rock. The trophy was said to be real gold, valued at $5,000. Originally it was intended to be a perpetual trophy with each winner's name inscribed but individual trophies were designed in later years. Miss America was to be invited back each year to protect her title. If she won three years in succession, the golden mermaid would be permanently hers.

In 1980, a story appeared in the Sunday edition of Atlantic City's *The Press* about a contestant during that 1922 Pageant. Eleanor DuQuesne, Eleanore Lindley at the time of the contest, was Miss Greater Camden, "the girl with the golden smile." The article describes the event: "It was called the Atlantic City Pageant and was part of the city's Great Fall Pageant, a series of baby parades, races, tournaments, banquets, balls, beauty contests and publicity stunts." The beauties were hurried from one event to another. They appeared at golf tournaments, yachting events, tennis matches, trap shooting contests and parades.

The highlight of the event was the afternoon Miss Pittsburgh was knocked unconscious when the chair she was standing on collapsed during a photo session at the Seaview Country Club. Miss Los Angeles had come the farthest distance. Fifty-seven contestants competed, compared to eight the previous year.

Lindley competed in the Inter-City Beauty Contest on the Million Dollar Pier. Miss Indianapolis won that portion of the contest, Miss Detroit was second, and Mary Katherine Campbell, Miss Ohio, was third.

Of the Bathers Revue Contest, held on the beach between Garden Pier and Steel Pier, Lindley recalls that "We just paraded across the sand like a bunch of dumb kids." Some of the contestants wore suits other than the modest, woolen bathing suits. "I wore this crazy green, rubber suit," she remembered. "I got $50 for wearing it in the parade and it got a lot of attention." Some of the other contestants were angry and organized a "beauty strike." The strike did not last long because Pageant officials agreed to re-judge the Inter-City Bathers Revue on the Steel Pier that night with everyone wearing "regulation" suits.

Much effort was made to get the contestants to entertain the people who had paid to watch the proceedings. Lindley said, "Most of us were not prepared to do anything. A nice little thing from New England did a dance and Miss Alabama, a real comic with broomstick legs, livened up everyone." The M.C. canvassed everyone for someone to sing the national anthem. Finally, Lindley volunteered. "I certainly wasn't shy like Mary Campbell!" She was well received, so much so that she added, "Columbia, the Gem of the Ocean." "My mother said I made a fool of myself," she chuckled, "but I had fun."

The three winners in the professional, amateur, and Inter-City divisions of the Bathers Revue were finalists. Miss Campbell, an Inter-City winner, won by a score of 6–2 before a noisy crowd of 12,000. The American Beauty Ball was held in the Ritz-Carlton Hotel in a beautiful ballroom.

Rules in those early years were not as strict as they are today. Eleanore Lindley was not technically a "Miss" since she had been married for a short time. Miss Alaska was really from New York City. She was lovely, though. She wore white a lot, but she never saw Alaska.

Many of the beauties were financed by commercial interests who gave them beautiful outfits and expensive gifts. Lindley received clothing from a local department store and an easy chair from a furniture store. All of the stores that contributed got a free ad in the newspapers. Of the new Miss America, Lindley said that Mary Katherine Campbell was gorgeous, but much too shy. Only sixteen, "she wouldn't go anywhere without me."

After the Pageant, talent scouts lured some contestants to movie studios for screen tests. Lindley appeared as an extra at Paramount. She made public appearances, attended business openings, and met celebrities of the day, including Gloria Swanson. She also was a model for photographers and fashion shows.

Although Mary Katherine Campbell was only sixteen years old, she had a well-developed figure that prompted many admiring glances. At five foot seven inches, she weighed 140 pounds with measurements of 35–26–36. In contrast to Margaret Gorman's blonde hair, Mary Katherine had bright auburn hair. She wore a size three shoe.

⁂

The tourist attraction in Atlantic City in 1922 was the Curtis Seaplane Hangar on the Boardwalk and Maine Avenue near Hackney's famous restaurant. My family often rode up to the Inlet to watch the seaplane take off and land in the ocean inlet. It was also an exciting event to watch the plane being rolled out of the hangar, across the Boardwalk and down a ramp to the water. As the plane took off it bounced roughly across the top of the waves causing tremendous splashing as it heavily rose into the wild blue yonder. Its return flight was equally thrilling as the plane hit the ocean with water flying high into the air. We marveled at the people foolhardy enough to pay for such dangerous experiences.

Years later I listened with much surprise as Adrian Phillips, hotel executive at the Chalfonte-Haddon Hall hotel and long-time Pageant official, told me about his first seaplane ride. Adrian and his wife, Emaline, left Atlantic City and landed on the Hudson River in New York on a promotional trip to introduce the service. His trip had been subsidized by the Atlantic City Hotelmen's

Association. Four passengers made the return trip with two pilots in a two-motored plane.

The population of Atlantic City in 1922 was 55,000. Among the stars who visited the city in that era were the great operatic tenor Enrico Caruso, Rudolph Valentino, the movie star heart throb of women Tom Mix, Bebe Daniels and Helen Hayes.

Mary Katherine Campbell did win the Miss America title a second time in 1923. She became the only two-time winner in Pageant history. The next year, the board of directors decided to have two additional golden mermaid trophies made, one for each of the first three Miss Americas. A limit was then placed on winning the title more than once. The original golden mermaid has disappeared without a trace.

There had been no rules prohibiting marriage in those first years. Mary Katherine Campbell's first runner-up, Ethelda Kenvin, turned out to be Mrs. Everett Barnes, wife of a Pittsburgh Pirates player. Miss Boston, Mildred Prendergast, had an attorney husband and a seven-month-old baby.

The first scandal touching the Pageant reared its ugly head a few years after Charlotte Nash, Miss St. Louis 1923, married theater magnate Frederick G. Nixon Nordlinger in 1924. He was shot to death in a hotel room in Paris in 1931. There was a long trial, which made sensational headlines in the news media on two continents. Charlotte Nash had been charged with murder, but eventually was acquitted. Endowed with prominent dimples, she had them insured for $100,000.

The first Pageant I attended to see the final judging was the 1924 Pageant held on the Million Dollar Pier in their huge ballroom. The pier is known today as Ocean One Mall with interesting stores, restaurants, and novelty shops. Like all the other piers of that day, the Million Dollar Pier extended far out into the ocean before it sustained damage from some of our disastrous storms. This year the pier was at the height of its popularity.

I remember the many times my mother used to walk me, as a small child, all the way out to the end of the pier where net hauls were held twice a day. The immense nets, which had been lowered into the water, were filled to overflowing with large, sometimes huge fish of many varieties, occasionally rare species. Turtles, seahorses and other marine life were abundant. It was fascinating for young and old to watch the fish jumping about as they were lowered into containers for sales to local and wholesale markets.

In the center of the pier was a large theater with a high balcony, commonly called the Hippodrome. I used to walk up the Boardwalk on warm summer evenings with my high school boyfriend, John Alton, later to become my husband, to see Welch's Minstrel Shows, which changed every week. The productions were always happily entertaining. Four end men were frequently hilarious with their antics, jokes and comic songs. The soloists had excellent voices, singing popular ballads of the day with voices ranging from tenor to bass.

Near the center of the pier was a white, attractive three-story house known as Captain Young's mansion. Surrounded by a garden of flowers, it was a real residence for John L. Young, owner of the pier. Its postal address was unique in the country, for it was known as Number One, Atlantic Ocean. *Ripley's Believe It or Not* listed it as the only address of its kind in the world.

When the minstrel show was over, John and I would walk back to the front of the pier to dance in the huge ballroom, where popular dance bands of the era played. The bandstand occupied one end of the ballroom. A large aquarium filled two side walls, containing some of the rare fish and turtles pulled in at the net haul.

Around the dance floor were wicker chairs and tall rocking chairs, several rows deep for watchers to watch and dancers to rest. It was also a boy-meets-girl place. Young women, including high school girls of my age, often gathered near or sat in the chairs. Any young man, or young at heart man, could and did approach possible female partners for a dance, which much of the time ended up being a date. This was not my cup of tea. I never went to the pier solo for that purpose.

A row of large boxes on the balcony surrounded three walls of the ballroom. The boxes were semi-circular in shape with half a dozen rows of elevated theater-style seats to accommodate thirty or forty people who could watch the activity of the dancers below. The ballroom ceiling was covered with electric light bulbs that flashed on and off continuously to reveal a huge, rippling American flag and an image of an eagle.

On the night of the selection and crowning of Miss America 1924, I went to the pier and found a seat in the front row of a box near the bandstand platform. My end seat was positioned so that I could have reached out and touched the person nearest me in the next box.

Armand T. Nichols, former secretary to the mayor, had succeeded Tom Endicott as director general. A new event for this Pageant was selecting the Most Beautiful Girl in Evening Dress for which only contestants in the Inter-City competition were eligible.

The judges who had been selected were famous artists: Norman Rockwell, Charles Chambers, Howard Chandler Christy, McClelland Barclay, Dean Cornwell, Haskell Coffin, John LaGatta and Arthur William Brown.

Unlike the Pageant of today, the 1924 and early Pageants were not a continuous production. After a fanfare of trumpets, contestants were introduced as they walked individually across the stage to be viewed by the judges. Since there were no chairs on the ballroom floor, the huge audience crowded around the stage filling the ballroom and squeezing each other together in the hot summer air. In a short time, an intermission was announced. Contestants were free to join their parents, relatives, and friends wherever they might be while there was dancing.

I noted that a very pretty contestant came to my adjoining box, where she embraced her parents and all the people there. I recognized her from newspaper publicity as Miss Philadelphia. Among the people in her box were the mayor of Philadelphia and his political aides. In a short while she was called back to the stage to continue in the competition. In between events, the band played and spectators danced.

Eventually, to my great surprise, Miss Philadelphia was announced the winner and was crowned by Armand Nichols. As I watched the crowd on the dance floor pressing forward for a closer look at Ruth Malcomson, Miss America 1924, it looked like a big jam of people, somewhat unruly. Adrian Phillips told me about it some years later. There had been an unpleasant protest that the selection had been rigged, with the choice having been made before the Pageant. Angry charges have sometimes been made during the years, but no shred of evidence has ever been presented. Phillips laughingly told me that Louis St. John abruptly left the platform and disappeared, leaving Phillips to handle the situation. The problem was solved with the band swinging into a lively musical number. Dancers began to dance, and all ended well. Miss America returned to her family and friends in her box where she received overwhelming congratulations and affection.

⁊⦁

As I rode home on the jitney, I felt a sense of disappointment in the contest. It wasn't anywhere near what I had expected. There hadn't been any show as such. The viewing of the finalist contests had been too short on stage. Nothing had been overly interesting or exciting, as far as I was concerned, except for the new Miss America herself. She had been a beautiful, charming contestant. I had special opportunities of observing her while she was enjoying her family. That was a memorable experience.

After the Pageant was over in those early years, contestants were free to come and go as they pleased; to mingle in the crowd, to dance with anyone who invited them, to go to the Ball, or to go out afterwards to any of the multitude of bars, cabarets and speakeasies that flourished wide open in the city. It was the beginning of the free-swinging, scandalous activity that gave the

Pageant such a bad reputation during the following years. The scandals eventually began affecting the hotel clientele to the point where prominent businessmen withdrew their support from the Pageant entirely in 1928.

During the 60th Anniversary of the Pageant, at a dinner for the board of directors, sponsors, and former Miss Americas, by chance my husband and I shared a table with Ruth Malcomson and her husband, Carl Schaubel, who was staff vice president at Pennsylvania Military College, now Widener University in Chester, Pennsylvania. Two of my brothers had been educated there. Ruth Malcomson in her maturity was even more beautiful: a gracious, charming woman, a delight to know. I couldn't help thinking with pride that the 1924 Pageant had indeed crowned a dignified lady with many fine qualities. Her beauty of character enhancing her beauty of face and form was even more evident.

In later years, members of Ruth Malcomson's family also competed in the national Pageant. Most recently her grand-niece, Jodi Graham, competed as Miss Delaware in 1981. Jodi's mother, Lorna Malcomson Ringler Graham, was Miss Pennsylvania 1956. Three generations of competitors in one family has been a Pageant record.

Chapter 8

The judging of contestants had become titillating gossip among many women during this period. Beginning in 1924, the contestants were taken to the Atlantic City High School where they were measured. A point system had been established for the seventeen judges, including Norman Rockwell, James Montgomery Flagg and Howard Chandler Christy. On a scale of 100, the construction of the head counted 15 points; the hair, nose and mouth each 5 points; facial expression, torso, legs, arms, hands and grace of bearing each 10 points.

Mother's friends used to laugh hilariously at the imagined picture of seventeen judges using tape measures with questionable, unbecoming familiarity in certain areas of the body in their search for a bathing beauty queen. How skilled were the men in measuring females? What standards were used for comparison, the mythological Venus? How tightly or how loosely was the tape measure drawn around delicate breasts, waists and hips? The women in many instances were either outraged at the judging system or just thought it was downright silly.

For many years, the Pageant continued to list, for publicity purposes, the measurements of contestants as they were reported by the girls. Eventually that practice was eliminated as not being of any relative importance. The girls frequently could, and often did, change their statistics to be more desirable.

The intent of those early judges was not only to select the fairest of the fair, the original Pageant goal, but also the most beautiful body. Perhaps some of the strong criticism of women through the years at the claimed Pageant's exploitation of women had its origin in some basis of fact back in the 1920s.

Ruth Malcomson, Miss America 1924, once described her trip to the high school with her mother for the judging, which she said consisted of casual and informal conversations with the judges. Jack Dempsey, the great boxing champion, was often a visitor to Atlantic City. As a friend of one of the judges, Dempsey sat down with them as an observer of the proceedings.

Miss America-to-be had won the bathing suit contest and also a prize in the parade as Betsy Ross. After her crowning, she returned to Philadelphia in a motorcade escorted by state police most of the way to Camden where they boarded the ferry across the Delaware River. The mayor and city officials orchestrated a tumultuous welcome upon her arrival in Philadelphia.

There is no evidence that Malcomson had any interest in a film career. At the end of her reign, she refused to return to crown her successor. She believed that professionals had infiltrated the Inter-City Beauty Contest, which had always been an amateur division. Dorothy Knapp, a famous beauty model, had arrived for the Pageant when the original titleholder became "sick." Kathryn Ray, a showgirl at Coney Island, also showed up. Earl Carroll had been one of the judges at Coney Island who also tried to involve himself in the new Pageant. The first title winner from a western state was Fay Lanphier, Miss California 1925. The first to represent a state rather than a city, she was also the first Miss America about which there was considerable controversy.

Before she arrived in Atlantic City, Lanphier had signed a contract with Paramount movie studios to have the role in a film called *The American Venus*. After she became Miss America, she was taken to New York for a special celebration by Paramount. Among the prominent guests were Will Rogers and Rudolph Valentino. For many women, Valentino was the man of their dreams during the 1920s, especially after his popular movie *The Sheik*.

Bernard McFadden in his newspaper *The New York Graphic*, had a series of articles stating that Fay Lanphier's winning had been fixed, a more than disturbing assertion for Atlantic City's prominent business leaders. Later on, McFadden was forced to issue a retraction, saying the information he had received had been inaccurate. Paramount eventually admitted it had sent a representative to sign up all the contenders for the title in order to get a cheap actress for the role. The Pageant had sued McFadden for three million dollars.

Lanphier went to Hollywood where she made *The American Venus* and a Laurel and Hardy film. The first had as its stars Vera Ralston, as a contestant from a fictitious city; Fay Lanphier as a stand-in for the crown of Miss America; and Douglas Fairbanks Jr., son of the great actor, as the leading man. Lanphier's acting was of such poor quality that her option was dropped. She finally married her childhood sweetheart.

⚜

Ernest Torrence, a prominent movie actor, assumed the role of King Neptune in 1925, replacing Hudson Maxim. Since Fairbanks Jr. was in town, he became Triton, the son of King Neptune. The 1926 Pageant had two contestants who were memorable. The first was Joan Blondell, Miss Dallas, who had entered the Pageant for the money her show-biz family needed to go to New York. As Miss Dallas she had already won $2,000.

In the Rolling Chair Parade, she was a startling picture. Dressed in a cowgirl outfit, her sombrero on the back of her head, but held in place by a leather strap around her neck, cowgirl chaps heavily bejeweled, tucked-into leather boots, she energetically and dramatically fired silver revolvers large enough to be 44's from her jeweled leather holster. She waved her guns around joyously, shooting everyone in sight while sounding forth with bloodcurdling yells. If her act was designed to attract attention to herself, she was highly successful. I'm sure no one who saw her that day forgot her. Even now I smile at the memory.

The other memorable contestant was Dorothy Lamour. An entirely different lady-like character, she was beautiful to behold. In future years, like a number of contestants through the Pageant's history, she achieved fame and fortune as the sarong girl with Bing Crosby and Bob Hope in their many movies together.

Miss America 1926 was Norma Smallwood. In my younger years I had thought Mary Katherine Campbell, our one-time queen, was the epitome of beauty, grace and charm. She was truly lovely. Now I added Norma Smallwood, who appealed to me as a queen for reasons I didn't understand. Perhaps it was her startling difference in appearance. While the preceding winners had worn their hair in a loose, curly coiffure, Norma's hair was straight, dark brown, parted in the middle, flat on top with coils of hair pinned in a round bun over each ear. She was intriguing. At 18, she was five foot four, weighed 118 pounds, and measured 33–25–34, more slender than her two predecessors. Ruth Malcomson had been 18, five foot six, weighed 139 pounds, and measured 34–25–34. Fay Lanphier was 19, five foot six, weighed 138 pounds, and measured 34–26–27.

In all the pictures of Miss Americas through the years, Norma's picture reveals an individuality in appearance unlike any other. She had her chance at the movies, but chose to marry a wealthy oil man in her home state of Oklahoma. In due time she was divorced after a messy, unpleasant public scandal. She then married a second oil man. She was the first to make a considerable amount of money from her title. She chose not to return to Atlantic City to crown her successor.

Lois Delander, Miss Illinois, was a sixteen-year-old high school junior when she won the title in 1927. She apparently didn't expect to win. All she really cared about was going back to school where she was an honor student. During her reign she met a number of prominent people, including President Calvin Coolidge and Charles Lindbergh. Her prizes were more than usual: four trophies, a screen test, a watch and an Oldsmobile car. When she graduated from high school, she went on to college and eventually married her college sweetheart.

Chapter 9
The 1930s

ohn and I had been married in October 1931 in the First Presbyterian Church at Pennsylvania and Pacific Avenues by Rev. Henry Merle Mellon, one of the city's prominent ministers. We had been going together since the seventh grade. Eventually we had lived together for 62 years in a more than happy marriage until he died in 1992.

Our wedding could be called a fashionable one. Scheduled for seven o'clock on a Saturday evening, the church was filled to capacity including the balcony. A dance reception was held at John Hollinger's Hotel Madison where everyone had been invited.

Mother and I had been buying our clothes for some years from Miss Clark, fashion manager of M. E. Blatt's department store at South Carolina and Atlantic Avenues, now an office building. Miss Clark took me to New York in the parlor car of a morning train. We visited the showrooms of several fashion designers where I picked out my lace wedding dress, a veil with a long train, and my trousseau along with velvet evening gowns for my six bridesmaids. Two wore lavender, two a peach color, and two a light green. The evening gowns were my gifts to my maid of honor and bridesmaids. John's attendants wore tuxedos. His brother, Clay, was best man. My two brothers, Harry and Joseph, wore their Pennsylvania Military College uniforms.

I speak about my wedding primarily because of an incident that took place. It was the era of prohibition. My father wore his swallow-tail suit. While Dad was not a drinking man, and liquor was not customarily served in our home except on special occasions, for whatever reason, my father forced a pint of liquor into the back pocket of his pants. As we stood in the church doorway ready to make our long walk down the aisle, waiting for the soloist to finish her songs, Dad suddenly remembered the liquor in his back pocket, which could have been plainly visible to the audience because of the cut of his swallow-tail coat. Dad began struggling to remove the pint, but it was stuck fast. The soloist finished singing. The organist began the traditional "Here Comes the Bride" music, but the bride was stuck in the doorway with a father who couldn't get that bottle out of his pocket. He struggled. People turned their heads to see what the delay was.

Finally the bottle was removed. Dad frantically handed it to the nearest of the policemen present for traffic duty as we began, late, our long walk to the altar.

John and I and our wedding party had a police escort to the Madison Hotel. There I learned that the policeman had returned father's liquor to him after the wedding. What happened to the contents I never knew. Although I discovered Dad had a private room in the hotel where his men friends, no women, could find liquid refreshment. Food and legal refreshments were available in the ballroom.

When John and I left the hotel for our honeymoon hideaway, it was late enough in the evening that by the time we arrived at our destination for that night, we were both physically and emotionally exhausted. All in all it has turned out to be a very good life.

We were blessed with the birth of a daughter, Elizabeth, in 1932, causing me to devote most of my time and energy to managing our home efficiently, providing for the welfare of my husband, and proper, loving care for our daughter in a warm and happy environment.

Chapter 10

The 1930s were not happy ones economically in our area. The stock market crash in 1929 was felt throughout this decade up until the beginning of World War II. Wall Street was having a difficult time recovering from its great losses. Real estate values plunged to a low level. There were not many sales transactions. Few people could afford high down payments. The construction industry, generally, and in Atlantic City, in particular, came to a halt. Businesses laid off unnecessary help.

In our area and all over the country, businesses continued to close their doors permanently. There was a general shortage of ready cash. Residents were reluctantly forced to accept scrip issued by our city and many other cities to pay bills and employees, for the scrip was widely circulated in the business community. In an effort to support and stimulate the economy, President Roosevelt had established the Civilian Conservation Corps, the CCC, in his New Deal. A CCC camp had been established nearby and paid wages of $15 a week to clear brush and debris from the woods.

My father had inherited a number of real estate properties in the center of the city, including a nine-story brick apartment house with mostly six-room apartments. All rental units, the lessees responded according to the strengths and weaknesses of people everywhere. Most paid regularly month by month, not always in full, but they paid or tried to pay. Some, including the wealthy renters of the apartment house, spent as much time as they could manage simply avoiding payment as long as possible.

※

An incident stands out from my early married life. When John and I moved into our Ventnor home after our marriage our four story house was heated by hot water fueled by coal. A large heater located in the rear section of the house had a bucket-a-day attached coal bin which automatically fed coal into the fire. As was customary, there was a large coal bin next to a window through which a ton of coal at a time was poured from the driveway. It was necessary to put a bucket of coal into the heater coal bin every day. When John was home there was no problem. But when he was away for a couple of days on business, I struggled to keep the house evenly heated. I had never tended a furnace before. Lifting buckets of coal was not my forte. I had considerable concern for my small daughter, whose hours spent on a drafty floor with uneven warmth was causing unnecessary colds. I felt something needed to be done. I did it.

I called our family plumber without telling John, who was out of town at the time, and had an oil burner installed in the heater, but first I had the heater moved entirely out of the house onto concrete under our back porch. There didn't happen to be a chimney there, or any enclosure. The weather was mild during fall days.

When John arrived home the next day he was considerably upset. A new chimney had to be built, a wall built around the furnace and such fireproofing as was necessary. My love was a good sport. Often exhausting himself, he arranged to have everything completed in two days. Our oil burner gave me total peace of mind. No more struggling with buckets of coal. Our home was evenly heated for the first time and, I suppose in a way, I had exercised my independent judgment as a woman. John and I were always equal partners, which may be why our marriage was such a happy one all those 62 years. I was never a clinging vine as so many women were. John liked me that way. I have always been my own woman.

Chapter 11
Rebuilding the Pageant

In 1935 Eddie Corcoran, promotion and publicity director for the Steel Pier, convinced the pier's owner, Frank Gravatt, on the idea of re-organizing the Pageant. I remember Frank Gravatt very well. Before he bought Steel Pier he had owned the Buick Automobile Agency at Missouri and Atlantic Avenues. When I was a sophomore at Syracuse University in 1927, I just couldn't live unless I had my own car. I coaxed my father until he gave in. He took me to his friend, Gravatt. What I really wanted was a roadster with a rumble seat. Father and Gravatt spent what seemed to impatient me hours chit-chatting, while I had made up my mind the moment I saw that sporty blue-green roadster in the window. After what, again, seemed like an eternity, I drove home the first car I had ever owned.

A veteran showman, Eddie Corcoran sold Gravatt on financing the reorganization of the Pageant. It was obvious that holding some events on Steel Pier would be a definite advantage for the Pier. Knowing the genius of his talented young showman, Gravatt was convinced that the Pageant could be re-established on sound business principles while making it a civic event of untold benefit for the entire resort as well as his amusement pier.

Tent 13, the Philadelphia chapter of the Variety Club, to which both Gravatt and Corcoran belonged, agreed to cooperate by assisting in establishing local contests in communities where Variety Clubs were located as well as through their other theatrical contacts.

A nucleus civic organization was formed, composed of John R. Hollinger, an owner of the Madison Hotel; William F. Casey, City Commissioner; and three representatives of the Variety Club of Philadelphia, including Gravatt. Hollinger was named president. Gravatt agreed to provide the necessary finances to promote the contests over the county and to stage the Pageant on his pier. The newly-formed board agreed to promote and finance a Boardwalk parade, necessary hotel accommodations for the contestants, and any special entertainment planned in their honor. Funds would be raised through subscriptions and tickets sold on a new automobile. Hollinger agreed to take over the financial campaign.

As the new organization's plans progressed, it became evident that someone was needed to coordinate civic activities and to sell the people of Atlantic City on supporting the newly organized Pageant. A search was undertaken to find the best person for the task. Eddie Corcoran had read an article about the only woman in the country running a beauty pageant. He contacted the St. Petersburg, Florida, Chamber of Commerce, where Lenora S. Slaughter was a staff member, and asked to borrow her for the job. She agreed to come on a temporary basis for $1,000. She proved to be an unusually well qualified person for such an important responsibility and assignment.

In future years she was to have an indelible impact on the growth and development of the Pageant. Her ideas, her untiring energy, wisdom, and good taste helped to build the firm foundations for the Pageant's successes in future years, its unequaled scholarship program, and its international reputation as the largest scholarship foundation for women in the world. She was an unforgettable executive of first class.

Plans were finally fully-prepared for the first Pageant of the new regime, newly named "The Showman's Variety Jubilee." Contests were underway in twenty states. Talent was included as a part of the attributes a contestant might display, but not a requisite, in seeking the crown. About half of the girls chose to present talent, while others relied on evening gown and swimsuit competition.

The program of the 1935 Pageant included a luncheon by Mayor White, Opening Day ceremonies on Steel Pier, followed by a formal dinner and reception. A small but curious audience saw the preliminary contests on Wednesday and Thursday evenings. The Boardwalk parade was held Friday afternoon, followed by the last preliminary contest that evening.

By Saturday, newspaper publicity had created great interest in the Pageant. The finals and the crowning found a packed house with a crowd of 5,000 visitors who stood throughout the entire three-hour performance. Henrietta Leaver, Miss Pittsburgh 1935, was crowned as the curtain went down on the first of the new Pageants.

Due to the creative genius of Eddie Corcoran, the business foresight of Frank P. Gravatt, the financial acumen of John Hollinger along with the support of civic leaders in Atlantic City and Philadelphia, this Pageant was the first meaningful success in its long history.

Unfortunately, some unpleasant publicity arose after the Pageant. The new Miss America, after much urging, had agreed to pose for sculptor Frank Vitter for a statue. She had declined to pose nude, insisting publicly later that she had worn a bathing suit with her mother present while posing. When the statue was unveiled it showed a nude Miss America. The statue went on display in the New York Sheraton Hotel Ballroom as decor. Henrietta Leaver was "Miss Model of America 1936." The Sheraton Hotel eventually wanted to donate the statue to the Pageant. It was delivered to Adrian Phillips where it stood in the woods around his country home for months. When the Pageant office staff came to Phillips' home for a party in the spring, the statue had deteriorated. Florence Miller, a local artist, took possession of it for the proposed Atlantic City Museum.

After the successful 1935 Pageant, Eddie Corcoran invited Lenora Slaughter to be his assistant at $3,000 a year. Lenora had been paid $5,000 in Florida, but she accepted the offer, seeing the potential future possibilities in the Pageant.

Eddie Corcoran didn't live to see his brainchild become a success. He died in the early spring of 1936 from a heart attack on his way home after meeting with motion picture executives in California.

On June 4, 1936, the Showman's Variety Jubilee was incorporated in the state of New Jersey. A board of trustees was established. John R. Hollinger, appointed General chairman, agreed to direct the financial campaign again. Frank Gravatt agreed to donate $5,000 to the budget and pay for staging the show on Steel Pier. George D. Tyson, a member of the Variety Club, was named executive director for a sixteen-week period during the summer. Lenora S. Slaughter was named Associate Director on a year-round basis. She returned to the Pageant from Florida to set up permanent residence.

A program of events was established for Pageant week. Definite policies for the handling of Miss America were decided, including a contract with the Showman's Variety Jubilee for the management of each Miss America during her reign. The Grand Prize would include an all-expense trip to Hollywood and a screen test by a major picture company. Sponsoring organizations included theaters, newspapers, amusement parks, state fairs and private promoters.

The contestants gathered in Philadelphia on Labor Day 1936 and were overnight guests of the Variety Club. They traveled in a group to Atlantic City on the American Beauty Special Tuesday, September 8th. The program of events for Pageant week included a Rotary Club luncheon, Variety Club luncheon, American beauty ball, bicycle parade, Boardwalk float parade, national fashion show, naval parade, championship ocean swim, three preliminary competitions and the final competition. That obviously was a very full, tiring series of events for contestants. Rose Coyle of Philadelphia was crowned Miss America 1936, a charming, beautiful girl with a wonderful smile.

The national fashion show, held in the Ballroom of Convention Hall on Friday evening, with contestants modeling "Around the Clock" fashions, had been an outstanding event. Many prominent New York fashion show editors and designers were in attendance. Local and Philadelphia society had boxes and reserved seats instead of standing every night in the Marine Ballroom on Steel Pier where the actual competition was being held. Thus was planted in the minds of the civic leaders the idea of staging the actual competition in the Main Auditorium of Convention Hall, a dream which was to come true four years later.

The Pageant was acknowledged to be a success. The budget of $21,000 had been met. One thousand dollars was contributed to the Variety Club of Philadelphia and $1,000 to the Community Chest of Atlantic City. The balance of the old budget deficit of $79,000 was paid in full.

Elizabeth B. Alton

Chapter 12

In the mid-1930s one Eastern Star friend was working in a busy center city yarn shop. Knitting and crocheting had become popular crafts for women, their popularity having been intensified during the First World War years. Then it had been considered a patriotic responsibility to knit khaki sweaters, caps, gloves or mittens for the soldiers on the field. Women carried their knitting in fancy knitting bags everywhere and would often knit, whatever the occasion.

My friend urged me to open a knitting shop where she would be the main instructor. I finally agreed, opening a yarn shop just off Atlantic Avenue on Pennsylvania. When Jane arrived for work the first day, she brought with her another instructor from their former shop. I didn't think she was necessary, since I was reasonably competent in that period. However, we did need her, for we soon had women sitting in the large store, knitting away at their intricate patterns much like a social sewing circle. It became a place to go to knit and chat.

Not long after we had opened, a man came to the shop to ask if we would supply a prominent wholesale company in New York with hand-knit jiffy sweaters. His financial presentation was attractive, so I agreed. Jiffy sweaters had become a strong fashion item.

I placed an ad in the local paper for knitters and was promptly swamped with applicants. I knew the depression years had been difficult ones, but I hadn't realized how many women welcomed a little extra money for their families. In some cases I was shocked, for women I knew were from financially substantial homes in former years were among the applicants. We supplied the yarn and simple instructions. An experienced knitter could make a jiffy sweater in an afternoon or evening.

I have always remembered a young couple who brought in a finished sweater that was unacceptable. They obviously needed the small cash we paid and seemed concerned about my accepting the sweater. I spent a little time apparently examining it, but really thinking about them. The sweater was of no use to us. It would have to be ripped out. So what, I thought, and paid the young woman the regular amount. Their happiness was satisfaction enough. Fortunately, they never came back.

We did a brisk business for several years. I recognized some of our sweaters in advertisements of major department stores in New York, Boston, Philadelphia and elsewhere. Eventually all good things come to an end. The International Garment Workers' Union of New York, disturbed that hand knitting was affecting their manufacturing, worked for the establishment of laws to prevent hand knitting in the home commercially. All yarn shops like ours were out of business in that field. I was sorry, not for our business, but for the hundred or so women who were being denied a little extra income for their families. I continued the yarn shop for a while, but I had lost interest in it. My father's failing health reminded me that I was needed in the family business.

The 1937 Pageant proved to be a remarkable year in many ways. It was a year of "growing pains." John Hollinger resigned as General chairman. Atlantic City considered adopting the project, but decided a politically directed Pageant would be unwise. The Chamber of Commerce discussed handling the event, but vetoed the idea. The Beachfront Hotel Association voted to lend its support only if the Showman's Variety Jubilee continued with its project.

On April 21, 1937, Mayor Charles D. White called a meeting of one hundred representative citizens "to discuss and decide whether the Pageant was an institution in Atlantic City which should be continued." Despite a downpour of rain, ninety-eight invited citizens met to make this important decision. The manner in which the Pageant was being operated, and the value of the publicity to the city were discussed. The Citizens Committee unanimously agreed that the Pageant must continue and under the same management.

John R. Hollinger presented a sound plan, which included the appointment by the mayor of

> 1. A board of governors composed of four members of the Variety Club of Philadelphia, four citizens of Atlantic City, and a representative of city government; the mayor to serve as honorary chairman;
> 2. An executive board, representing each beachfront hotel, eight leading avenue hotels and the presidents of important service, civic and fraternal organizations;
> 3. A finance committee of successful businessmen;
> 4. A general committee of carefully selected citizens.

While the mayor should appoint members of all committees keeping their prestige in mind, their duties should be cleared through the board of governors.

The citizens committee unanimously agreed and adopted the recommended program. John R. Hollinger was drafted again to serve as general chairman. Headlines in the *Atlantic City Press* the next day praised the Pageant's fortitude in overcoming the crisis.

Mrs. Charles D. White accepted the board's invitation to serve as chairman of the new hostess committee to supervise all of the contestants' activities and accompany them to all Pageant events. Thus was laid the foundation for the organization of similar groups of volunteer women all over the country in local and state Pageants.

When Lenora Slaughter arrived in Atlantic City in 1935, she realized that something had to be done to control the activities of contestants while they were in attendance. They had to be kept out of bars, saloons and gambling halls. They had to be unable to date any man, known or unknown, who asked for a date. They had to live a sedate, regulated, chaperoned life from the time they arrived in Atlantic City until they left.

In order to organize a chaperon committee, Lenora had turned to Mrs. Charles D. White, whose husband was not only mayor, but more importantly an owner of the famous Marlborough-Blenheim Hotel on the Boardwalk. The hotel catered to an exclusive clientele, people famous in the business world, society leaders of metropolitan cities and celebrities of distinction. A devout worker, Mrs. White was a fine lady in every sense of the word, highly respected, of impeccable reputation and gracious charm.

Mrs. White had agreed to serve as chairman of the hostess committee only under certain conditions: that she could

1. Establish the rules governing the conduct of contestants;
2. Select the women who would form the committee;
3. Be free from any political influence or any other influence from the Pageant.

In a nutshell, the committee originated as a reasonably autonomous committee, a precedent continued to this present time. Lenora readily agreed, happy to have a woman of Mrs. White's social stature in the community as a co-associate in the Pageant organization. Mrs. White chose as the first hostesses the wives and daughters of the area's most prestigious hotel, business and professional men, a policy that remained intact for many years.

Lenora had been influenced by the poor reputation the Pageant had received in the past. She had also been disturbed that the New Jersey State Federation of Women's Clubs, the largest organization of women in the state, had passed a resolution during a convention in 1927 condemning the Pageant for its scandalous operation. When I became a hostess in later years, she often spoke to me about it. She knew I was a state officer of the Federation.

The story was a simple one. The husband of a club woman up state had become too friendly with a contestant. Intensely angry, the wife had persuaded her women's club to present a resolution to the state organization condemning the Pageant. The resolution, unanimously approved by convention delegates, remained a policy for many years.

Nineteen thirty-seven also inaugurated the establishment of the Miss Atlantic City Pageant under the chairmanship of Isora B. Somers (Mrs. Warren Somers), a prominent resort club woman. Civic, service and social clubs were invited to nominate candidates for Miss Atlantic City to be the official hostess to Pageant contestants.

George D. Tyson returned to the city to organize state Pageants. Hundreds of local civic leaders were now involved in the planning and successful completion of Pageant events, which had finally won community approval. The Boardwalk parade became the big outdoor attraction. The beautiful Miss America Ball was held in the Ballroom of Convention Hall. Morris Guardsmen had served as official escorts for contestants for a few years. Atlantic City bachelors furnished the necessary transportation for contestants, hostesses and chaperons. Seats were now provided on Steel Pier for parents and important dignitaries. Others stood during the competition, as in the past.

New rules were inaugurated, including the point system for judging five contestants from each of the three divisions and preliminaries who were selected to compete in the final competition. At the request of the hostess committee, contestants would no longer be permitted to visit nightclubs, bars, inns, taverns and any places where liquor would be served. Curfew was called for 1 a.m.

Twenty-eight states were represented this year with forty-nine contestants seeking the crown. An enthusiastic audience packed the ballroom of Steel Pier and cheered the decision of the judges. Sixteen-year-old Elizabeth "Bette" Cooper, Miss Bertrand Island, New Jersey, was crowned Miss America 1937.

The biggest publicity story in Pageant history occurred the next morning when newsmen and photographers gathered for the traditional pictures re-enacting the coronation. The throne was empty. Nowhere was Miss America to be found. She had simply disappeared.

Betty Cooper has probably been the most-remembered Miss America of all queens who have won the title, at least by the news media. She was a top student, active in athletics, and was attending Centenary Collegiate Institute, now known as Centenary College, as a Junior.

A quiet, conservative family, the Coopers had been reluctant to allow Bette to enter the Miss America competition. She had won the title of Miss Bertrand Island on a dare when she had attended a fair near Lake Hopatcong. Finally the family decided a week in Atlantic City would be a good vacation for them all.

This was not a good year for the name and reputation of Atlantic City. A wide-open town for years, federal law enforcement authorities had descended en masse upon the city, closing up houses of prostitution, gambling and unlawful businesses. The sins of Atlantic City became front-page headlines all over the country.

One of the prominent young bachelors assigned to chauffeur Miss Bertrand Island was Lou Off, son of Frank Off, owner of the Brighton Hotel, an orchid farm in Linwood, and also a city commissioner. Lou Off had a car and a biplane. He was also known as a handsome, steady, responsible young man of excellent character.

When Miss America could not be found by police and state police searching all over the state, rumors began to fly of a possible romance between Bette and Lou Off. Lenora thought that Bette, only sixteen, had developed a crush on Lou who had sent her orchids every day and entertained her 'round about town. Some thought her parents had simply thought it best for Bette to return to school. Whatever the reason, it was many years before Lou Off broke the silence.

In a featured article in *The Press of Atlantic City*, Off told the story. Aside from being chauffeur for Bette, his privileges and duties had included dancing every night with her on Steel Pier, sending her orchids from his father's nursery and a luncheon date at Harry's Restaurant in Somers Point on the day of final competition.

Bette had done well in competition all week. She had sung "When the Poppies Bloom Again" in the talent contest and had won the evening gown competition the following night.

During the luncheon at Harry's, Off asked Bette what she was going to do if she won the title that night. Bette replied that there was no chance of her winning. It wasn't possible. Off told Bette that if she won, he had no intention of becoming Mr. America and was not going to follow her around the country on her coat tails. Bette seemed affected by that decision.

As Off had predicted, Bette was crowned that night by the outgoing Miss America, Rose Coyle. About 2 a.m., following the crowning, Bette telephoned Off in tears, protesting her unwillingness to become Miss America. Off decided to help her. He telephoned two of his friends, George and Robert Pennington, who helped Off smuggle Bette out of her room down a fire escape and took her to Margate where Off's boat was tied up. They drove out into the ocean and dropped anchor off the end of Steel Pier deciding no one could search the ocean very well, the safest place to be.

Bette was exhausted. She had been suffering from a heavy cold and had not been feeling well. She slept soundly below deck while Off and his friends fished, watching the commotion on the pier. Angry photographers, dismayed Pageant officials and a paying public anxiously awaited Miss America's public appearance.

Meanwhile, it was first thought that Off and Bette had eloped. Bette's father believed Off was an awfully nice young man and Bette's first fancy. Lenora described Bette as "pretty as a picture with her blonde hair and dimples."

Before sunset the boat returned to shore and the young men drove Bette to her home in Hackettstown in North Jersey. They heard a radio announcement by Walter Winchell that Bette and Lou had been secretly married; it was one of the few times the prominent radio commentator was wrong. A few days later Miss

America accepted her trophy and the $1,000 fur coat that was her Grand Prize. She returned to school.

Pageant historians have claimed that Bette was the only Miss America to refuse her title. That apparently wasn't true. Off said that her father trusted him to take care of her, adding that he often slept on the floor outside her hotel room for her protection during public appearances. He also said there was no "hanky panky" between them although they cared for each other for some time. Theirs was a comfortable relationship.

Their association continued for about three years until Off enlisted as a navy pilot in World War II and she took a job in Kentucky. Their last meeting was in 1952 when Bette and her successful stockbroker husband visited Off and his wife.

Off believes she found the life she wanted, probably looking back on the Pageant as an objectionable thing. He was sorry to see her so distressed at the time when she should have been so happy.

Lou Off has run the well-known Brighton Orchid Farm in Linwood across the meadows from Atlantic City for many years.

Two people of celebrity status visited the Pageant in 1937: Mrs. Nellie Ross, who was the first woman governor in the country, and Rudy Vallée, the popular and famous crooner.

Chapter 13

An empty throne did not discourage future Pageant planning. A week after the 1937 national finals, the board of governors and chairmen of committees met to improve their program and correct their mistakes.

The financial outlook was excellent. All bills had been paid and all charity contributions made. Funds were available to start organizing state and local Pageants immediately, instead of waiting three months before the national finals. Better sponsors could be secured and more time devoted to local competitions. Everyone agreed that the coordinated efforts of its citizens fostered a successful civic promotion. In three months the resort had received an estimated 670 pages of publicity in 1900 dailies; that represented $482,400 in free publicity. And this before inflation.

Under Lenora Slaughter's guidance, radical changes in rules governing contestants were inaugurated. The Pageant became a manless week for contestants. Taxis only were to be used for transportation. Talent must be performed by all contestants who competed in the finals. Contestants must compete under the title of a state, key city or a geographical division of a state. Amusement park or commercial firm titles were taboo. A contestant's age must be between 18 and 28 on opening day of the Pageant. Birth certificates were required. Contestants were limited to single girls who had never been married, divorced or had their marriage annulled.

Not only were the rules governing contestants tightened, but state and key contest sponsors were more thoroughly investigated. Legitimate theaters or business organizations were approved.

Private promoters were discouraged. George Tyson was instructed to endeavor to secure state representation and to accept key city representation only when a state Pageant could not be organized.

Mayor White reappointed all former members of the board, and increased membership from seven to nine, adding Paul J. O'Neill Sr., chairman of the executive committee, and Hugh Riddle, president of the Chamber of Commerce.

Earle W. Sweigert, of the Philadelphia Variety Club, recommended that the Pageant be staged in Convention Hall. Sufficient seats would then be available to accommodate the patrons. The proposed changes were studied, but the board ruled to continue the Pageant on Steel Pier. More seats were to be made available for important personages.

Financial offers poured into Pageant headquarters for promotional tie-ins, including dance marathons, Junior Miss and Mr. America competitions. The board declined all and steadfastly concentrated on improving the Miss America competition.

A real effort was made to secure more valuable prizes. The grand prize for Miss America continued to be an all-expense trip to Hollywood and a screen test, but a $500 tweed wardrobe was added. Ned Weyburn offered the runner-up a $1,500 scholarship to his School of Dance in New York.

The contests across the country showed considerable improvement. Thirty-one states with 41 contestants were represented at the national finals.

The Pageant week program of 1938 began in Philadelphia on Labor Day with entertainment provided by the Variety Club. Contestants arrived on Tuesday morning in Atlantic City on the Pennsylvania Railroad. The train made its customary stop in Absecon to take on the women of the hostess committee who would chaperone them during the week.

After welcoming ceremonies on Steel Pier, the Variety Club luncheon was held. A fur fashion show was staged in the evening in a theater on Steel Pier. This provided a special event where the audience could be seated. Wednesday's program included the Rotary Club luncheon and the first preliminary that night. Thursday an Exchange Club luncheon was inaugurated where each contestant was presented with a sterling silver compact. A nautical parade followed in the afternoon and the second preliminary at night. Friday was the big Boardwalk parade, with the last preliminary that night.

On Saturday morning a private beach party was given for the contestants. The Steel Pier ballroom was packed to capacity in the evening when the fifteen finalists, selected from the preliminaries, competed for the title. Emphasis on talent had proved most popular. A lovely young dancing school instructor, Marilyn Meseke from Marion, Ohio, captured the Miss America 1938 crown.

Showman Earl Carroll, famous for his Vanities stage shows, had arrived during the performance and protested his displeasure with the judges' decision. He insisted that Miss California should have been the judges' choice. He announced to the press that he would personally crown her at Broadway and 42nd Street in New York City the following Monday. Pageant officials merely shrugged their shoulders and began planning the 1939 event. They had again achieved a balanced budget of $27,000.

Earl Carroll had been annoyed that he had not been invited to be a judge. He was reported to have sent letters to a few top contenders offering them a contract. Miss California, Claire James, had signed the contract. Claire had won the evening gown competition but did not do well dancing in the talent competition.

Miss California went to New York with Carroll on Sunday morning where she was duly crowned Miss America the next day. In later years she claimed to be a former Miss America. Once she represented herself to a TV producer as such. But she chose the wrong producer, Harry Koplan, who was married to Rosemary LaPlanche, Miss America 1941.

She wasn't the first non-Pageant winner who had claimed the title Miss America. In August 1935 a Miss America had been crowned by two men who ran a midget and nudist concession at fairs. Since the title "Miss America" was not copyrighted until

1950, there was nothing the Pageant could do about it. San Diego's Miss America had won as her prize the right to pose in the nude for two years.

The year 1939 proved to be a turning point in Pageant history. Two new members were added to the board: Ed Curtis, manager of the local telephone company, who had been chairman of the judges' committee for three years; and J. Howard Buzby, vice president of the Dennis Hotel. Buzby, a member of the Atlantic City auditorium commission, prepared an excellent artist's conception of the Pageant staged in Convention Hall. This idea caught the interest of more than 500 civic leaders now serving on pageant committees. The resort adopted the slogan, "On to Convention Hall."

On April 12th, 1939, Mayor White called the board of governors to a meeting in his offices. A proposed plan and budget for operating the Pageant in Convention Hall was presented by Howard Buzby and Arthur Chenoweth. It was the consensus of the board that the Pageant was now sufficiently strong to make the change to Convention Hall. Frank Gravatt, originator of the renewed Pageant, presented his plan. He requested that the Pageant be staged one more year on the Pier, while all Atlantic City worked together to build an even stronger foundation. He pointed out more time was needed to prepare a Pageant for Convention Hall. He promised to support the Pageant with the same enthusiasm and finances that he had given during its five years on Steel Pier. Everyone agreed that with eighteen more months for planning and financing, the move to Convention Hall had a greater chance for success. The board of governors unanimously passed a resolution to hold the 1939 Pageant on Steel Pier and the 1940 Pageant in Convention Hall. As a result everyone worked long and diligently and succeeded in staging the most successful Pageant to date.

The year 1939 was special for me as well. John and I were blessed with the birth of our son Robert, who along with our daughter, made our family complete. I was happy to have produced a son, for my daughter had been the first girl in the Alton family for a couple of generations. Both children, in their youth and in their maturity, have richly filled our lives with much love and have given us two fine grandchildren.

⁂

During this year Sally Rand was a popular fan dancer. Whether she danced nude under her large, feathered fans was an object of speculation. I saw her dance here in Atlantic City and couldn't really tell. I suspect she wore a nude body stocking. For a while she danced under the title Miss America at the Golden Gate Exposition in San Francisco. The Pageant strongly objected. Sally Rand finally dropped the title.

This year, also, the development of western state pageants was inaugurated. Miss Atlantic City flew to the San Francisco Exposition to meet contestants from Montana, California, Idaho and Washington to escort them back East.

A change in preliminary competition was made. One third of contestants competed in evening gown, one third in swimsuit and one third in talent in each preliminary, which gave the girls more time for talent rehearsals.

The Variety Club luncheon was changed to a beautiful banquet. Rudy Vallée served as emcee with many important celebrities present.

Miss America received a cash prize for the first time when a hat company agreed to pay her $2,000 for endorsing its products. The screen test in Hollywood was replaced by a voice and screen test in New York for both Miss America and the first runner-up. The Ned Weyburn Dancing School scholarship was again offered.

Contestants appeared in decorated rolling chairs in the Boardwalk parade instead of private cars, which was popular with the on-lookers. On the final night at Steel Pier the reserved seats available for important people were filled with celebrities. The hostess committee, seated in a group, formed a glittering picture in their magnificent ball gowns, worn at the request of the chairman, Mrs. White.

A tall, graceful brunette from Detroit, Michigan, captured the hearts of the audience and the judges as she appeared on the runway in evening gown and swimsuit competition. In the talent division of the Pageant she was to steal the show with her stylized singing of "Man Mose is Dead" while playing the bass fiddle. The audience roared its approval as the crown of Miss America 1939 was placed on the head of Pat Donnelly, Miss Michigan.

The audience also sang "Auld Lang Syne" as the curtain went down on the last of the Pageants to be held on the word famous Steel Pier.

Chapter 14
The 1940s

The 1940s proved to be a decade of unusual events, new growth and development, new governing board procedures, and new rules and regulations. The first membership meeting of the Showman's Variety Jubilee was held in 1940. Civic and sustaining members were elected to represent the corporation. Bylaws were adopted establishing proper procedures for electing future boards of directors and Pageant officers. Hereafter, the board would consist of eighteen members, fifteen from Atlantic City and three from the Philadelphia Variety Club. Atlantic City members were to serve three years, one third of the membership being re-elected or replaced at each annual meeting. Variety Club members were to be appointed by that organization. Officers of the Pageant were to be elected by the board, which would also appoint all Pageant committees.

At the first board meeting, Bennett Tousley was elected president, Joseph Wagenheim and J. Howard Buzby, vice presidents. Through drawing of names, the members who were to serve one, two, and three years were determined. Buzby was named producer of events in Convention Hall, and George D. Tyson executive director. Thus were established the parliamentary procedures, most of which have lasted through the years.

The finance committee, headed by Joseph Wagenheim, performed miracles in advance sale of tickets. Box seats were sold by a special committee of local socialites. No free tickets for the board of directors, committees, or any Pageant supporters were given, a policy still in effect today. The city of Atlantic City loaned the Pageant $10,000 with the understanding that it would be repaid at the end of the Pageant.

The advertising committee, composed of some of the largest advertising agencies in this section of the country, assumed the responsibility of advertising the Pageant through billboards, posters, window cards, heralds, newsreel trailers, restaurant menus and newspapers. Much of the advertising was secured gratis or at cost.

The program of events committee, headed by Harry Godshall, inaugurated many new attractions, including a baby parade, navy maneuvers, Mardi Gras, fireworks, mummers frolic and a public dance in Convention Hall ballroom. Public events were planned to please tourists.

The Miss America sorority, Mu Alpha Sigma, was organized by Lenora. All national contestants from 1935 became charter members. Each new Miss America would serve as president, Miss Congeniality as vice president, Miss Atlantic City as secretary. Rosemary Corcoran, daughter of the Pageant founder, Eddie Corcoran, designed the beautiful sorority pin.

The contestants arrived in Atlantic City on Labor Day for the first time. The parade was changed to Tuesday, with each contestant riding on her own beautifully decorated float. An official Pageant program book was published for the first time. A Variety Club banquet, Rotary and Exchange Club luncheons, and a private beach party gave contestants an opportunity to relax.

Finally the longest anticipated moment in Pageant history arrived with the largest number of patrons ever to attend a Miss America competition seated in the main auditorium of Convention Hall. The huge curtains of the great stage opened to reveal a veritable fairyland of beautiful flowers while lovely girls came into view. The audience expressed enthusiastic approval by their thunderous applause as the show opened with the "Parade of States" down the 110-foot runway. Forty-six contestants from 30 states and the District of Columbia made their first formal appearance in Convention Hall.

Pageant audiences grew each night until Saturday night's final performance when a sell-out crowd filled the gigantic auditorium, a tradition which has continued throughout the years. Lovely Frances Burke of Philadelphia was crowned Miss America 1940.

When the second annual membership meeting was called on December 9, the board of directors reported that the $45,000 budget had been met and the city of Atlantic City repaid for its $10,000 loan, as well as charitable contributions made. There was still a balance in the bank of $3,373.22 to start the 1941 Pageant program.

Through my family and various civic activities, I came to meet or to know personally almost all of the local members of the board of directors. Arthur Chenoweth had been my Latin teacher in Atlantic City High School before he became the superintendent of schools and a Pageant official.

Local and state contest promotions were given top scrutiny in 1941. Emphasis was placed on issuing franchises only to responsible sponsors who would direct dignified pageants worthy of association with the national event. George Tyson had been named managing director of Ice Capades. In his travels to every state, he would have a better opportunity to interview personally the promoters and amusement men directing state and local competitions.

The Pageant's operating budget was raised to $53,000. Atlantic City again loaned $10,000 to the board for advance operating expenses, with the understanding that it would be repaid after the Pageant.

Rules for judging the national competition were changed. The panel of judges was limited to a minimum of nine and a maximum of eleven. National judges would be required to be present at all three preliminary competitions as well as the finals. A special breakfast meeting was arranged for judges and contestants so that the five finalists would no longer be interviewed in the judges' box during the actual competition.

Arrangements were made for Miss America to receive $1,000 for endorsing a swimsuit and a soap manufacturer's product.

Requests for personal appearances at theaters, fairs and nightclubs began coming in advance to the Pageant office. Miss America was thus assured an income. Motion picture executives sent their scouts to the resort. National advertisers sent portable radios and wristwatches to each of the contestants.

Once again, the Pageant was a happy, exciting time for Atlantic City visitors. Plans had been made to both lure visitors to the resort and entertain them with parades, Mardi Gras, fireworks, civic luncheons and the Variety Club banquet. All had capacity attendances. Every night, enthusiastic audiences poured into Convention Hall to watch the 43 lovely contestants from 32 states compete for the Miss America title. On the final evening, glamorous Rosemary LaPlanche, Miss California, captured the title in her second year of competition on the national level. She had been first runner-up the previous year.

Rosemary was only fifteen when she first entered pageant competitions. She had won baby contests and others throughout the years, having won 30 by the time she became Miss America. She had been well endowed physically, although her measurements were similar to others at five foot five-and-one-half inches tall, weighing 120 pounds with a measurement listing of 34-24-36. Nevertheless, she was strongly accused of having padded her swimsuit. The controversy became so unpleasant that hostesses took her aside to check. They reported back that Rosemary was all girl.

She had a successful movie career, including films with famous Fatty Arbuckle and other prominent stars, making 84 films for RKO. Surprisingly, Rosemary became nationally famous as a portrait artist in oils. She married Harry Koplan, a TV and movie producer.

At the conclusion of the Pageant, the board met once again to consider its financial status. The budget was balanced, the city loan repaid, contributions to charity made, and a working capital of $9,298.03 was in the bank to start the next year.

The months of October and November were spent studying both the praise and criticism of the 1941 Pageant. The bylaws were amended to change the name of the corporation from Showman's

Variety Jubilee to the Miss America Pageant, a suggestion made the previous year by Nick Carter, a representative of the press club. The change was welcomed with warm approval all over the country.

The system of judging used at the national finals would be required by local and state pageants in the future. A new rule was established. A former contestant who had competed once in Atlantic City for the title would not be permitted to return to competition a second time. The rule did not affect contestants competing a second time at local and state pageants.

A full-time pageant director was needed to concentrate on developing better local and state pageants. Lenora S. Slaughter was named executive director to replace George Tyson who had to resign because of his Ice Capades commitments. She was given authority to change state pageant franchise holders to civic and service organizations when expedient. J. Howard Buzby was elected president.

On December 7, 1941, the Japanese attacked Pearl Harbor and our nation went to war. One of my brothers was in Pearl Harbor at the time, on a military mission for the Navy. Fortunately, he was unhurt.

The 1942 Pageant was set in a different mood and tempo from its predecessors. Keyed to a nation at war, it was presented with almost insurmountable obstacles. Much thought had been given to discontinuing the Pageant for the duration. The board of directors decided, as well as the community generally, that the Pageant was emblematic of the spirit of America, a spirit that continued through war and peace, good and bad.

In 1942, I was worthy district deputy of the Eastern Star, a state office requiring supervision over eleven chapters in Atlantic County and nearby Cape May County. Aside from frequent visits to those chapters, I was also required to make an official visit. An especially poignant moment arrived one night when I was officially visiting Keystone Chapter in the Linwood Masonic Temple. I was in the process of making a speech to the members and visitors when the air raid sirens sounded and suddenly the lights all went out. It is quite an experience for anyone to be in a room without windows in absolute darkness, unable to see even one's hand before one's face.

Everyone sat perfectly still while I had to adjust my remarks in order to keep their attention and be in control of the situation. It was quite an experience to speak to people I couldn't see. I couldn't judge their reactions to my speech and I couldn't know whether or not I was receiving a favorable response. In a few minutes, the lights came back on and the applause when I finished was generous. All had ended well.

There was gasoline and food rationing in 1942. My father had given me power of attorney to collect rents and pay bills because of his failing health. Our attorney had determined that I was performing real estate business and needed a real estate license. He tutored me in some of the law. I passed the broker's license test, which allowed me a few more gasoline coupons as a business needed more than the average amount. The extra coupons proved helpful in my travels to Eastern Star chapters. In addition, the men of the chapters used to provide me with extra coupons occasionally. As usual, there was black market gasoline available from certain stations, although I didn't patronize them.

There were also certain food shortages because of the large amount of food being shipped overseas. We were given ration books for butter, meat and other items. Diabetics were allowed an extra ration.

Soldiers could now be seen everywhere in town on their training maneuvers. I remember being surprised to find soldiers running down my street in Ventnor, rushing up driveways and alleys and, as at our home, over the back fence to the next street. The former Haddon Hall Hotel became England General Hospital where the war wounded were returned home for treatment. Many local women volunteered to push wounded men in wheel chairs on the Boardwalk and help cheer up the bedridden in the hospital.

The soldiers were also a strong economic stimulant to the local economy, particularly to the bars and taverns of the area.

I've forgotten why my father had acquired a popular bar on a corner of Atlantic Avenue located in a property he owned. My hazy recollection seems to be that the former owner was in trouble with the law and wanted to leave town, sacrificing the bar. Because of a purely business decision my father had made, I became involved in managing the business end of a jumping, jiving bar. Father kept a check on the bar manager.

In retrospect, it was a pretty funny situation. I have been a lifelong teetotaler. Psychologists would say that I had been conditioned by a most difficult, traumatic experience as a very small child. Unexpectedly, I had been a witness to a horrible situation, for my young mind, involving an irrational drunk. I never really forgot it and subconsciously, at least, could not touch alcoholic drinks. What I've tasted I haven't really liked much anyway.

So there I was, buying liquor for a bar open 24 hours, filled with soldiers, day and night. I didn't know one brand of liquor from another. Because I refused to walk in the front door of the bar and walk back to the stockroom, I had a door built at the far end of the building so I could enter unseen from the driveway. This way I could control the liquor inventory, check on the cash register receipts, and pay obligatory taxes.

Dealing with liquor salesmen became an early problem, especially when whiskey was being rationed because of the war. One couldn't run such a busy bar without hard liquor. My ignorance was helped a little by advice from my husband as far as brands were concerned. One day a liquor salesman, who was a Masonic friend of my father's, sat down with me and began teaching me the intricacies of buying liquor. It was not a simple system then, complicated by war and rationing.

My youngest brother, Charles, had sailed from New York on the Queen Mary, then a troopship, during this period. He had landed with allied troops in the first invasion of Africa, planned to overcome Rommel's German troops. I've always remembered the date of that October 1942 invasion, for I was presiding over a district meeting of our eleven Eastern Star chapters in our Masonic

Temple. The stage backdrop was a large hand-painted aeroplane landing, in simulation, on our stage. The word of the successful landing in Africa had reached us during that meeting and was especially meaningful to us all.

Atlantic City played host to the men of the Air Force on their way to the battlefront and at the same time to the beautiful women of America who would one day welcome them back home.

The Convention Hall auditorium, where nearly 25,000 visitors had watched the 1941 Pageant, was taken over by the Air Force for military training. The most beautiful, ornate theater on the Boardwalk, the Warner Theater, with a seating capacity of 4,185, became the Pageant's wartime home. Originally built by Warren Weilland, who was a Pageant board member for many years, the theater had been designed for the legitimate stage and for Broadway shows being tried out in Atlantic City before opening on Broadway in New York.

The Pageant budget was cut to $17,500. No longer would business interests be solicited for subscriptions. Instead the Pageant relied solely upon the sale of tickets to events to meet the budget. Atlantic City loaned the Pageant $5,000 to carry on its work until revenue from ticket sales would be available.

The famous Boardwalk, where glittering floats, bands, and contestants had paraded so happily in former years, was now the scene of thousands of marching men. The parade had to be canceled.

The lights of Atlantic City were now dim and at times completely dark when air raid sirens sounded periodically. The fabulous hotels, which had housed contestants in the past, now housed a great army of flyers and technicians of the Air Force. All of the contestants were now housed in one available hotel, the Morton Hotel, on South Virginia Avenue. Ezra Bell, hotel owner, made a lasting contribution to Pageant history.

The Pageant presented a picture of hope to the fighting men stationed in Atlantic City. Fifteen hundred men joined enthusiastically in the song "Deep in the Heart of Texas" as Jo-Carroll

Dennison, Miss Texas, sang and danced her way into their hearts as well as the hearts of the judges to become Miss America 1942.

Twenty-nine contestants from 24 states, along with Miss America, carried a message of hope all over the country. They served our military men in camps, hospitals, defense factories, USO clubs and Red Cross canteens, and wore the uniforms of women in the armed services.

Some of the board members resigned to perform necessary war services. New local business leaders came to the Pageant's board assuming many needed responsibilities. For the first time in the new Pageant's history, a deficit of $5,312.29 was faced. The city of Atlantic City canceled its debt by an exchange of checks for repayment of the loan and authorized a donation of $5,000 to the Pageant to continue in 1943.

This war year also brought to an end the many civic activities that had been a part of the Pageant from its beginning, limiting public events to the competition itself. Only the Around the Island Swim has remained during the succeeding Pageant years.

Again, the Pageant considered canceling the 1943 Pageant for the duration of the war. Protests poured in from local and state pageant organizations that were already working closely with the war effort in their own locales. Business firms booking Miss America for personal appearances, or using her endorsements in advertising, joined the protest. The War Finance Department in Washington advised that such activities were approved, provided they did not conflict with the war program. Pageant officials were commended for the war contributions the contestants were making by their sales of war bonds and their appearances at service camps and hospitals.

Financing the Pageant was a difficult problem calling for master planning. It had to stand on its own merit and the sale of tickets for events in the Warner Theater. The board deliberated over facts and figures. Then promoters in Madison Square Garden, New York City, indicated they were planning to take over if Atlantic City gave up the event. A decision was quickly reached.

"The show must go on." Never again has canceling the Pageant been considered.

Howard Buzby resigned as president to serve as chairman of production. His valuable artistic talents were most needed in producing a beautiful stage show at a minimum cost. Harry Godshall, whose experience with the Pageant dated back to the first one in 1921, became president.

Mrs. Charles D. White, chairman of the hostess committee, resigned. Her co-chairman, Mrs. Malcom Shermer, was named chairman. Mrs. White received much admiration and praise for her important services in protecting the image of the Pageant. Continued support was pledged for the committee she had organized.

A booster committee was formed in the city. Hugh L. Wathen, advertising and promotion manager of the South Jersey Gas Company, became chairman. Under his leadership, civic and service clubs joined in a summer-long campaign of ticket sales so that a budget of $22,500 could be met. Wathen was elected to the board of directors to replace Fisher White who had resigned to become an officer in the Navy.

Lever Brothers offered the Pageant $5,000 to aid in meeting the budget if Miss America 1943, accompanied by Pageant executive director Lenora Slaughter, could go on a nationwide War Bond tour. Miss America would receive a fee of $2,500 and would work in cooperation with local War Finance committees. The offer was accepted. While selling bonds for Uncle Sam, Miss America could be presented to the nation under proper Pageant supervision by Lenora Slaughter.

When Pageant Week arrived, 33 lovely contestants from 27 states cheerfully accepted whatever inconveniences had become necessary. Miss Cincinnati, Joan Hyldoft, later to become a great ice skating star, refused to be dismayed when her mock ice rink was ruined. Instead, she skated on a wooden floor to the delight of her audience. Similar improvisations were necessary throughout the week. The show provided the relief so needed during those difficult times of stress and sorrow.

The panel of judges had selected a beautiful and talented lyric soprano, Jean Bartel, Miss Los Angeles, to be Miss America 1943. This charming and poised member of Kappa Kappa Gamma sorority on the campus of the University of California at Los Angeles (UCLA) was destined to change the pattern of future Miss America Pageants, the first step toward becoming the renowned Pageant of today.

Jean Bartel unselfishly gave up the opportunity to profit financially from public appearances by being the first traveling Miss America, touring the country from coast to coast in an effort to sell war bonds in a patriotic zeal. Accompanied by Lenora Slaughter, she made 469 appearances during her year, many of them entertaining service men, visiting soldiers' hospitals and visiting workers in war industries. She is the one who established the concept of the traveling, public-speaking Miss America that we see and know today.

The three-month War Bond tour included appearances in 53 key cities from the east to the west coast. Millions of dollars of Series E war bonds were sold. Hundreds of service camps and hospitals were visited. Thousands of service men and women were entertained by this gifted artist who sang her way into their hearts.

During her War Bond tour with Lenora, she sold 2.5 million dollars of bonds in 100 appearances, more than any other person in the country. She is also reported to have done espionage work for the CIA in Lebanon on the side.

During her busy year for the war effort, Kappa Kappa Gamma sororities in various colleges and universities invited Jean Bartel to visit. In one of these visits, Lenora Slaughter learned the answer to a proper Pageant award for Miss America. Student leaders voiced their approval of a competition embodying beauty, brains and talent. They had also voiced a strong desire to have an opportunity for higher education in the form of scholarships. That's how the Miss America scholarship program was developed by Lenora Slaughter, a dream of inestimable value to young women of our country.

The idea and plans required another year to prepare and execute. Meanwhile, Jean Bartel went on to an outstanding musical career on Broadway. She had the lead in a number of popular productions: *Of Thee I Sing, The Desert Song, The Merry Widow*, and *Vagabond King*. She also sang in smart supper clubs in Brazil, Paris, London and the Middle East. In later years, she developed her own international travel business and became international chairman for the Television Academy, Hollywood Chapter.

Like Jean Bartel, many of our Miss Americas have been exceptional young women: beautiful, brainy and talented. Have they been exploited, as some women's organizations like to claim? I firmly believe otherwise. These are fine young women whose ideals, goals, and purpose in life have been richly fulfilled by the opportunities provided to them through Pageant guidance, direction and scholarships. In my experience, all of them have been thankful for the experiences and for the opportunities they have had.

A working capital of $10,211.40 was available for the 1944 Pageant. Nationwide good will toward the Pageant was much more evident as improved state pageants were being developed by Lenora. Anxious to have local civic and state sponsors that were both respect-worthy and important, she secured the acceptance of the North Carolina Junior Chamber of Commerce to sponsor the Miss North Carolina Pageant. She was establishing a pattern so that Jaycees across the country might undertake a similar project in their home states. Two months later, the Texas Jaycees accepted the same challenge, eventually followed by the Georgia Jaycees. Other Jaycee organizations soon followed.

Lenora has always given credit to the Junior Chamber of Commerce, known as the Jaycees, for saving the Pageant when their organizations became local and state sponsors. Their prestige and responsible business organizations gave stature to their sponsored pageants, encouraging fine young women to compete. Previously, sponsors had been state fairs, theaters, even a boxing firm in Delaware.

Lenora advised the Jaycees to talk with parents and tell them about the scholarship program before even approaching girls to become contestants. Both parents and the public needed to know that the Pageant was "morally sound." She says she "owes the Jaycees a debt of gratitude, for more than anyone they helped build the Pageant" by selecting the type of contestant they would be proud to sponsor.

Lenora believed it was important to build a good reputation for the Pageant with big business. She worked constantly to secure respect for Miss America, booking her in better places and always traveling first class befitting a fine lady. She never allowed Miss America to smoke in public, nor contestants at the Pageant.

During these war years, the roles of women in the workplace had been undergoing significant change. Of necessity, women had been assuming more and more positions formerly held by men fighting overseas. Positions in manufacturing, the construction industry, and in ship building had been filled, among others. I especially remember the Philadelphia and Navy shipyards where a female friend of our family worked, riveting in the construction of a large ship. "Rosie the Riveter" became a publicly-touted name to describe women doing men's work in the shipyards.

When soldiers began coming home after the war to resume their means of livelihood, they found many of their jobs had been filled by women who were either reluctant to, or simply refused to surrender them to the men who had formerly filled those positions. Some of those men had been promised their jobs back on their return. It became a difficult economic issue for several years as women fought to retain their economic gains.

Two important events were instrumental in the future growth of the Miss America Pageant. One week after the finals, a hurricane struck our shores, creating tremendous damage to our city. The hurricane of 1944 was an unforgettable experience. We didn't have hurricane warnings in those days. We native residents of long standing had experienced many damaging storms to our shore areas, but nothing like this. I have lived all my married life in Ventnor

City in a four-story, well-built house located about halfway between the ocean and the bay. The island is only three blocks wide here in this suburban community adjacent to Atlantic City.

As the storm grew more ferocious hour by hour, the waters began rising in the streets closer and closer to our house and others. My husband, who had come home, built a protective device in front of our basement doors to keep the water out and used throw rug carpets to protect inside the doors. At the height of the storm, one of our brick chimneys collapsed with several bricks crashing through a window on our stairway landing. The house was shaking. The ocean and bay met not only in our neighborhood, but in the center of Atlantic City at South Carolina and Atlantic Avenues, the widest part of the island.

Powerfully high waves destroyed almost all of the Boardwalk in Margate and all of it in Longport, washed away most of Ventnor Pier and fishing piers, and damaged large areas of Atlantic City's Boardwalk and hotels. Much of the Boardwalk down-beach was never rebuilt. The approaches to the Boardwalk were washed down side streets to or near Atlantic Avenue, tearing down front stairs and damaging front porches of houses as they washed up the street.

The high ocean waves carried with them tons of beach sand which piled up into sand dunes several feet high on Atlantic Avenue in lower Ventnor, Margate and Longport. There was so much damage to houses and property—our main traffic artery blocked with sand—that the National Guard was sent in to prevent looting and to control the movements of people. When the storm finally moved up the coast, Absecon Island's communities looked like a war zone in many places.

There had been no thought of leaving the island for sanctuary inland as we have been advised in more recent years. In those days, it would have been especially difficult, for there were only two bridges in Atlantic City for crossing by more than fifty thousand people. For the substantial population of down-beach residents, there was one bridge in Ventnor, one in Margate and one in Longport. These are not sufficient exits from the ten-mile long island to accommodate people leaving the city at nearly the same time.

It was the most disastrous hurricane to strike our shores in my memory. The catastrophe pointed to the fact that a weather problem could bring financial disaster to this non-profit civic corporation. In order to meet such problems, a guarantors committee was organized to subscribe $25,000 annually toward any Pageant deficit that might be incurred. This guarantors group existed for a number of years and disbanded when the Pageant was financially protected by other sources of income.

There was another important event this year. Lenora Slaughter met W. R. MacIntyre, executive vice president and chairman of the board of the Joseph Bancroft and Sons Company. Mr. Mac, as he came to be affectionately called, became the godfather of the Pageant's scholarship program.

Lenora's dream of scholarships for Pageant contestants included a vision of a nationwide scholarship program for girls. Lenora had the ability to promote her ideas with tremendous energy and drive when she believed strongly she was right. Mr. Mac not only understood her vision, but demonstrated his faith in the Pageant and his desire to give assistance to talented American girls by being the first contributor to a scholarship fund. Other national sponsors, following Mr. Mac's lead, have helped build the largest educational scholarship in the world for girls through local, state and national finals.

W. Ralph MacIntyre was recognized internationally as one of the leaders in the textile industry. His firm was widely recognized under the trade names of "Everglaze" and "Ban Lon." Lenora has said of Mr. Mac, "The Pageant is deeply indebted to W. R. MacIntyre for his leadership in building the Miss America Scholarship Program; for his inspired use of Miss America and her gift wardrobe in the fashion markets of the world; for his leadership and support in every phase of the Pageant program. The Miss America Pageant has never had a greater friend." My personal contacts with Mr. Mac in later years revealed a caring, compassionate individual who had a sincere interest in developing educational opportunities for smart, intelligent, talented young women.

In due time, a committee of university women was appointed to establish the rules governing the scholarships and to guide the recipients in their use. Dr. Guy E. Snavely, executive director of the Association of American Colleges, agreed to serve as national counselor. Dr. Snavely had a distinguished background in higher education, the recipient of 23 honorary degrees, the George Washington Honor Medal, and the Huguenot Cross. He had been a faculty member of New York University, dean of Lafayette College, and president of Franklin and Marshall College.

One by one the beachfront hotels were being mustered out of the service. The resort was regaining some normalcy. In planning the program of events, a patriotic parade was found feasible and acceptable. Cooperation of the military stationed in Atlantic City was assured. The parade became one of the highlights of Pageant week. Resort business leaders sponsored magnificent floats, paying tribute to each branch of the armed services as well as auxiliary service organizations. Marching units of thousands of men and women in full dress uniform, stirring military bands, and the lovely Miss America contestants won much applause and cheering. Thirty-three contestants represented 27 states.

The state productions each night brought an enthusiastic audience to fill the magnificent Warner Theater. The first redhead to capture the title was beautiful Venus Ramey, Miss Washington, D.C.

Another War Bond tour for Miss America was proposed, but Venus Ramey preferred to make personal appearances in theaters and accept a motion picture contract. She would still sell war bonds, however.

At the annual membership meeting, the board announced that the budget had been met with $809.19 working capital left.

Chapter 15
The Pageant 1945–1947

The Variety Club of Philadelphia requested that the board of directors be confined to Atlantic City business leaders who could perform more actively. At the board's request, however, Earl Sweigert agreed to serve another year.

Arthur L. Chenoweth, superintendent of public schools, a former Rhodes Scholar, Oxford University graduate, and my high school Latin teacher, became president of the Pageant in 1945. He was the perfect person to head the beginning of the Pageant's scholarship program.

Before the first meeting of the board, Lenora Slaughter had submitted a written proposal to each board member recommending that Miss America be awarded a $5,000 educational scholarship. She proposed that five national advertisers be given endorsement rights to the title for a contribution of $1,000 to the scholarship fund. After her proposal had been carefully studied, the board authorized her to try to raise the money. The accent was on "try," for their approval was a reluctant decision. However, she was not permitted to raise funds locally because area business men had been asked too often. Lenora's question to the board was that if they didn't believe in scholarships, how could she interest big business?

Letters were quickly sent to a group of 269 desirable national advertisers by Lenora explaining the program and requesting contributions. By return mail, a $1,000 check arrived by Joseph Bancroft and Sons Company along with a personal note from W. R. MacIntyre congratulating the Pageant on its wisdom and foresight. A second check arrived two weeks later from Catalina,

Inc. Third to respond was the F. W. Fitch Company, followed shortly by Harvel Watch Company. The Sandy Valley Grocery Company completed the list of contributors to the first Miss America Scholarship Program.

A week prior to the Pageant, two scholarships of $1,000 and $750 were donated for the first runner-up and the most talented non-finalist.

Civic leaders in communities around the country became seriously interested in the scholarship program when new awards were announced by newspapers and over radio stations nationwide. Lenora Slaughter prepared a campaign manual showing how to organize and execute a successful civic promotion with scholarships in the offering. Many new Jaycee organizations joined the program. Three universities directed pageants. The Grace Downs School of New York joined the official family.

Forty contestants competed for the title and scholarships. Thirty-two states were represented, the largest since war had been declared.

The guarantors fund of $25,000 was subscribed by local business interests. The bylaws were changed to make guarantors voting members of the corporation.

Not many people knew it, but I was indirectly responsible for disbanding the guarantors committee. I had become a member of the board of directors in 1955. Shortly afterward, the president of the Charity League, a guarantors committee member, attended a board meeting and spoke by invitation during the meeting. She had the right to vote on board business. The Charity League president was a friend of mine that I later appointed to the hostess committee. Eventually she became the first woman president of the Pageant.

Through my presidencies of a number of diverse organizations, I was reasonably expert in writing bylaws and knowledgeable about parliamentary procedures. During the meeting, I entertained myself by thinking how easy it would be for anyone who really wanted to be president of the Pageant to be elected to that position without any difficulty. For instance, I was president of the 300-member Woman's Research Club. If I brought to an election meeting a few more club members than board members who were present, my guarantors club could have nominated and elected me president of the board. Obviously that was not my ambition, but it was possible for any person from any guarantors organization to take over governing the Pageant's board of directors, based upon the board's organizational structure and bylaws at that time.

I made the comment to a Pageant associate as a humorous possibility. The comment apparently found its way to Al Marks, then president of the board, for a short time later the bylaws were changed, eliminating guarantor organizations entirely as they were no longer needed.

⚜

But I am getting ahead of myself. I accepted Mrs. Shermer's invitation to serve as a hostess to contestants in 1945. Membership on the committee was by written invitation. The term of service was one year only. It was necessary to receive a written invitation each year. If no invitation arrived, one was no longer a hostess. No reason or explanation was ever given.

The Friday before Labor Day each year, the hostess committee was entertained at a social luncheon in a beachfront hotel. The first luncheon I attended was at Haddon Hall Hotel. Most of the women I had known for some time. The few I didn't know were particularly friendly, so that I felt quite comfortable in the company of women who were considered the socially elite.

In accordance with the standards set by Mrs. White, I suppose I was eligible to join that august committee. Ours was one of the early families to reside in Atlantic City. My father's father, Joseph Abridge Barstow, made his home here in 1856, two years after the city was incorporated. He came from his home in Damariscotta, Maine, and eventually married Elizabeth Turner of Port Republic.

Grandfather became a builder in those early years. Heston's *Histories* names him as a contractor-builder of some of the early hotels, including Chalfonte House, a boarding house run by Mrs. Sarah W. Leeds, and the Shelburne Hotel. Chalfonte House was not built where the large Chalfonte Hotel was eventually built on the Boardwalk, but closer to Pacific Avenue on North Carolina Avenue.

Eventually, grandfather became president of the Atlantic City Gas and Water Company, the local utility, until he died in 1898. He was also a member of City Council, indirectly responsible for the establishment of the first paid fire department. Up until that time, Atlantic City had volunteer firemen who rushed to their horse-drawn hand pumping vehicles whenever the city fire bell rang. I had for many years a fireman's helmet from U.S. Company Number One which belonged to my father's brother, Charles.

Grandfather had strongly opposed the movement to have a paid fire department established. It was his Yankee prudence for the dollar, I suppose. One day, the home he had built on the corner of Pennsylvania and Atlantic Avenues caught fire. The city fire bell rang. The volunteer firemen arrived with the equipment, but no one raised a hand to fight the fire. The house burned to the ground. Grandfather got the message. The city got a paid fire department. The Barstows got a new seven-bedroom home on Pennsylvania Avenue to accommodate a family of six children: three boys and three girls.

Grandfather also had a hand in another civic event. He was a member of the city council at the time that plans to build a Boardwalk were under consideration. His name can be seen today on a bronze plaque at Park Place on the Boardwalk as one of the founders.

As a builder, he helped build some of the new narrow Board-walk that was taken up in sections every fall and stored, some of it in grandfather's storage building. Each spring, the Boardwalk was put back in place on the sand.

One other member of the Barstow family had a part in lasting community service. My father's sister, Georgiana Barstow Wright,

Mrs. William Wright, was an active member and president of the Woman's Research Club, a group of well-educated, influential women civic leaders of the community. Aunt Georgie had once been principal of a school in Paterson, New Jersey.

This group of women had decided that Atlantic City should have a library. They rented a store on Atlantic Avenue, near our city hall today, donated appropriate books, and volunteered to serve in the library gratis. Thus began the civic movement to establish a library building in the city. A handful of local citizens, including Aunt Georgie, succeeded in receiving a grant of $50,000 from Andrew Carnegie to build a library at Illinois and Pacific Avenues. Aunt Georgie's name was on a bronze plaque just inside the doorway as a library founder. The city has since built a new library near city hall. I've often wondered what became of the original plaque. It was probably abandoned with the building.

I could not have dreamed in 1945 that my name would one day be found on a bronze plaque in the library of The Richard Stockton College of New Jersey as a founder of the college, and that a building would have my name in recognition of my efforts to establish the college.

Before hostess committee luncheons, Betty Gore, social editor of *The Press of Atlantic City*, always arranged for a photographer to be present to take the pictures of all the hostesses. We were grouped together six or seven or so to a picture. For years, the Sunday *Press* had all six pictures of the women completely filling the front page of the society section of the paper and a long write-up.

Following luncheon, Lenora Slaughter always spoke enthusiastically about the coming pageant, the contestants who would arrive, and the importance of the committee in protecting the image of the Pageant. Mrs. Malcolm Shermer, whom we affectionately called Ted, followed Lenora with particular emphasis on the rules which contestants were required to observe, such as their contacts with the news media in general. She warned about photographers who might pose contestants in front of billboards or other kinds of unsuitable advertising in the background, especially those promoting liquor, cigarettes or other subject matters inappropriate for the Pageant's image.

We also were given a number of tokens to pay for taxi rides as we escorted contestants to and from their appointed responsibilities. We were not permitted to drive our own cars because the Pageant was not insured for that purpose.

I had been assigned Miss New Orleans and Miss California. Contestants were required to register upon their arrival in Atlantic City on Labor Day. Headquarters for registration that year was in the Traymore Hotel.

I had volunteered for registration duty. After signing in, contestants were taken to a special room where they received bathing suits to try on for fit. Catalina, Inc., as a national sponsor, provided one-piece suits in a variety of colors with a tight skirt across the front. One of the girls I escorted to their assigned hotels was Bess Myerson, Miss New York 1945, who had arrived with her sister as a chaperone. From that first day, Bess was an outstanding young woman, tall, dignified, and on this day, wide-eyed, as she looked out her bedroom window of the Brighton Hotel at the ocean, Boardwalk, and beautifully landscaped, spacious grounds of her hotel. She had graduated from Hunter College in New York.

The story has been told many times that her white assigned swimsuit was too tight for her. She was given another suit in lime green in a larger size. This suit did nothing for her fine figure. In an effort to stretch the suit, her sister, a little larger in size, put on the suit and slept in it. The next day when Bess put on the suit, her sister sewed the straps together on the shoulder and Bess wore it under her evening gown during her competition. The effort was successful, for Bess won swimsuit. Contestants have occasionally been sewn in their clothes during emergencies. In later years, Bert Parks was sewn into his pants when a faulty zipper gave way.

Bess Myerson has been recognized as the first Jewish Miss America. In her room at the Brighton Hotel, I was aware that some of our finest hotels on the Boardwalk, so exclusive in their clientele, did not accept Jewish guests. That sounds as offensive in today's world as it was in the 1940s, but it was a fact of life not limited to hotels.

I first experienced this exclusion when I became president of the Woman's Research Club. For years, our club had held a reciprocity day meeting with another of our city's largest and finest organizations of Jewish women. This year it was the Research Club's turn to be hostess. At a joint committee meeting, I suggested our joint meeting be held at the Dennis Hotel where we met regularly. I went personally to the hotel manager, husband of one of our members, to make arrangements. I was astonished to be told the hotel would not be available for that event. These were fine, outstanding women civic leaders in the community. The answer was "No." I was considerably embarrassed to have to report to the planning committee my inability to find an appropriate meeting place. They accepted my tactfully careful explanation in good grace, knowing, I later believed, what the answer would be. The event was held in happy association with our Jewish friends in their meeting place as usual, the Jewish Community Center.

⁂

In later years, Lenora changed the term bathing suit to swimsuit as a more dignified designation. Her girls didn't bathe in their suits. Swimsuit was more appropriate for its ultimate use.

One of my most exciting days as a volunteer at registration came in 1949 when Kathleen Crowley, recently crowned Miss New Jersey, arrived. There had been much interest in her locally for she was a resident of nearby Green Bank, a small, sleepy community along the Mullica River. She was the first woman from southern New Jersey to win the title. Egg Harbor City had held a big parade for her as a send-off to the Pageant. The Exchange Club had raised $350 to give her a new set of luggage.

What I found exciting was an event I hadn't experienced before. I became aware that a large band was playing foot-stomping music as it came marching down the street to the hotel, its rhythmic beat growing louder and louder as it reached the hotel. The band was followed by the mayor and city officials of Green Bank and a caravan of cars following a flower be-decked limousine transporting Miss New Jersey. Local and area support for her was especially strong. Kathleen Crowley was a doll of female pulchritude in all her 5' 2½" and 110 pounds. She was a down-home country girl type with all the charm and lovable characteristics that brought her so much admiration and affection. In her demure, self-effacing way, she made a grand entrance into the hotel where she quickly became a crowd-pleasing favorite during the Pageant.

When she was taken to her particular hotel, the Claridge, her mother had brought along with her an ironing board which she used during the week to press the clothes of the girls. While Miss Arizona was rumored to have paid $3,000 for her evening gown, Kathleen had paid nineteen dollars or so for the material her mother had made into a gown for her.

Kathleen won not only Miss Congeniality, but succeeded in making the top ten. In later years, she became a well-known movie and television actress. She has appeared in *Batman, Bonanza, Jane Eyre, 77 Sunset Strip*, and *Westward to the Wagons*. At the time I'm writing this, she lives less than a mile from her childhood home with the responsibility of opening and closing the bridge over the Mullica River.

Hostesses had been given working schedules prepared by Lenora. The schedules were invaluable for all Pageant officials, committees, and the working press, reciting in exact detail the times for rehearsals, judging, press events, parade, and competition each night. Included were the kinds of attire necessary for each event, the handling of talent props, and instructions on the proper placement of Pageant badges and ribbons.

When the time came for my first Pageant event in 1945, I was driven to the Morton Hotel to meet Miss New Orleans and Miss California and to escort them to Convention Hall. Miss New Orleans was a tall, dignified brunette who considered herself to be a lady of culture and refinement. She was friendly to me so that we got along very well, but she just couldn't stand Miss California, a short, very pretty, bleached blonde with curled, bushy hair falling well down her back, dressed demurely in little-girl style clothes. Her outward appearance was that of a sweet young thing, but that was far from the real character of Miss California. She was actually a show girl; a chorus girl type, somewhat tough and brassy, as many chorus girls were in that era. She bleached her hair every night.

Miss New Orleans flatly refused to travel with or be associated in any way with Miss California. It took all my skills of persuasion to assure her that we positively had to travel in taxis together.

When I called for a taxi this Labor Day, I soon discovered there was an unpleasant problem in using taxis. Our tokens had a set price for the ride and a built-in tip. Taxis were inevitably slow in arriving, especially over the holiday. If there were other calls from more lucrative hotel patrons or visitors to the city, we waited and waited, sometimes causing real concern that we would arrive late for our schedule.

It was also difficult getting home at night. I was required as a hostess to go to the girls' rooms when I arrived, telephone for a taxi, and take the girls to the hotel entrance for the taxi ride to the Hall. At night after competition, I had to take the girls to their rooms, then return, hopefully, to a waiting taxi. Often the taxi didn't wait, and I was stranded at midnight or later with no transportation.

Mrs. White and Mrs. Shermer had required that hostesses wear full evening gown attire when escorting their contestants at night. That meant public transportation was out of the question. I called taxis and sometimes called several times before one arrived rather than get my husband out of bed. He was an early riser.

After the war, the 1945 Pageant was held for the last time in the beautiful Warner Theater. I was experiencing my first rehearsal while various contestants performed. One lovely girl was dancing for her talent, not with any particular skill. Her dance ended in

113

what I think was a buck-and-wing where one ends on one foot with the other leg thrust back. The only problem was that she couldn't keep her balance. She rehearsed over and over with the same result. That night I needn't have felt such concern for her. At the very last moment, the master of ceremonies playfully reached out and caught her ankle preventing her from toppling over. It looked like part of the act, so all ended well.

Miss New Orleans had a fashion display for talent, clothes she had designed and made. The day Miss California was scheduled for talent, I was sure it would be my first and last year as a hostess. When I arrived in her room after lunch, I discovered a man in her room down on his knees carefully cutting fringe on a long leather jacket reaching below her knees. A man! In her room!! Her chaperone was present, but I was flabbergasted. Before I ordered him out I wanted to know what he was doing.

Miss California was singing a cowboy song for her talent. She had gone a short distance up the Boardwalk with her chaperone to Tom Endicott's Dude Ranch, a western store. Endicott had loaned her a valuable western leather short coat with the understanding that the coat be returned unharmed. The man in the room was a newsman cutting the coat shorter and cutting fringe around it. The coat was not returned.

I was considerably upset and urged him to leave. I felt certain I would be quickly relieved of my hostess duties. A Man in her Room!!! The worst possible happening.

That night I was astonished at Miss California's performance. She sang "Ragtime Cowboy Joe" with such a rhythmic beat, personality, and strutting, that she won the talent contest. Bess Myerson had also won talent the night she had competed, playing both the flute and a difficult piano concerto. She had also won swimsuit, becoming a popular choice to become the new Miss America as well as the first scholarship winner of the Pageant with a $5,000 award.

One unusual event occurred during that Pageant that I believe has not been repeated. Two girls who appeared to be identical

twins competed together as Miss Tennessee. I was quite taken with
their special beauty and naturally blonde curls, dressed in lovely
light blue evening gowns. As I watched them walking down the
runway built out over the theater seats, I thought either one had
an excellent chance.

After the crowning on Saturday night, we proceeded to the
ballroom of Convention Hall for an evening of dancing and
recreation for the contestants and an opportunity for local residents
to view the girls. Food and refreshments were available, but I
didn't manage to get either very well in that crowd. Besides, it was
difficult keeping an eye on two contestants who never seemed to
be near each other. It was well into early morning before I reached
home and the comfort, at last, of my bed.

On Sunday morning, the working schedule had directed us
to take our contestants to the Brighton Hotel. We spent an hour
or two wandering around the spacious, beautifully landscaped
gardens of the hotel. As a new hostess, I wasn't sure what was
supposed to be happening until I realized the purpose of our
presence. Motion picture scouts were interviewing possible movie
prospects. Neither of my contestants had much attention.

My first year as a Pageant hostess had been an exciting new
venture into the world of beauty and show business. The hours
from early morning to late at night all week had been long and
tiring. Watching the mechanics of putting a show together in a
few days had been fascinating; the responses of contestants had
been interesting to watch. There had been challenges to meet
and a few frustrations. Sharing experiences with other hostesses
had been a good learning process for me. All in all, my first year
as hostess had been an unforgettable new chapter in my life. I
was glad I had finally joined the committee. Apparently, no one
had heard about that man in the room and I didn't tell, so I was
invited back the next year.

I was greatly impressed with the executive ability and
management skills of Lenora S. Slaughter, whom I had not met
before the Pageant. Watching her overcome the myriad details that

filled every minute, monitoring production activities, handling public relations with national and state sponsors, answering questions of the news media, and solving the problems that arose provided me with a kind of education in itself. In an era when women were not often recognized for their abilities and achievements, Lenora was far ahead of her times. Perhaps because she was a woman during a period of male dominance, she was not given sufficient recognition for her successes.

Lenora almost single-handedly changed the Pageant from a bathing beauty contest of somewhat questionable reputation into a scholarship pageant which has provided millions of dollars to thousands and thousands of smart, intelligent young women, many of whom have secured masters, doctoral, and professional degrees. By her own words she "begged, pleaded, argued, persuaded, and struggled" to convince the board of directors of the changes she proposed from time to time.

Scholarship opportunities changed the character of contestants from star-struck, would-be movie and stage stars, often chorus girls, to the average college girl whose goals in life were primarily accomplished through a college education. It took a few years for me to understand fully the powerful impact of Lenora's efforts to convert the Pageant from a beauty pageant to one of world renown.

What was she like as a person? She was an unforgettable woman. It wasn't just her height, taller than average, close to six feet in the high heels she always wore; nor was it her pretty auburn hair which reflected the occasional temperament of her personality; nor the bearing of her body, ramrod straight from head to toe. It was rather the animated enthusiasm and dynamic energy she exuded to everyone she met, the quick toss of her head, the frequent gestures to illustrate the points she wanted to make, her strength of character.

She had a warm smile that made people instinctively like her, a kind of charisma entirely her own. Her voice was normally soft with a southern drawl which years of living in the north had modified only slightly. When aroused in anger, her voice was strident, emphatic and sometimes filled with plainly expressed language.

She was a woman of insatiable ambition, not for herself, but for the Miss America she directed and the young women whose future lives she had the power and the will to influence so greatly. As executive director of the Pageant, she had a vision for the future but could be tough and indomitable when it was necessary, a woman of unusual determination, courage and wisdom.

Her decisions were based upon what she believed was right for the Pageant, rather than how they affected her personal reputation. Even to casual observers it was clear that she was an opinionated woman, used to associating with men who were important corporate leaders in the world of big business. She had the kind of personality that drew people to her and, at the same time, a way of laying down the law which could infuriate those who felt her wrath. In her private life, she was soft, sentimental, and entirely feminine, a pushover for compliments and an occasional tale of woe. Socially she was just one of the girls, easy to know, fun-loving, popular, not yet married: she was a romantic at heart.

She was a woman of many talents, with a clear understanding of how to improve and expand the Pageant operations. Her personal dedication to providing educational opportunities for the young women of America has influenced the lives of countless young women for the better. In her unique way she was a woman of exceptional achievements which became the firm foundation on which the Pageant has grown into its international reputation for the excellence of its scholarship foundation. Lenora Slaughter was a one of a kind, very special woman.

In later years, she has refused to accept credit for the development of the Pageant leading to its present day successes. She claims the successful credit belongs to the civic leaders in Atlantic City and the thousands of people and representatives across the country for their support.

In a letter to me, she says,

I was borrowed from the St. Petersburg (Florida) Chamber of Commerce for six weeks in 1935 to build Atlantic City's faith in a civic event which, if properly handled, could prove a valuable tourist attraction for the resort. I was able to build a Boardwalk parade to give Atlantic City a part of the event promoted by the Steel Pier and thus create a civic flavor for the event.

I had no idea what I was facing including the ban by the Federated Women's Clubs of New Jersey. But when I arrived in Atlantic City, I saw a potential civic event which could surpass our Festival of States in St. Pete, for we were local and the Miss America Pageant had national possibilities. At the conclusion of the 1935 Showman's Variety Jubilee, Mr. Hollinger asked me to remain on a year round basis as Associate Director. I accepted the challenge. I worked the next seven years for $3,000 a year and in 1942 I was made executive director at a salary of $4,000 a year. The former executive director George Tyson was paid $7,500 for 3 months, June 15 to Sept. 15. I was only interested in the necessary money to live. I was consumed with ambition to build a Pageant worthy of its existence. I had found my goal in life and for 33 years I gave my heart to accomplish that goal. The only credit I deserve was my faith in the project and my ability to sell capable people in having faith in our goals and contributing their knowledge, ability and money to building a civic event for young women through unselfish endeavors of civic leaders in Atlantic City as well as local and state civic leaders throughout our country.

She mentions a testimonial presented to her by the board of directors on the occasion of her retirement dinner in December 1964, when I was present. She says,

I treasure that beautiful testimonial more than anything I own. It hangs in my den over my TV where I can look at it constantly and I relive the memories of my years of association with an American Institution. The Pageant has grown by leaps and bounds since my retirement and will continue to do so as long as its goals are more important than individual acclaim, thus your goals and mine are assured.

We lived in an era when discrimination against women in the workplace, and in general, was the way of life. It's not really surprising; in fact, it was almost inevitable that women would begin demanding equality in the workplace and elsewhere. What is surprising is that it took so long.

Lenora, in her own words, agreed to work for seven years at $3,000 a year and for $4,000 as executive director because she had a consuming ambition to build a Pageant worthy of its existence. The Pageant board thought Lenora, as a woman, was worth less than half of the $7,500 they paid George Tyson for three months. Nevertheless, she had the goal and ambition that superseded monetary rewards. This was the real driving force behind her great success.

I've often thought that even today, the role of female success in the community is much less important than that of male success. For example, Atlantic City recently established a hall of fame. Named among the first to be inducted was Albert A. Marks Jr. for his years as chief executive officer of the Pageant and chairman of the board. Al Marks deserved every bit of credit he was given, for he brought the Pageant into television fame with many outstanding achievements to his credit. The hall of fame simply ignored the woman who had built the Pageant into a television commodity in the first place by her years of experience in building the firm foundation on which the Pageant exists today. She should have been included also.

In my long years in active association with the Pageant, I have sometimes met the painful experiences of female discrimination not only in the Pageant, but in many other places.

In 1946, the Pageant was making plans to return to Convention Hall after the war. Atlantic City had been gradually returning to its seashore vacation status. Hotels had refurbished after the Air Force left. The Boardwalk had been rebuilt in Atlantic City and partially down-beach. The shore had returned to normal as far as possible.

Lenora strongly believed that the first Pageant scholarship of $5,000 should be increased. While the board had been reluctant in the beginning, this time she was able to persuade these prominent businessmen that the goal of $25,000 for her scholarship program should be set. Under MacIntyre's guidance, the Bancroft firm increased their contribution to $5,000. Catalina and F. W. Fitch Company followed. F. L. Jacobs Company replaced one sponsor and Bancroft added another $5,000 to replace another sponsor, making their total $10,000.

The price of tickets for Pageant events was increased while an intense advertising and publicity campaign began in order to meet the budget of $50,000.

I had learned during my first year as hostess that there was scarcely time to rush home long enough to eat hastily and dress in evening gown before the necessity of dashing off again to meet my contestants. I therefore had prepared all of my clothes to be worn for the entire week and their accessories well in advance. An organized person, I began with the clothes to be worn on the first day and night, placing them in one end of the closet and placing each day's outfit and evening gown adjacent to them in order, as they would be worn. Plans for my family's food and comfort had also been made well in advance.

This year, the hostess committee consisted of women who would escort and chaperone 51 girls from 38 states, 25 women who would escort the state chaperones, who had traveled here with the contestants, and six substitute hostesses.

I noted in my working schedule for that year that, besides the 38 states represented, there were contestants from Greater Philadelphia, New York City, Memphis, Detroit, Chattanooga, Los Angeles County, Omaha, Canada, Pittsburgh, Washington, D.C., Brooklyn, Miami Beach, Louisville, and the Philippines.

A typical program of events began on Labor Day with contestants registering at a hotel on their arrival. A business meeting was held in Convention Hall at 7:45 p.m., followed by a meeting on stage with the producer at 8:45 p.m.

On Tuesday, beginning at 9:00 a.m., contestants appeared in swimsuits at the Atlantic City Press Bureau on the Boardwalk at Convention Hall for the panorama picture of all contestants. A meeting with the press, newsreel, and radio broadcasters followed. Luncheon was scheduled for 12:30 p.m. The Boardwalk parade was held at 3:00 p.m. Dinner was 5:30 p.m. A general rehearsal on stage at Convention Hall began at 7:00 p.m. for several hours.

On Wednesday, Thursday, and Friday, the schedule was basically the same. General rehearsal at 9:00 a.m. Luncheon 12:30 p.m. At 2:00 p.m., general rehearsal followed by talent rehearsals lasted often until the dinner hour. Contestants would arrive at Convention Hall at 8:00 p.m. for the first, second, and third preliminary competitions. On Thursday and Saturday mornings, contestants had a breakfast conference with the judges at a beachfront hotel at 10:00 a.m.

On Saturday afternoon at 2:00 p.m., there was a general rehearsal for some changes in the show because of the finals. Talent rehearsal would follow for those who wanted to rehearse their talent in case they were in the finals. Miss America was crowned at 11:30 p.m. and then was available to the press and radio reporters at midnight. The coronation ball was held at a Boardwalk hotel for a couple of hours or so.

On Sunday, there were conferences all day from 11:00 a.m. until 2:00 p.m. for scholarship winners, Miss America and runners-up, with Dr. Snavely and the Pageant scholarship committee. At 2:00 p.m., all contestants would meet with talent scouts and the press, bringing their swimsuits with them. At 3:00 p.m., they would meet with photographers. At 4:00 p.m., there was a tea for Miss America and contestants.

On Monday, all contestants were to say farewell except for those selected by the national broadcasters to audition before the network chains of America. Two of the most talented would have been selected for the auditions.

Hostesses had been instructed to help contestants with their plan for departure to see that the hotel managements were properly thanked for their hospitality and personal hotel bills had been paid. They also had to be sure that all talent props had been removed from Convention Hall.

The Pageant production, on its return to Convention Hall, had been a smash hit. Miss America, Bess Myerson, had made her royal entrance on stage in a beautiful Everglaze fashion creation. The contestants making their glamorous walk down the 110-foot runway created such an enthusiastic response from the audience that they received a standing ovation.

The second winner of the Pageant's $5,000 scholarship was lovely Marilyn Buford of Los Angeles. I had admired her expensive wardrobe. She went to Italy sometime after the Pageant and is reported to have been associated with the famous director, Roberto Roselini, prior to his meeting Ingrid Bergman.

My third year as a hostess proved to be more than an exciting year for me. The Pageant continued to grow that year of 1947. New sets and scenery had been bought for production in Convention Hall and new equipment for the parade.

The judging had been reviewed and a fourth ballot inaugurated for the judges. Along with the criteria of judging contestants in evening gown, swimsuit, and talent, the judges were now to consider personality and intelligence. That made a great deal of sense to me. I had long believed that beauty alone was not enough. Beauty in my opinion is much more than skin deep and the body beautiful. Contestants on that basis only had to be walking dolls with talent. While the poets have said that "beauty is in the eyes of the beholder," it is true that we all have our own standards of beauty. It was a common expression in that era that "blondes were dumb," or "she's a dumb blonde." Beauties were not looked upon as having brains.

I've often thought that the old myth that the Pageant exploits women had its origin in those early days before brains and intelligence became the most important part of the judging process. Women, I think, either consciously or subconsciously resented having beauty upheld as a standard in their lives. Every woman likes to think that she has a touch of beauty whether it be visible or not. She also likes to think that she is not only an intelligent woman, but has that extra something that makes her a likable, unique person to her family and friends, possibly her community and workplace.

Including personality and intelligence in the judging process, along with the new scholarship program, continued to change the character of the Miss America Pageant contestants. In the early years, those who came to the Pageant were mostly girls interested in a show business career, drawn by scouts from the motion picture industry and the opportunity to have a screen test. After the scholarship program had been introduced, a new kind of contestant began coming to Atlantic City: college girls whose primary interest was securing a college education as a basis for their future lives.

※

In my early years as a hostess, I was assigned Miss Iowa. One night during a preliminary competition, I was called backstage to the dressing room where Miss Iowa was alone in a corner of the room, her face washed with tears as she cried. I tried to comfort her, thinking she had been upset by her talent performance that night. A fine, lyric soprano with a well-trained, beautiful voice, clear, true to pitch, she could have a successful future ahead of her as a singer. The reason for her tears surprised me. As I hugged her she cried, "Oh, Mrs. Alton, I'm so happy," the tears streaming down her face, "I'm so happy. I've just won a non-finalist scholarship of $1,000 and now I can go back to college next week. I didn't have the money for tuition, now I can complete my education and get my degree." Miss Iowa's tears had been tears of joy. Her education had been most important to her.

If I had ever had any reservations about the value of the Miss America Pageant in the lives of thousands of young women in our country, it vanished then and there. The scholarship program provides a multitude of opportunities not only for the girls who compete in Atlantic City, but for the unseen, unknown, thousands of young women who enter local and state pageants to secure the scholarship money available. Opportunities are not solely financial. They come in many ways as doors open to successful careers that would not have been available otherwise. At that unforgettable moment, there was no question in my mind that the Pageant was providing a valuable service to smart young women and I was at last proud to be a small part of it.

I confess I had had a few reservations about joining the Pageant family. There had been so much scandal in the early years. Sometimes when people disliked the final winner's choice, casual comments that the winning had been rigged occurred. I am a careful observer of events. I had watched and looked and listened, but I had been unable to find any reason for concern. Lenora Slaughter was so dedicated and determined to establish a first-rate Pageant that would have significant importance in the lives of young women across the country, their education, families, and careers, that her enthusiasm was contagious. I was sold. I am still sold on the value of the Pageant in today's world.

Many uninformed people still contend that the Pageant exploits women. In my opinion, based upon many years of experience, the Pageant does just the opposite by creating doors of opportunity to many young women who never reach Atlantic City but are awarded scholarships at regional pageants. They otherwise might not have had the opportunities given to them.

Educational scholarships are an important key to success. If my Miss Iowa of the early years had been exploited, she had welcomed it with open arms, for her dreams of a scholarship had come true.

Elizabeth B. Alton

Chapter 16

My personal life had become more of a civic one from 1945 through the 1950s. In retrospect, I was developing leadership skills and organizational contacts valuable in later years. Many different doors of opportunity opened for me, gradually leading me from one position to another. My children were in school or college. My household ran like a charm, thoroughly organized in detail. I had free hours that needed filling with more than hobby crafts and reading. I began filling my free hours with activities outside the home.

My years in elected offices and state positions in women's Masonic organizations had provided friends who recommended me to fill offices in other organizations. I first became president of the Woman's Research Club of Atlantic City. The extensive publicity of the club's civic activities in *The Press of Atlantic City* resulted in my accepting chairmanship of the Ventnor City Cancer Drive, in a city of some 10,000 population, and becoming a member of the board of directors of the Atlantic County Cancer Society.

For the several years I ran the Ventnor Cancer Drive, it was not only a real challenge for me, but one I struggled with. The hardest part of the job was securing workers who would canvass one entire street in their neighborhoods. Finding the names of people to ask was easy. The hard part was the asking. There were hours when I physically forced myself to sit at the telephone and dial. I always found someone for each street, but it was a job I disliked doing very much.

We placed containers for donations in stores and businesses, sold chances for articles with a public drawing on Ventnor Pier, and held other events. Our donation cans were collected and officially counted in the city hall office of the city clerk.

With my interest in mental illness, I also became a member of the board of directors of the Atlantic County Mental Health Association.

A group of women representing several clubs asked me to organize the Atlantic City League of Women Voters. The effort was successful. I became the first president with a reasonably strong league in operation. I accepted a state committee position within the state league which allowed attendance at state league board meetings. For a while, I drove to the northern part of the state for meetings which proved burdensome in addition to my driving for the State Federation of Women's Clubs.

I was invited to become a charter member of the auxiliary to the Betty Bacharach Home in Longport. Eventually I became president of what is known today as the Betty Bacharach Rehabilitation Hospital Auxiliary in Pomona. Originally, the Bacharach Home in Longport had been organized as a child care facility for child victims of infantile paralysis. When that disease was pretty well eliminated by the Salk vaccine, the rehabilitation hospital became a project.

Some twenty years later, the Atlantic City Medical Center and the Betty Bacharach Rehabilitation Hospital sought to build two separate but adjoining facilities on the campus of Stockton State College in Pomona. The approval of the trustees of Stockton was required before state approval. Fortunately, I was the second chairman of the board of trustees at the time. Adrian Phillips was the representative of the two medical institutions and a long-time Pageant associate. I was able and privileged to guide proposals which secured the approval of the board of trustees and the state. On the day of ground breaking, I was proud to represent Stockton College. Today, two large, prestigious medical hospitals have been serving a growing population very well.

During those early years, I had been president of several other organizations. My young son, John, had generously donated my services to both his elementary and upper level schools, without my permission, as his home room mother. In that capacity, I was required to collect 50 cents from parents as dues in the Parents and Teachers Association. Later, I became president of the Ventnor PTA, pleased that for the first time our membership drive had reached 1,000 members.

I was also president of the Atlantic City Woman's Club, the Atlantic City Business and Professional Women's Club, which later named me their Woman of Achievement for the year, and the Ventnor Civic Club. In future years, my activities outside the home were primarily on a state level.

In those early years, Lenora liked the first view of Convention Hall by contestants to be a dramatic one. Hostesses were instructed to have their taxis arrive in the garage area under Convention Hall. Contestants would be taken up the long ramp to the Boardwalk entrance into the main auditorium. As the girls entered the Hall, there were always gasps of surprise and awe at seeing the size of the place where they would be performing. After that, our usual entrance was on Pacific Avenue, the stage entrance.

Rehearsals were always long and tiring for everyone. Contestants were limited to a three-minute talent presentation, but there were always problems to be solved and unnecessary delays. Sometimes the talent presentation exceeded the three-minute limit. Extra rehearsal time had to be taken to make the necessary cuts. Sometimes material was being used that had been copyrighted and permission had not been given for its use. Sometimes there were problems with props, or the orchestration for musical numbers was not immediately available, especially when last minute changes in talent had been made unexpectedly. Sometimes girls had to sit around and wait while professional talent rehearsed. Always there were problems. Hostesses became involved in solving many of them. I remember spending several hours on the telephone trying to locate a long slip for an evening gown which had inconveniently been left at home. Another time, locating a particular swimsuit in an emergency was most difficult after the season. There was never a dull moment. The shows took hours and hours of preparation and rehearsals.

Stage shows and theme settings in those days were always magnificent to behold. J. Howard Buzby, vice president of the Pageant and later owner of the prestigious Dennis Hotel, and Robert Leeds, later an owner of Haddon Hall Hotel, were producers. Buzby was a man of considerable ability and artistry.

The masters of ceremony that year were a surprise. Ted Malone and Phil Regan were popular in their field, but they apparently misunderstood their roles as emcee. They performed as though the Pageant was located in a huge nightclub or cabaret. They told stories and jokes that were often off-color, leaving the audience properly shocked. Their performances on succeeding nights were entirely subdued.

Most of our days were spent in rehearsals on stage. The main auditorium was so immense that it claimed to seat 25,000 people on its main floor and balcony. Convention Hall was built with exceptionally long and high arches thirteen stories high, upholding the roof, an architectural gem. In 1971, a helicopter had flown Miss America, Phyllis George, inside the hall, which was 635 feet long and 350 feet wide, before an equally large addition named West Hall was built. The stage area is huge, large enough for basketball games, boxing and wrestling matches, and seats for the audience. The main hall has been used for a variety of sporting events, professional hockey games, collegiate football competitions between well-known colleges, and concerts. Ice Capades was a summer-long event of interest for some years. Most unusual, perhaps, was greyhound racing on a large track in an era when dog racing was illegal. Gambling on the races was easily available as well as illegal, too.

The large organ was the brainchild of Arthur Brooks who planned, designed, and supervised its installation. The organ was said to be the largest in the world with enough wiring to circle the earth. Brooks played the organ for some years at special events. Lois Miller succeeded him. Not many were capable of playing that great instrument. Once, one contestant played a simple piece on the organ in her talent competition.

Perhaps the most nationally noteworthy use of the Hall was the Democratic political party convention when Lyndon Johnson and Hubert Humphrey were nominated president and vice president of the United States.

Lenora had been working hard to establish state pageants only, with the goal of eliminating key city and other miscellaneous sponsors. With her scholarship program, she was beginning to succeed in her goal. She attended 21 organizational meetings of state pageants. Meetings with the chambers of commerce of Santa Cruz, California, and Seaside, Oregon, resulted in establishing new pageants there. Colleges were visited to explain the scholarship program.

Inspired by the success of the National Scholarship Program, state Pageant leaders devised ways and means of establishing scholarships for their state finalists. With some $16,500 raised by local civic leaders, many contestants received $250 to $500 scholarship awards at their own local and state pageants. The largest number of college students in history had competed in the 1947 Pageant.

I had been assigned Miss Illinois and Miss Memphis, both especially charming, intelligent, and beautiful women, so different in character from my first two contestants that I was delighted with them. They were assigned to the Colton Manor Hotel, a popular high-rise hotel on North Carolina Avenue. Both were college students.

I was feeling more comfortable as a hostess as this pageant opened. One of the first events, the panorama picture in swimsuits and individual and group pictures of girls from neighboring states, was taken on the Boardwalk in front of Convention Hall. The girls assembled at the Atlantic City Press Bureau run by Mall Dodson in a store in the Hall. The few publicity pictures taken in the Press

Bureau before going out on the Boardwalk always tickled my sense of humor. The girls assembled there for the pictures.

It was a long, narrow store with a room in the back on a lower level which required going down a small flight of stairs. In that room were 51 contestants, 26 hostesses, some Pageant officials, and a host of photographers. There wasn't room to breathe adequately, as we were squeezed together. What used to amuse me was watching the photographers coming and going, squeezing their way through the contestants, holding their cameras necessarily high over their heads. The obvious enjoyment of such pleasant body contacts as the men wormed their way through was more than evident. Every one of them had wide smiles and grins on their faces from ear to ear. One could easily say that they found their assignments especially pleasurable, not at all hard to complete.

The afternoon parade held on the Boardwalk was always a colorful event. The girls wore evening gowns. Hostesses delivered their contestants to the Breakers Hotel in a large room overlooking the beach and ocean. When it was time for them to be taken to the Garden Pier where they were placed on rolling chair floats, hostesses traveled down to a reviewing stand in front of Convention Hall. Reserved seats were available in a front row.

There was only one trouble with an afternoon parade. In early September, the sun at our seashore can be very hot in the mid afternoon. As I had learned in the 1920 parade, the girls got sunburned even though sunburn lotion had been advised. Contestants in those days were not always as tanned as they are today. Some of them had quite light skin and did suffer from sunburn which concealing cosmetics didn't quite help.

My Miss Memphis became a popular contestant. The night she performed talent, she was the picture of a beautiful, poised, ladylike Southern belle. Her evening gown, with a tight bodice and flowing bouffant skirt, enhanced her dignity and charm. She sat at the piano playing accompaniment as she sang softly, a picture of elegance. I was delighted when she won talent.

During the week, she received such good attention from the press that we were kept busy. Then, I began hearing that she might be a winner. When that great moment finally arrived, my Miss Memphis, Barbara Jo Walker, was crowned Miss America 1947. I couldn't believe my good luck.

When the curtain came down, I went backstage to be with Barbara Jo during the publicity picture taking and interviews. In those days, the press still simply stampeded onto the stage, creating a kind of pandemonium after the curtain went down.

When it was time to leave for the Ball, Lenora ushered us into a police car which had been driven into the Hall and positioned near the stage. Captain Joe Lodovico was the driver. He had been in charge of the police detail. A tall well-built man, he was my idea of a really tough cop with a heart of gold. Not having had much association with the police, I suppose I was somewhat intimidated simply by the air of authority he exuded.

Lenora and Captain Joe sat in the front seat, Barbara Jo and I in the back. Within seconds, Lenora and Captain Joe were having a really heated discussion. As best I can remember, it had to do with our route of transportation to the nearby Claridge Hotel. I thought it might be a continuation of a former discussion. At any rate, in my state of excitement, I was both shocked and highly amused. As the discussion became more heated, their words became less polite. Lenora is a lady to her fingertips, but she is also, at times, one of the most determined women I have ever met. Backing down was not her style, and her language, when or if the occasion demanded, could be quite plain. When she was right, by golly, she was right. As Barbara Jo and I sat entranced, Lenora minced no words in response to Captain Joe's blasts of equally tough police opinions. But they were always good friends.

Eventually Captain Joe did what Lenora had apparently wanted in the first place. He drove us from the stage area out the front door of Convention Hall onto the Boardwalk and up the Walk several blocks to the Claridge Hotel. We made our grand entrance into the Ballroom with a fanfare of trumpets and tremendous applause for our new Miss America. Escorts had been provided to all contestants for dancing. It was well into the wee hours of the morning before I got home.

Our Sunday morning began at nine o'clock; Barbara Jo and I were on the beach where the press photographers were taking her picture in swimsuit, dipping her toes into the Atlantic Ocean. A press conference with reporters followed at ten o'clock. Unlike former years, there were no talent scout interviews any more on Sundays.

It had been customary for Lenora to take Miss America to New York on Sunday afternoons for fittings for a Pageant wardrobe and for the interviews and appearances required for publicity purposes. This year was different. Lenora kept Barbara Jo in town for a week after the Pageant so that my hostess duties had been extended for that period. It was a happy, memorable, more relaxed experience than I ever had in later years. I had the great good fortune to show Barbara Jo around town, to take her with my husband and young son to our famous Hackney's Sea Food Restaurant for dinner and bathing in the ocean from the Traymore Hotel. Mostly, we went around privately without publicity hoopla. Sometimes she was recognized, as she was at Hackney's, where their only intrusion into our privacy was snapping her picture for their gallery of celebrities on their walls. I have one of us all in my books of memories.

The one time I can remember that we had police protection was when we went bathing in the ocean. Police escorted us down the beach to the water's edge. Lifeguard boats were waiting for us in the ocean. It was like having one's own private life boat for protection. Both of us were good swimmers, but like lifeguards all up and down our beaches, they cautioned us when we were deeper than they wanted. There were, of course, publicity pictures for Barbara Jo.

Our new Miss America was the kind of young woman that parents would have desired as a daughter. A smart, intelligent, beautiful woman with none of the airs, temperamental reactions, or burning show business ambitions. She was a normal, happy, considerate person in every respect. I admired her as a person who wasn't letting the title go to her head, also finding in her a friend for whom I had much affection.

At her first press conference after her crowning, she had calmly announced that she would not be interested in motion picture or theatrical offers. It was her plan to return to college, graduate, marry her fiancé, a pre-med student, teach until he completed his medical education and training as a pediatrician, raise a family, and be a good wife and mother.

She willingly devoted her weekends and special holidays to keeping Pageant engagements. She spoke at religious conferences, State Education Association meetings, and the National Education Association Convention. She served as a Goodwill ambassador to Johannesburg, South Africa, and was guest of honor at the Annual Fiesta in Mexico.

In later years, the Scholarship Committee set up a special trust fund so that the unspent portion of her scholarship fund could be used for the education of her first born, John Andrew.

Barbara Jo was the first Miss America to marry during her year of reign. There had been a great deal of publicity, especially during the honeymoon. Jacque Mercer was second.

I have always remembered what a Pageant judge had said to Barbara Jo as a brief glimpse into the judging system. He had said that she had been his choice from the first time he saw her. There have been Miss Americas who have had the same kind of effect on judges. They just stand out above the crowd.

The year of 1947 had been an exciting and difficult one for me personally. In May of that year, I had been appointed second district vice president of the New Jersey State Federation of Women's Clubs when the incumbent moved out of state with her husband. In that position, I had 25 women's clubs in Atlantic, Cape May, and Cumberland Counties to visit and supervise. The following year, I was elected to the position. It became the first step toward leadership of the largest women's organization in the state.

The difficult part of the year arrived in July when my father suddenly died. Many changes in my parental family took place. Two of my brothers lived in San Diego, California, and one in Miami, Florida. My mother lived alone in the ancestral seven-bedroom home on Pennsylvania Avenue. Settling the estate was a long process. The Miss America Pageant in September, with the unexpected experience of having a Miss America, had been a happy event coloring some of my life with new interests and activities.

I had had what some people would call a premonition of my father's death six months previously. I have learned to call it a "word of knowledge" as described in First Corinthians, chapter 12 verse 8, of the Bible.

We were having Christmas dinner in our parents' home that winter of 1946, a happy occasion with all of my brothers, my husband, our children, and me joining my parents at a table filled with turkey and all the festive goodies. Conversation was light and fun-filled. I was simply enjoying a memorable family holiday when suddenly I heard the words in my mind as though they had been spoken aloud: "This is his last Christmas." I was stunned. I knew instantly my father was enjoying his last Christmas dinner. He appeared to be in good health generally although we didn't know that he had cancer. The knowledge that he would not be with us much longer caused me so much indescribable sadness that I had to struggle to maintain my normal composure.

It was not the first time I believe God has spoken to me, nor has it been the last. The first time was so sudden, so startling, so clear and so powerful that I was physically controlled by it.

I had been faced with a serious problem in my family which I believed with all my heart, knowledge, and experience was the wrong course of action. I had tried in every way I could to change the plans I knew were wrong. Finally, I realized that I had done all I could and could do no more. I was defeated, but more importantly, the course of action was unchangeable as well as disturbingly wrong. That night, in my despair, I cried out to the Lord, "I give up, Lord. I surrender. I put the problem in your hands. I have tried. The answer must lie with you. I give up."

The next morning, I was walking to a neighborhood grocery store with thoughts of the food requirements for the day filling my mind. Unexpectedly, a tremendous voice filled not only my head but my entire body. I was physically stopped in my tracks, transfixed for several minutes by the voice I had heard. "Let not your heart be troubled." I had my answer to our family problem. God was in control.

When I got home, I looked up God's words. The first place I found them was John, chapter 14, verses 1 and 27. Many times in my life when there have been deep, troubling concerns, God's message always returns: "Let not your heart be troubled."

⅍

For the Pageant office, 1947 was a good year. Ruth Mccandliss, who eventually became executive secretary of the Pageant for years, had joined the Pageant family.

Barbara Jo Walker's recognition by education associations had spurred state sponsors to increase their efforts to secure scholarships for their contestants. They raised $50,000 in scholarships to augment the national awards of $25,000. Catalina, Inc. and Joseph Bancroft and Sons Company became the sole national sponsors.

Catalina, for years, had been providing swimsuits for the contestants. When Barbara Jo returned as Miss America for the 1948 Pageant, the swimsuits were no longer in various colors to suit the coloring of each girl. Instead, every girl wore a black and white zebra striped suit which did absolutely nothing for the most perfectly formed and shapely contestants. In the eyes of the outraged hostesses and other women viewers, the suits detracted from the beauty of the girls. Lenora was upset. She didn't hesitate to make her displeasure known to E. W. Stewart of Catalina, Inc.

Thus began, I am convinced, a three-year period of disagreement between two strong-willed people. I believe that Catalina's monetary contributions toward the scholarship from its beginning gave them the impression that they could dominate decision making concerning their product. On the other hand, Lenora allowed no one to dictate any decision that she believed was not in the best interests of "her girls." For Catalina, "money talks." For Lenora, "only in the best interests of the Pageant." I'm convinced the fires of discord simmered slowly on both sides for some time.

I've also always believed the difficult, well publicized battle with the press that year arose as a result of those zebra striped suits. In a continuous effort to upgrade the Pageant image, Lenora had announced that Miss America would no longer be crowned in a swimsuit with her red royal robe, scepter, and crown. Henceforth, she would be crowned in evening gown attire as a dignified Queen should be, a lady of royal refinement.

The decision to crown Miss America in an evening gown was an exceptionally difficult one for Lenora to achieve. The all-male board members were not favorable. They liked seeing contestants in swimsuits as a public attraction. In a recent TV interview, Lenora said she got down on her knees to the board to allow her to crown Miss America in evening gown. Constantly striving to upgrade and dignify the Pageant with good taste, the board was finally persuaded and supported her when it became necessary.

The announcement created a battle royal with the working press. They were outraged. "Positively no," they vociferously said, "No way." The battle raged all day. Lenora refused to surrender. They refused to submit. They wanted a swimsuit picture or else. Or else meant folding up their cameras, taking down the newsreel stands, platforms, and lights and leaving the Hall. Lenora held firm. Pageant officials supported Lenora. Word of the impasse went around the building like wildfire. Lenora continued her refusal to give in. Rehearsals continued as usual. The press walked out and disappeared.

I am personally satisfied that Lenora was so convinced that her decision had been the right one, and she had such personal strength of will and character, that she would have crowned Miss America in an evening gown if no representative of any of the press had been present. She was establishing a precedent that she believed presented the right image for the Pageant. It was her belief that the Pageant was not crowning a bathing beauty. It was crowing a beautiful girl representing the finest of American young womanhood in our country. She was not permitting the exploitation of a woman's body as cheesecake. Instead, she was presenting a young woman who was beautiful mentally, morally, and physically, an ideal the young women of America would emulate.

The photographers stayed out of the Hall all day. When people began lining up outside Convention Hall, a transition took place inside. A transition as dramatic as the show itself. Back came the cameras. Back came the newsreel platforms and spotlights. Back came the press.

The most gratifying scene for Lenora came backstage at midnight. Here, the old timers of the press and newsreels congratulated Lenora and Pageant officials and said, "Now we'd be proud to have our own daughters take part in your contest." Vivacious and talented BeBe Shopp, Miss Minnesota, found her dimpled smile on the front pages of newspapers the next morning as Miss America 1948 in evening gown.

I am satisfied that the editors of many newspapers simply instructed their press representatives to return for the story and the pictures. One has only to look at the pictures of Miss America that year to see the silent story of BeBe Shopp in a lovely evening gown, her four runners-up in zebra striped swimsuits. They really do look ridiculous.

Beatrice Bella Shopp, commonly called BeBe Shopp, was an exemplification of the All-American Girl. Although just eighteen, she was a picture of physical fitness, perhaps because she had been raised as a farm girl. She was five foot nine, weighed 140 pounds and measured 37-27-36. With an ebullient, outgoing personality, and a contagious grin, she was an interesting personality. She was also an excellent musician, playing the vibraharp. BeBe Shopp has been one of the outstanding Miss Americas, a vital influence for many years on the young women of our country and our Pageant.

BeBe graduated from the Manhattan School of Music after her year as Miss America and emceed the Miss Minnesota Pageant. She was the first Miss America to go abroad during her reign. For a while, she toured the country with her own trio of musicians, had her own TV show in Minneapolis, and eventually became the national director of the New England state pageants. She married Lt. Bayard David Waring, had four daughters, and became involved in her music, church, community chorus, and percussionist work with the Cape Ann Symphony. She made the cover of *Active Years* magazine in 1990 and at that time was known for her skits and performances as a Vista Volunteer for a Drug Free Youth Program.

Nineteen forty-eight was the year Vera Ralston, Miss Kansas, became third runner-up to Miss America, later becoming movie star Vera Miles. It was also the year that two-piece swimsuits were worn by contestants; the only year, in fact. The bare bellies were not considered attractive on every girl. Their sizes and shapes made quite a difference in body symmetry. One more reason, I feel sure, that Lenora disagreed with E. W. Stewart of Catalina, Inc.

The Fox Movietone News produced a ten minute short entitled "Talented Beauties," featuring BeBe Shopp as Miss America and five contestants of the 1948 Pageant. The film was translated into many languages and shown throughout the world, necessitating personal appearances for other Miss Americas. Requests began pouring in to the Pageant office for Miss America 1949 before she was even selected.

Jacque Mercer, Miss Arizona, became Miss America 1949. She was the exact opposite of BeBe Shopp in every way, at five foot one inch, the second shortest of the title holders after the first Queen, Margaret Gorman, in 1925. She weighed 105 pounds. Hers was an unmatched determination to win the title. She had begun at fifteen training her qualifications. She had four coaches to teach her in various fields, including dramatic and fashion presentations. She studied the judges and their selections. She became so skilled that she wrote a popular book, *How to Win a Beauty Contest*.

The Pageant had reached the stage where a business manager for Miss America was needed. Bradford H. Frapart was appointed to this position in 1949 and to direct the Boardwalk parade. He would investigate requests for bookings for Miss America, approve schedules, arrange transportation, and supply necessary advance publicity. He would keep financial records of all bookings, collect Miss America's fees, and turn them over to her or her parents.

This policy for handling Miss America continued throughout the years. While the Pageant spent thousands of dollars managing Miss America, she did not pay any fees or commissions. Instead, she was expected and required to abide by a supervised program of appearances that reflected credit on her and her title.

The Pageant had gradually built up $20,408.48 working capital. The city commission had again decided to pay the Pageant $10,000 for their work in publicizing the city. At the end of 1949's fiscal year, the board waived their rights to the payment, for the budget had been met. Twenty-six wagons for float building had been purchased. The building's mortgage had been paid off.

In those years, before he became a judge, Earl Wilson attended the Pageant as a well-known syndicated columnist for a New York newspaper. It was fun to watch him talking with the girls for his interviews. He always asked one question without fail year after year. "Have you any foibles?" It was surprising how many girls didn't really know what a foible is. He got some very surprising answers. I always felt he was having a ball.

Nash Motors was accepted as a third contributor to the Scholarship Foundation along with Catalina, Inc. and Joseph Bancroft and Sons Company. Scholarships in local and state Pageants increased to $75,000. The board ruled that key city representation be eliminated under Lenora's recommendation. Exceptions were New York, Chicago, Philadelphia, and the District of Columbia.

Talent competition had much improved. Some of the best talent performed at the Pageant then included popular and classical singers, musicians, artists, actresses, dress designers, pets and dancers. One entrant, Miss Montana, was a champion horsewoman from Billings. She rode her horse on the huge stage of Convention Hall. The spellbound audience gasped when the horse stumbled on a mat at the edge of the orchestra pit, although Miss Montana kept perfect control. Hers had been a superb act, but the board ruled that, for safety's sake, animals would not be permitted on stage.

An unusual event happened that night in Convention Hall during the show. Eddie Cantor, at the height of his popularity, had been recognized in the audience. Thunderous applause continued until he consented to go on stage. His words of encouragement to all Pageant committees were, "Where but in America could we find such a representative gathering of citizens, thrill to a competition among such representative youth and for such educational opportunities as you are offering." He then entertained the audience with the songs he had sung over the years. I'll not forget the great pleasure he gave us all as he came out onto the long runway while he sang. It was an unplanned, unrehearsed, spontaneous presentation. One of that era's truly great entertainers who gave willingly of his time and talent to entertain us all. When he was thanked for his generosity, he modestly replied, "I thank you for giving me this opportunity to perform before such a large and receptive audience."

Chapter 17
The 1950s

he spotlight in 1950 was turned on Birmingham, Alabama, and the *Birmingham News*, the oldest sponsoring organization associated with the national Pageant. This newspaper had annually sent a contestant to Atlantic City. Lily Mae Caldwell, their music, art, and drama critic, had guided the Alabama Pageant from its inception. Lily Mae was a gem, beloved by other state sponsors, members of the press, and Pageant officials. Me, too.

Lily Mae, as we came to call her affectionately, had kept the Alabama Pageant abreast of national Pageant developments. When our first $5,000 scholarship was given in 1945, Birmingham Southern College provided a four-year scholarship for Miss Alabama. When our scholarships were increased to include many contestants, the Alabama pageant did the same. By 1950, Alabama was offering three college scholarships as well as scholarships for the study of drama, voice, piano, violin, ballet and art. The Alabama Federation of Women's Clubs joined the list of scholarship donors. Eventually, Lily Mae's scholarship program included every college and university in the state, several out-of-state schools, and thousands of dollars in cash. Seventy-five girls benefited in 1950 with over $40,000 in scholarships.

Alabama's contestants had constantly been selected as semi-finalists or finalists. Lily Mae came to Atlantic City to cover the Pageant for her newspaper every year, but she had not been able to take home a winner.

I became involved with Miss Alabama 1950 by chance. It was Lenora's custom to ask the hostess committee chairman, Ted Shermer, to appoint some of the more experienced hostesses to girls Lenora had reason to believe would be top contenders. Lily Mae, at last, was bringing a contestant to the Pageant she firmly believed could be the next Miss America. After consulting in advance with Lenora about the qualities and characteristics of the reigning Miss Alabama, a particular type of hostess was desired. I had had Miss America 1947. I am by nature a calm, deliberate and organized person. It was decided that I should be Miss Alabama's hostess.

I soon discovered why I had been assigned to Yolande Betbeze at one of the first Pageant events. All of the contestants and hostesses were together in Haddon Hall Hotel. Lenora spoke to me while I was watching Yolande and said, "Don't let her out of your sight." "Ah hah," my intuition told me, "you have a problem girl." Lenora's admonition had meant, I felt sure, stick to her like glue. My intuition has always been fairly reliable. It proved to be so a short time later when I saw Yolande headed down the hall in the direction of the powder room. I hastily followed her, to her plainly expressed displeasure. "Do you have to follow me everywhere I go?" she angrily asked. My reply was short, courteous, and to the point, so that she could understand exactly what our relationship was going to be, and was: "Yes, I do."

I had come into contact with independent women like Yolande during my years of speaking at women's clubs and traveling to Newark where the board of directors of the Federation had their state board meetings. In 1950, I had been elected recording secretary and a member of the executive committee of the New Jersey State Federation of Women's Clubs' 46,000 members. As a state officer, I came to understand well the women who insisted on having things their own way, not our way. I understood Yolande very well.

Early in the Pageant, Yolande became the popular favorite as she alphabetically led the parade of states down the runway.

She won swimsuit. For talent, she had a really fine lyric soprano voice. She had been trained by a retired Italian opera star in the hope of a singing career on the concert stage or in the opera. She chose to sing "Sempre Libera" from *La Traviata*. By the end of the week, she was developing a throat problem. Lenora arranged for me to take her to a prominent ear, nose, and throat specialist who sprayed her throat. Yolande decided to change her aria to "Cara Nome" from *Rigoletto*, accompanied by a pianist rather than the orchestra. This necessitated sending notice to Philadelphia to have the musical score delivered in time for Saturday night.

As beautiful as Yolande was, and she really did have an outward appearance of beauty, she had some personality traits that did not endear her to the contestants backstage. She exhibited an air of superiority that was offensive to other contestants, as though no one else had any chance of winning. She apparently didn't care about being friendly and her interests appeared to be solely self-interest. The girls not only disliked her, but they wrote unpleasant things in lipstick on her mirror. I thought she was headstrong, determined to have her own way as much as possible, with a greatly enlarged ego.

By the time the finals began, it was pretty well expected by the press and the public that Miss Alabama was going to be the winner. Everyone, including the hostesses, was rooting for Lily Mae. That year was the first time the five finalists were required to talk on stage, to be judged for the ability to speak extemporaneously.

When Lily Mae's Miss Alabama was crowned, press row went wild and hailed Lily Mae as the Woman of the Year. At long last she had a winner. It was a wonderful celebration.

I thought about Lily Mae during the 1994 Pageant year when another Miss Alabama became Miss America 1995. One of the most outstanding of recent title winners, Heather Whitestone is proving to be exceptionally popular. She has overcome almost total deafness from her early childhood in ways that are a fine example of self-determination and achievement.

Our three National Scholarship Foundation sponsors were joined by Lane, a furniture company known for years for its cedar chests. State and local pageants increased scholarships to $125,000.

Although Yolande Betbeze won her title at the 1950 pageant, her title as Miss America was postdated to 1951, the first to be treated in this manner. At this time the title was finally copyrighted.

I attended the photography and news interview events on stage with the new Miss America when the curtain went down. It was always a wild few minutes after the curtain was raised to allow the press on stage. It had been Mall Dodson's policy to issue press badges to anyone who had what appeared to be a letter from a publication or had a camera. As a result, the prominent important newsmen of newspapers, press associations, and magazines had to fight their way to the new Queen through many whose right to be on stage at that time was always questionable. One was smart to be out of the way when the great rush began.

I accompanied Yolande to the ball in the Claridge Hotel. Hostesses were always separated from those attending the ball by being seated in a small conference room overlooking the main ballroom. On Sunday morning, the press conference was held in the Shelburne Hotel where Yolande was a guest. By courtesy of the management, her room had been changed to the penthouse suite overlooking the ocean, one of many luxurious new rooms.

After Yolande's press conference, I took her to a private meeting with Lenora and MacIntyre, president of Bancroft. The purpose of the meeting was to impress upon Yolande the importance of accepting the Pageant's guidance in her public appearances and protecting the Pageant's image. Mr. Mac, in his kindly, gentle way, was low-key and tactful in his statements. He surprised me by telling Yolande that if at the end of her reign she had performed well to the satisfaction of the Pageant, he would provide an additional $5,000 to the scholarship of $5,000 she had already won.

It had been customary through the years for a hostess to Miss America to be her official hostess when she returned the following year. In this way, I was assigned to Yolande again. We had a young, handsome police driver who drove me around town in our police car at breakneck speed, passing red lights and up and down side avenues to miss some of the red lights. When I remarked on his law breaking of traffic regulations he laughed and said something to the effect of "What's the use being a policeman if you can't break the law?" Then he indicated he was not going to be a cop much longer. I had certainly hoped not.

Yolande was not any more cooperative as Miss America than she had been the year before. I particularly remember the day we were both to be guests of the Kiwanis Club for luncheon. Our driver was to pick me up at the time I had designated in order to meet Yolande at her hotel. The arrangements had been agreed. When the appointed time came, no driver showed. I went out front, then to the nearby corner to wait. Still, no pageant car. I waited and waited. Finally, I went to the phone and called Hackney's Restaurant where the luncheon was. Yes, Miss America had arrived. They had simply ditched me.

I had my pound of flesh, though, from the driver, with quite a bit of personal satisfaction. Yolande went to parties after the Pageant each night. This night it was a party for the judges. Deems Taylor, one of New York's top music critics, was a judge that Yolande singled out and talked with almost to the point of monopolizing his time for quite a while. Since she was interested in a musical career, he was able to open doors of opportunity for her. Time went by.

The hour got later and later. Our policeman driver was waiting in his car. It must have been a monotonous, boring, tiresome wait at that hour of the morning. The policeman made half a dozen trips to complain to me about leaving. I confess I didn't hurry Yolande one bit. He had made me wait, knowing I was required by the Pageant to accompany Miss America to the Kiwanis Luncheon and everywhere else she went. He simply ignored me. After all, it was a chance to have Miss America all to himself for a while. So I'd waited in mental discomfort. Now it was his turn. He could wait as I had waited. And he did.

During a recent pre-Pageant program on NBC, I heard Yolande Betbeze say that because she had refused to appear in a swimsuit at Catalina's swimsuit fashion shows, the Miss Universe Pageant had been established. She may believe that is true, for Catalina and the Pageant came to an official parting of the ways during her reign. Catalina had demanded that the Pageant compel Yolande to model their suits or disqualify her. The Pageant board had declined. Catalina withdrew as a sponsor. The Pageant board, I suspect, was not that happy with Catalina anyway.

However, that version of the story is a long way from being the true story in my opinion. My personal experiences and personal knowledge attest differently. I am convinced that the parting of the ways actually began three years earlier during Barbara Jo Walker's regime when the zebra striped swimsuits created such unfavorable publicity. E. W. Stewart and Lenora had strongly disagreed on the styles of swimsuits which Lenora had not approved. The following year, Catalina had introduced the new two-piece swimsuit which also had detracted substantially from the physical beauty of contestants.

Knowing Lenora's temperament when she was displeased with anything that could possibly reflect upon the Pageant and "her girls" unfavorably, I can almost hear her telling E. W. Stewart to go form his own pageant. That would have been her normal reaction. Yolande's personal preferences of doing what would promote her own career first in place of cooperating with Pageant sponsors gave both Lenora and Stewart a good excuse to part company. It was just that, an excuse. Not the real cause for establishing the Miss Universe Pageant. Three years of swimsuit disagreements were enough. Besides, Lenora detested the swimsuit competition, which in her eyes lowered the standards of the Pageant to a bathing beauty contest.

It was Yolande's excuse to Lenora that she preferred devoting her time to furthering her singing career rather than modeling swimsuits in fashion shows for a Pageant sponsor. Her first priority appeared to be doing what was best for Yolande rather than serving the Pageant's interests. Lenora was asked in an interview if there was anyone she thought should not have become Miss America. She replied that there had been only one in her opinion.

I don't know which one Lenora had in mind. For my part, I would have no difficulty whatsoever in my personal selection. Of all the Miss Americas I have seen, known, and been associated with through the years, one stands out as being least representative, in my opinion, of what the ideals and purposes of the Miss America Pageant have been, and are.

However, Yolande was responsible for something else. Previous Miss Americas have supplied their own chaperones, usually their mothers or family members. Yolande's traveling companions had been considered unsuitable for the Pageant's image by the sponsors. As a result, Nash Motors and the Bancroft Company decided to employ official traveling companions who would assist at press conferences and supervise the appearances of Miss America. Her schedules were arranged by the business manager, Brad Frapart.

I never knew whether Yolande received the additional $5,000 that Mr. Mac had promised her if her performance as Miss America received satisfactory approval. She had been an individual who I believe was not overly willing to abide by Pageant guidance. The sponsors' willingness to employ official traveling companions gives the appearance of some disapproval of her performance.

I've often wondered if the many years Yolande had spent publicly criticizing the Pageant and ridiculing it had their origin here. Sort of like biting the hand that fed her the many opportunities she received as Miss America, opportunities that she may not have had otherwise.

Through the Pageant she had met Deems Taylor, the famous music critic, who introduced her to his friend, Howard Fox, a wealth producer, who became her husband. He was able to provide her with career opportunities and a good life.

⁂

The Pageant was still growing and expanding in 1952. Working capital had reached $44,444.86. Executive director Lenora spent three months in the West, helping state pageants develop better local pageants where scholarships had reached $150,000. Many more former contestants had been graduating from colleges and universities.

More scenery and stage equipment had been purchased. Nash Motors provided 55 Rambler convertibles for the parade because of difficulty in securing an adequate number of rolling chairs. Bancroft and Nash Motors again provided the National Scholarship Foundation. Lane withdrew as a national advertiser and Florida Citrus Commission was granted television spot announcement rights to the title.

Of great personal and public interest had been the grand marshal of the parade, Marilyn Monroe, then a rising young star. I happened to see her in the parking lot of the Warner Theater for publicity pictures the afternoon of the parade. She was seated on the folded down top of a convertible, certainly in no personal danger for she was surrounded by the largest number of policemen I had ever seen together. She obviously had their full, professional attention. It was said that Marilyn wore no underwear. I could well believe it, for she was a stunning picture of beautiful body perfection as well as beauty of face. She drew people to her like a moth to the flame, especially in the parade, wearing a black sheath cut to the navel.

Bob Russell had been retired as master of ceremonies in favor of an unknown from South Carolina, Robert Evans, who had performed in his home area pageant. On the first night of competition, Evans not only got thoroughly mixed up with the names of contestants as they appeared on stage for the first time, but he came apart at the seams in his nervous frustration. The first night program was a real mess.

Al Owens, executive secretary of the Atlantic City Chamber of Commerce, and a long time WFPG radio announcer, was quickly hired as a last minute "pinch hitter." Without enough adequate rehearsal time, Owens did a successfully good job right through the finals, even handling the necessary vocals. He was a local hero in the eyes of his many friends.

As a result of the request to the board from Jacque Mercer, Miss America 1949, a new rule was established that Miss Americas were not permitted to marry during their regime without approval from the board. Based on her own experiences, she thought hasty decisions should not be made at a time when they should be devoting their plans and thoughts to their obligations to the title.

It became desirable to shorten the competition on the final night from fifteen contestants to ten. The board agreed. For this year, five of the semi-finalists who did not place in the top ten would receive $1,000 scholarships as usual. In future years, only ten semi-finalists would be selected. For the first time, all other contestants would receive $100 cash scholarships. Miss Congeniality and the most talented non-finalists would still receive $1,000 scholarships.

In the talent segment, Miss Utah 1952, Colleen Kay Hutchins, captivated the judges and the audience from the moment she appeared on stage as Elizabeth, in Maxwell Anderson's famous play, *Elizabeth The Queen*. One of the tallest of our contestants, this University of Utah graduate not only became Miss America, but was much sought after as a public speaker.

Early contestants had had showgirl experience. In the 1940s and 1950s, the singers and dancers were joined by drama performances. There were always girls with different skills: performing magic, riding a horse, ice skating, designing and making clothes, ventriloquists, to name a few. One year, Miss Nebraska tossed a flaming baton into the judges' box. Another girl had doves in her act which became startled and took off into the auditorium. Some of the audience had physical reminders of their presence. There have been contestants with bows and arrows. One aimed at balloons in her father's hands. And swords. One walked on glass.

When Colleen Hutchins, Miss America 1952, performed with excellent skill the role of Elizabeth and won, other contestants followed her lead the next years. We listened to Lady MacBeth,

Joan of Arc, the Massacre at Lidice, and other heart-wrenching tragedies, not always well done. Occasionally, they were awful.

It soon became a pattern that whatever the skill, talent, appearance, and characteristics the title winner had displayed the year before, the states thought that was what was needed to win in Atlantic City. They chose contestants who resembled carbon copies of Miss America at times.

Lenora began instructing the judges each year so that they would not select a Miss America on anything other than her individual qualities and characteristics. Miss Americas, even the two succeeding Miss Mississippi state winners who won the title, always have been unique young women.

The advent of television developed talent presentations into even more skilled and trained showcases of sometimes exceptional performances. There is a surprising history of young women, not always winners, who had achieved national prominence on the concert and opera stages, in popular singing and dancing careers, in films, as TV anchor women, as professional speakers, or with their own programs. Many have succeeded in business ventures of their own or have become well known in various professions. Some have become lawyers, judges in various courts, doctors of medicine, and corporation CEOs.

Miss Americas and many contestants have become collegiate members of Phi Beta Kappa, and have a surprising number of masters and doctoral degrees. Unfortunately, the TV shows haven't been able to portray to the general public the brains, intellectual capacity, and motivated drive of the average contestant.

I remember some of those early years when contestants were mostly show girls. In striving to upgrade the qualities of the young woman who would wear the crown, Lenora used to tell the judges, "Just pick me a lady, a girl with poise, evidence of good breeding, able to handle any situation in good taste, with good carriage, style and grace." The Pageant really has come a long way since those days.

On occasion, Lenora would invite a guest to make an appearance at the Pageant. For several years, Miss Indian America would walk our runway to the interest of spectators. A typical guest was Miss Indian America II, Mary Louise Defender, whose long Indian name meant Woman of the Red Earth People. She was a full-blooded Yanktonais Sioux, a graduate of Haskell Institute, Lawrence, Kansas. She spoke several Sioux dialects fluently, as well as excellent English. Employed by Standing Rock Sioux Tribe, she managed the land division of the U.S. Agency at Fort Yates, North Dakota.

She wore a typical Sioux Tribe costume valued at $1,000. The necklace was of Sioux design composed of pipes. Each one of the "pipes" was a shank bone of a deer. The leather costume was hand tanned and hand sewn with deer sinew. Defender had been chosen Miss Indian America II from 70 contestants in seventeen states representing 33 tribes at All American Indian Days at Sheridan, Wyoming. The contest was sponsored by the Mandan Indian Shriners Unit of El Zagal Temple, Fargo, North Dakota.

When Nash became a sponsor, the Nash automobiles had become the form of transportation for hostesses and Pageant officials. I had been greatly relieved to have a convertible and driver pick me up every morning, drive me to meet my contestants, take us to Pageant events and then, how wonderful, drive me home at night after the show. Our hostesses were really enjoying this sponsor. I was happy not to have to rely on taxis any more.

This year there was an interesting experience for contestants in the dressing room. Elizabeth Arden, famous for her cosmetics and beauty products throughout the world, served as a Pageant judge. She brought members of her staff to Atlantic City and placed them at the service of contestants. The girls arrived backstage early to learn her basic rules for a careful makeup program emphasizing the "natural look." The winner of the title in 1953 had all of the essence of beauty required for a natural look with her natural curls, peaches-and-cream complexion, a perfect figure, and exceptional talent as a concert pianist. Neva Jane Langley of Georgia became Miss America 1953.

Neva Jane was well endowed physically. Once again, the mothers of contestants protested that she was padded. She proved to be all girl, too. As a concert artist, Neva Jane was featured at some of the finest music festivals in the country. She was a cheerleader for the University of Georgia at all their major football games, appeared at the Tournament of Roses and other festivals, and visited over half of the state pageants. The greatest appearance of all was the invitation to attend President Eisenhower's inauguration.

After her reign ended, she preferred to return to Wesleyan College in Macon, Georgia, for her senior year rather than accept the many offers from the world of entertainment. She later married her college sweetheart to become a successful wife and mother.

Howard Buzby, producer of the Pageant for thirteen years, resigned. He had been training his son from 1946 in every phase of the production. Each year, George Buzby had assumed more and more responsibility, being permitted to design the stage sets in 1950. In 1951, he had been assistant producer. The following year, he was co-producer with his father. The board immediately appointed him producer in 1953.

Howard Buzby's stage productions had been artistic masterpieces, beautiful fountains, waterfalls, natural flowers, and woodland scenes all created in architecturally perfect sets. George Buzby introduced themes for his productions. The first was "Gems of the Ocean," with all events presented against a nautical and marine background.

On occasion, Lenora would invite a special guest to appear with contestants. Miss Sweden, Anita Ekberg, walked the runway one year, although she did not compete.

Eddie Fisher appeared at Registration Day activities for contestants and Pageant events, courtesy of Pepsi-Cola. At the height of his singing career, the girls enjoyed him as they sang along in an informal get-together. He dated tall Miss America, Evelyn Ay, who had to wear flat shoes when with him.

Chapter 18

At the end of my three-year term as second district vice president of the Federation in 1950, I had no ambition to seek further office. Quite frankly I didn't think I could be elected. The largest number of club memberships were in North Jersey. A woman from South Jersey required support from northern club women to win.

My Master Planner opened another door of opportunity. One day, I had a call from Frances Gaskill, southern vice president, who lived in Moorestown, South Jersey, near Philadelphia. Frances asked me if I would run for state recording secretary of the Federation. I voiced disinterest in doing so because if there was competition from North Jersey I couldn't possibly win. She assured me that my candidacy was needed, for she was the only woman from South Jersey on the executive committee of the Federation. At that time, the president, two vice presidents, recording, corresponding and financial secretaries, and the treasurer made up the executive committee. With tongue in cheek, I allowed my club to nominate me for the position, not really believing I could win. Surprisingly, no candidate rose to contest my election. I presume the state officers had had some influence or my election was part of a master plan for me. Anyway, I was elected.

Another door of opportunity opened for me in 1954 during the Federation of Women's Clubs convention here in Atlantic City at Haddon Hall Hotel where I was staying. A telephone call from Lenora invited me to meet her and Hugh Wathen, president of the Pageant, at the hotel. Olive Rundstrom had also been invited.

During the meeting, I was more than surprised to hear that Olive and I were being invited to become co-chairmen of the hostess committee since Ted Shermer had resigned to further her career as a teacher. Olive had been chairman of the prestigious Miss Atlantic City Pageant for a few years, but voiced some reluctance in accepting. I was not concerned with leading a group of fine women as hostesses, but I did have some concern about dealing with the news media. I had been interviewed a number of times by the press as a state officer of the Federation. Olive and I were promised strong support and we agreed to the assignment.

Olive had been an active member and supporter of the Atlantic County Historical Society. In an era when membership in the Daughters of the American Revolution was considered prestigious, she was registrar of our local chapter, expert in tracing genealogical records. My father's sisters had long been members. Olive decided to bring our family's history up to date so that I could become a member.

In doing so, she discovered that we had a common ancestry way back when. Our ancestry had been traced to Pieter Wolfertsen Van Couwenhoven who emigrated from Holland in 1630, sailing on the ship DE ENDRACT, which landed in New Amsterdam, now New York City, where he settled. Descendants were the first to own land in Atlantic City. The Van Couwenhoven-Conover Family Association has members in every state, Canada, and foreign lands. The Sooy, Leeds, Turner, Higbee, Johnson, Smith and Bowen families are among the descendants locally.

When the hostess committee luncheon had been held the Friday before the Pageant in 1954, Olive and I presided for the first time as co-chairmen. I had been given the privilege of presenting a beautiful diamond ring to Ted Shermer in recognition of her excellent service as chairman of the committee. Lenora, as always, provided all of the interesting tidbits of information about contestants, as well as new plans for the Pageant. Hostess instructions were presented.

During the summer months, the idea of televising the Pageant had been discussed with Hugh Wathen, Pageant president. Paul Whiteman, one of our country's most successful band leaders, had been a 1953 judge and a Pageant fan. He was also a vice president of the American Broadcasting Company's radio and television network.

One day, he had luncheon with Wathen at the popular Penn Atlantic Hotel where businessmen frequently lunched. Wathen was impressed with his suggestion to broadcast the Pageant on TV. He arranged with Al Marks, then a recent past president of the Atlantic City Chamber of Commerce, to discuss the matter with Whiteman and some executives.

When Lenora was first approached with the plan being proposed, she was hesitant to agree. She feared that television might affect attendance, thus affecting Pageant income. Respecting Marks' business acumen, she eventually agreed. The Pageant board granted contractual rights to televise the Pageant for $10,000 to the Philco Corporation. The first live broadcast was televised from 10:30 p.m. to midnight.

Television did not adversely affect attendance. Instead, it created increased national, state, and local interest in the Pageant, and resulted in the establishment of additional new state pageants and a waiting list of national sponsors.

President Hugh Wathen had also met with the parade committee that summer to consider changing the parade to an illuminated night parade. Every mayor in South Jersey agreed to enter an illuminated float representing each community. Generators were purchased by the Pageant and loaned to participating communities. The parade, when it occurred, was acknowledged to be the greatest outdoor spectacle ever staged in the resort in spite of heavy rain.

I've not forgotten that night. Lenora had instructed me to go to the end of the parade at Albany Avenue and check on every contestant as she left the Boardwalk on her return to her hotel. I stood there in the pouring rain for a long time until I was told that the girls were being taken off their floats or cars directly into the Convention Hall about halfway in the line of march.

I particularly remember Mr. Kane, a prominent Boardwalk furrier, who lived on my street. He told his tale of woe one day. His firm had loaned each contestant a beautiful mink stole. Rain does not damage fur. But some of the girls actually dragged their fur capes directly across the Boardwalk boards into the Hall. This ruined linings and soiled the furs. He had considerable damage financially. He was more than disturbed; he was angry.

Olive and I didn't really understand our positions as co-chairmen of the hostess committee that first year, playing it by ear as each day progressed. Up to that time, the only role of women had been a minor one of simply escorting the girls and keeping them out of trouble. No female voice had ever actually been heard in any capacity, other than Lenora's, within the Pageant organization.

All I really knew was that hostesses were required to be present at all media contacts with the press when contestants were being interviewed or photographed. I assumed that Olive and I were expected to monitor, supervise, and oversee all press activities with contestants for Pageant protection, among other escort duties.

What I didn't know at the time was that Ted Shermer had always deferred press requests to Lenora for decision making. They used to sit together on a corner of the stage and confer. Lenora was in control.

My first experience as co-chairman was being seated with Lenora in the same corner of the stage. When Lenora had to leave on other business temporarily, a member of the stage crew invited me to leave the stage. I told him I had been instructed to sit there. I suppose I could also have said that when Lenora said "sit," I sat.

When members of the press came to me for approval of their plans—if Lenora was elsewhere involved—I gave approval, disapproval, or deferment of decision for Lenora to decide. Since I didn't know any differently, I proceeded to assume this type of decision making was one of our duties. Little by little, Olive and I became more deeply involved with press activities.

Lenora supported our beginning efforts with encouragement, taking personal charge of special events and photography. A great deal of her time, though, and her energy were spent overseeing production of the show, watching rehearsals, and dealing with national sponsors and state Pageant officials, plus a myriad of business details and problems. Only her great energy, ambition for the Pageant, and dynamic drive made it possible for her to do so much.

Dealing with the press was the biggest problem Olive and I had. One serious problem I soon realized was the fact that rules established by the hostess committee were only by word of mouth. This created misunderstandings when new press representatives came into town. Olive and I were very careful with the press those first couple of years, more so than some desired. One day, an Associated Press reporter of stature came to see me backstage after a rehearsal to discuss easing our relations generally. I told him that with the several hundred reporters and photographers Mall Dodson presented with badges, Olive and I had no way of knowing who was who. We needed help recognizing the reputable press from the not so reputable. I plainly asked for his help. It was quickly forthcoming. A number of men and women of the press would stop a moment to warn me about some reporter or publication. I soon felt a sense of protective camaraderie from time to time.

We had another problem those first few years, one of organization behind the scenes, little details no committee was actively involved in solving. As I watched the many activities taking place around me in Convention Hall, I observed a host of minor details that needed better organization, so simple to achieve, but apparently unnoticed by those actively involved in putting a show together. Many involved the comfort, safety, and talent performance of the girls. I felt motivated to try to correct them.

As a first step I carried a small notebook and a pen everywhere to record the simple matters I believed could be easily improved. By the end of Pageant week, I had a couple of notebooks filled with suggestions. I prepared a written report for Lenora and the

Pageant president who were always supportive. Little by little and step by step, I began changing some of the conditions that upset my understanding of good Pageant management.

One of the biggest problems in Convention Hall was the handling of the press after the show each night. The stage was overcrowded with news media, all contestants, hostesses and Pageant officials. There seemed no system in place. Everyone was doing his or her thing while many girls were being interviewed or photographed and many were just standing around waiting. I couldn't find anyone who appeared to be in charge. There was no one calling a halt to the proceedings. Time went on and on.

I wrote a letter to the president asking who was in charge so I'd know whom to contact for a heart-to-heart talk on better and easier stage management with less confusion and stress with the news media.

Needless to say, my efforts to change some of the status quo were not always acceptable to the prominent men used to doing the same things in the same way for years. The reasons were simple. Women had not ever had any standing or participation in any of the Pageant operations in Convention Hall. It was an era when women were more to be seen than heard.

Lenora supported our efforts with encouragement. She always took personal charge of the panorama picture of contestants in evening gowns taken on stage after Wednesday night competition. Much of her time and energy were spent overseeing production of the show, watching rehearsals, dealing with sponsors and state Pageant officials, and the myriad of business details. Only her great energy and drive made it possible for her to do so much.

Since dealing with the press was the biggest problem Olive and I had, I began studying what was happening on stage during rehearsals. Photographers were allowed on stage while rehearsals were in progress, often being in the way. I realized publicity was publicity, but certainly it could be more efficiently managed. A new rule was established allowing interviews and pictures on stage only during rehearsal breaks.

I can't say that all of the working press was happy with the new changes. The top professionals were. New press in town, unused to the hostess restrictions, occasionally griped, but accepted our ways of operation. Personal popularity was not and never has been my goal. The success of the endeavor worth doing was all important to me and worth doing well.

I really wasn't aware of it at the time in those early years, but what I was doing to improve conditions in Convention Hall was different in every respect from what the hostess committee had been. Mrs. White and Mrs. Shermer had cultivated and preserved the image of the hostess committee as socially elite women chaperoning contestants to Pageant events during the week. Olive and I sensed, on a number of occasions, that my efforts to help improve conditions for contestants were not particularly welcome. Women had their inactive place in society in general and the Pageant in particular. I quickly learned we women were supposed to stay there in our place, more or less unheard, even unseen.

I couldn't do it. I couldn't watch the difficult, often unnecessary problems facing the girls, be personally responsible for their safety and well-being, without calling these matters to the attention of those who could or should correct them. Some Pageant officials accepted my information and suggestions and acted on them. Some listened respectfully but simply ignored me. There were times when I felt as though I was supposed to fold my tent and slip quietly away. I couldn't do that either. With notebooks filled with situations and conditions that needed changing, and after informing Lenora, the president, and production staff, I began step by step to bring a better sense of order to press activities, to the dressing room, to rehearsal time, and to security for contestants.

Happily my efforts were accepted by top-ranking officials. Unhappily there were a couple of new members of the board of directors who generally disagreed with my activities all eighteen years I was a member of the board.

I am satisfied that whatever opposition or disagreement I aroused in changing the role of the hostess committee from an escort service to one of useful, effective management was the result of two basic factors. One, there was no real understanding of the problems faced by both the hostess committee and the contestants in those "everything goes" days by the men running the Pageant. Not many men understand women.

I used to wish I could have one of my two dissenters spend a day, or even half a day, with me. Present as they were backstage, they never really saw what was happening even in their presence, or were too busy.

Second, the role of women in the man's world of the Pageant had been nonexistent. I had a recognized choice to make if my chairmanship was to have any value. Be a "yes" girl and receive nice pats on the head, or forego popularity per se and do what I knew needed to be done. I decided I had the know-how, based upon my knowledge and management experience with large organizations, to make useful and effective and changes. The difficult part was getting the men on board.

To some of the board members, the women volunteer workers did not count as worthy of recognition. Today we would call it discrimination. But then it was a way of life for women in business, in civic activities, and in the Pageant. I used to laugh privately a few years later at the thought that the women's liberation protests at the Pageant had been for the wrong reasons.

Olive and I simply began the process of adding new dimension to the responsibilities of the hostess committee while retaining the best of the escort-chaperone image. We had not been seeking it, but we were beginning to have a small but meaningful voice being heard for the first time in some of the Pageant's operations; a voice never heard before and destined to be heard more often in the future whenever we could make it heard. That was not easily done. Whatever improvements we made, either with pageant support or arbitrarily, were made item by item from the notebooks I filled every pageant.

Chapter 19

During our first years, Lenora's working schedule had been more efficiently arranged. The girls were required to register on Labor Day in the west room of Haddon Hall. Lenora and I sat together in an alcove of the room while she talked with each contestant. Olive was the official greeter as each girl arrived at various times. Rehearsals began that night.

A breakfast meeting was held on Wednesday morning with the judges in Haddon Hall, their headquarters. For the first time, I was present during the judging. Hostesses always had to wait in another room. It was an interesting procedure to watch. The girls were seated at small tables in groups of five. The judges rotated from table to table every few minutes when the signal was given. I not only had a chance to watch the girls' reactions to the judges, but also view judges well-known nationally in their particular fields. Some girls wanted to be in the spotlight, claiming as much of the attention of the judges for themselves as possible, which I'm sure detracted from their scores. Some were able to turn on and off their charm. Some had a gimmick of some sort to create conversation and personal attention. A psychologist would have enjoyed watching human nature at work. I did.

With the exception of a second judge's meeting with contestants on Friday mornings, the next days were spent rehearsing for the show and talent. The evenings had preliminary competition Wednesday through Friday. Saturday morning at the rehearsal for the finals, contestants turned in their ballots for the selection of Miss Congeniality. The winner of the $1,000 scholarship was announced by Lenora with attendant picture taking. Later, rehearsal for the crowning of Miss America and the necessary changes in the show were held. Girls who expected or hoped to be in the final ten could rehearse talent if they desired.

As hostess co-chairman, I spent much of my time either on stage during rehearsals or in the dressing room during competition. Olive Rundstrom and I always seemed to have a dozen things to do which kept us busy and often separate.

The stage area in Convention Hall is immense, located in the center of a wall facing Pacific Avenue. There are two large, open rooms on each side of the stage. Room A, where the girls' dressing room was located, was on the left of the stage. Room B was located on the right, and was used by Miss America and professional talent, as well as Pageant officials, for various purposes.

The dressing room was set up with rows of dressing tables and mirrors for six girls at each long table. Contestants were assigned alphabetically, beginning with Alabama and ending with Wyoming. There was a fairly large unused open area on one audience side of the room where a few chairs were available. There were food tables containing danish and sweet rolls at the breakfast hours and a variety of sandwiches during lunch time and periods of the day, plus coffee and soft drinks. Contestants and hostesses often needed a quick snack or even lunch, too.

Aside from the lack of clothes racks to hang up their outfits and evening gowns, the room also lacked a telephone. It did have a nurse's station—a small alcove with a cot—and a registered nurse to care for the occasional health needs of contestants or anyone else backstage. The Pageant had a local medical doctor, Dr. David B. Allman, a past president of the American Medical Association, and member of the board of directors. We had no microphone yet in the dressing room.

Pageant officials, when needed, if not on stage, could usually be found in Room B, which was a long hike, the best part of a city block in a corridor, behind the stage from Room A.

We had fine police protection. Police were stationed in various areas of the stage and at stage entrances, we also had policemen outside our dressing room doors. An inconvenience that couldn't be changed was the location of the powder room on the second floor with entrances possible, but closed, from the balcony. There was a staircase inside the dressing room where a Convention Hall guard was usually seated up on the landing.

Our Nash Rambler convertibles were driven by off-duty firemen under the leadership of William Peterson. Each Pageant official and hostess had been assigned a car and driver. By the time the week was over, we had usually developed a fine rapport. Firemen were also on duty in the stage area where high voltage electrical equipment and heavy stage curtains were located. I thought the Pageant was very well organized and it was. I didn't realize then how much more needed to be accomplished in Convention Hall.

Evelyn Ay, Miss America the first year I was hostess chairman, was the first to graduate from an Ivy League university, the University of Pennsylvania. Evelyn had that first important characteristic present-day winners must have—brains. Her articulate and intellectual capacities were revealed in the way she presented her talent. She chose to recite "Leaves From a Glass House" by Don Blanding. The poem exceeded the three-minute time limit, forcing her to rearrange the order of some verses and eliminate others after she arrived in Atlantic City.

She was scheduled for talent on the last night of preliminary competition. She never did recite it during rehearsal as she would be forced to do today. Since she didn't need music, she convinced the production staff that she was prepared, although she wasn't, and didn't need to rehearse. Actually, when Saturday night came, she went on cold, performing so well that her talent points combined with her swimsuit win placed her high enough to secure the title.

For years, Evelyn was sought after as a highly popular public speaker, delivering her message in a warm, friendly, often humorous manner. Her traveling companion, Mary Korey, often used to tell about Evelyn's interesting public appearances. One time, they were the only women present at a large luncheon meeting of men. Billy Graham had preceded her as speaker. Since Evelyn had thought they were attending a small affair, she hadn't been prepared. When her turn came, she spoke off the cuff for a long time. When she finished, she received an enthusiastic standing ovation in recognition of her personal character and excellent, thoughtful remarks. Billy Graham's office called her for weeks to ask her to speak many places.

My first year as hostess co-chairman was also the first year of the televised show in 1954. Lenora, who used to crown the new Miss America backstage, invited a cameraman backstage to film the winner's reaction during the first telecast. As the first three runners-up were being taken on stage, the TV director leaned toward Lee Ann Meriwether and said "Congratulations! You are Miss America."

Lenora placed the robe and banner on Lee Ann and ushered her to the entrance through the curtains. Lee Ann paused for a minute, gazed toward heaven and whispered, "You know I know how happy you are." Lenora said later that was the first they knew that Lee Ann's father had died just two weeks before.

ABC won the prize that year for the best television shot on the air. Lee Ann hadn't known she was on TV. She wept copious tears of joy as she walked the runway.

From that time, for the benefit of television, finalists were seated on stage to await the judges' decision. Bert Parks would announce the runners-up until only two were still seated. Occasionally, in the excitement of the moment, there was confusion in the minds of the two remaining finalists about which one had won.

On Sunday morning after the crowning, a press conference was held at 9:30 a.m. in the new Miss America's Hotel Dennis. The Pageant had begun screening the photographers and working press, establishing a period of time for each group. At one o'clock, Lee Ann would be photographed in color. At two o'clock, she made appearances at Boardwalk stores to receive gifts of jewelry and furs and her first official Miss America "Everglaze" evening gown. She was to spend fifteen minutes each at DuPont's, Yamrons, Koff's and Polonsky-Kane-Shuman's. The scholarship winners had met with the Scholarship Committee earlier. At five o'clock, Lenora left with Miss America for the Waldorf Astoria Hotel in New York.

Not long after Brad Frapart had become business manager of the Pageant, a romance had developed with Lenora. The hostesses used to be interested, watching and hoping for her happiness in her new association. In due time, wedding bells had sounded when Lenora became the bride of Brad Frapart to everyone's great pleasure. It was a good marriage lasting many years until Brad died.

Nash Motors resigned as a scholarship contributor due to changes in management. Bancroft became the only original scholarship supporter. The Camay Division of Proctor and Gamble Company joined the Philco Corporation and the Florida Citrus Commission as advertising contributors.

Bert Parks, a popular television and stage personality, well known for starring on Broadway in *The Music Man*, was engaged as master of ceremonies in 1955. He had a long, popular, memorable association with the Pageant, unforgettable by many. Kirk Browning, an experienced director of television shows, became director and Glen Osser, musical director.

Bert Parks was not only highly popular as emcee, in fact, the most popular of all emcees, but he was equally popular with everyone behind the scenes and backstage. With the girls, he was always helpful, encouraging, full of good humor, making everyone feel comfortable during rehearsals. Whatever his personal opinions and misgivings may have been at times, no one could guess from his outwardly jovial disposition. The production staff found him professional in their associations. With the stage hands, drivers, police, and others, he was just one of the "boys." With Pageant officials and hostesses, he was a gentleman of first class. If problems existed, and I'm sure there were some, they were not generally known. He was an excellent emcee, having a special charisma with the public unequaled by his successors.

When the Pageant first began being televised in 1954, Al Marks had become the official Pageant representative. He certainly was no favorite of the television people in the beginning. They were accustomed to the rough and tumble of network competition, but they were inclined to stick together in the presence of outsiders. This was true where Al Marks was concerned, for he was no shrinking violet, willing to be "talked down to." He was a tough negotiator. He was elected to the board in 1955.

When he negotiated the second year with the Philco Corporation, his asking price was increased from $10,000 to $25,000, to which Philco objected. When Marks pointed out the advantages of TV, Philco finally agreed and Marks won much praise locally. His first appointive position was the beginning of many responsible leadership offices with the Pageant, always as a volunteer, until he retired in 1987.

In following years, Marks never hesitated to switch to other networks, using all three, but staying with NBC in recent years. Television executives admitted that Marks made "hard decisions." The one thing he always insisted upon controlling was having artistic control of the television show. He used to say to me with glee, I think, that he wore the hat of executive producer of the TV show because he could have absolute control and veto power. That he did.

He was under extreme tension in those early TV years in his determination to produce a TV show in the best possible taste and in the best interests of the Pageant. I well remember the day in an early TV year when Adrian Phillips escorted Marks in nervous tension tears out to the Boardwalk for a short time to restore his equilibrium.

I never told him so but I remember Al Marks from the time when he was quite a young man, not too many years out of college in the early years of his business career. He lived with his parents across Ventnor Avenue near my home in Ventnor. I used to see him almost every morning walking to Atlantic Avenue to the trolley car when I was driving my children to school. Even then there was something noticeable about him.

Marks was a graduate of Ivy League universities with post graduate degrees, articulate always in his expression of views and completely logical in his presentation of facts for any audience. In his business career with Newburger and Company and later Advest Inc., stock brokers and investment advisers, he was recognized as an important community leader, holding positions of responsibility on a variety of boards and agencies on a volunteer basis. Governmental leaders sought his services and advice. He once told me in later years that local and state political leaders had wanted him to run for a seat in Congress. He had declined because of financial responsibilities to his family.

His outspoken public opinions when he was president of the Chamber of Commerce, and later with the Pageant, brought him many requests to speak at civic and service clubs, some of which he served as president. The news media interviewed him frequently on matters of public interest.

Marks was always popular with men and women alike, an individual who was outgoing and easy to know. He was always fun to be with, his wit and good humor bubbling over frequently in his social and business contacts with people.

I first met him in his early forties when he joined the board of directors of the Pageant a year after me. He still had and continued to have throughout the years, a tall, reasonably slender build. His dark hair had a suspicion of thinning a bit over his forehead. His round face was a happy face with brown eyes expressively revealing both the contentment and passions within him. His mouth seemed perpetually turned up in a smile with laugh lines developing near the corners of his mouth.

As a business executive and with the Pageant he was the dominant male, totally in control of any situation in which he was involved. He brooked no interference or questioning of any decisions he made for public relations in difficult problems, giving completely logical explanations with a touch of humor when the situation warranted. With Pageant officials, he had a ready ear and would listen well to differing points of view. He really listened.

Like many corporate executives, he could be tough, arbitrary on occasion, determined to carry out what he believed to be in the best interests of all concerned. At times, he was entirely satisfied that he knew best what the course of action was, better than anyone else. In his own words, said often to me, he was "the most autocratic of autocrats."

Marks was also a creative thinker, constantly striving to find new ways and more modern or efficient means to handle or improve whatever business was at hand. The juices of his creativity were always flowing in the direction of both the artistic and executive management of the Pageant.

He was an unusual man, talented, witty, wise, honest, lovable, understanding, sociable, tough, determined and dominant. The unique qualities of his character supplied the Pageant with the courage, integrity, and good sense it needed to build on the lasting accomplishments of the retired executive director, Lenora Slaughter.

When he became the new chief operating officer and chairman of the executive committee, Al Marks gave much of his life in volunteer service to the Pageant, developing television programs and TV associations, opening new levels of Pageant interest and acceptance throughout the world. Some members of the press used to call Al Marks "Mr. America." Whatever title one gives him, he well deserves the accolades of praise that have been given to him.

Ours was a good working relationship. Al Marks respected the developing role of the hostess committee as an asset to the Pageant's operations, was always willing to accept our ideas and suggestions in general, and supported our efforts to improve the Pageant image. On the other hand, I was a silent repository of personal frustrations, secrets, and confidences when he felt the need to get something off his chest. As the Pageant continued to grow and develop, he extended my role as hostess chairman to instructing state pageant sponsors on national Pageant regulations during regional conferences in the country. On occasion, I was a speaker for the Pageant at civic clubs in and out of state and on television. Al Marks really understood the importance of the hostess committee to the Pageant, ahead of his time.

Elizabeth B. Alton

Chapter 20

I never gave much thought about the mechanics of getting contestants on stage on time during the shows in those early years of the revived Pageant. When I became co-chairman, Howard Buzby, producer, had asked me to assign two hostesses to the dressing room to assist the production staff. I chose the Bross twins, two lovely young women who had once competed in the Miss Atlantic City Pageant. That was the first organized supervision within the dressing room by hostesses.

In looking back over those years, I also realize it was the first step toward organizing the transition of the hostess committee from socially elite women whose duties were limited to being chaperones with the sole responsibility of preventing scandal or poor publicity from damaging the Pageant's reputation.

Arrangements were made to provide Miss America with hotel headquarters in New York, to facilitate her travel schedule. Her extensive wardrobe would be kept at the New York headquarters where it could be properly supervised and augmented.

When the Pageant became televised, I spent most of my time backstage in and out of the dressing room with cues when girls had to be on stage and seeing that they went where they belonged at the time needed. There were many times when instructions had to be given to everyone at once. Since the room was large, it was necessary to project my voice so all could hear. I was used to doing this since I often addressed two or three hundred people without a microphone in the days when they were not yet popularly used. I saw no reason, however, to exert myself or expend further energy, and asked to have a microphone in the dressing room. What I was given was a bull horn. It weighed a ton. It was all I could do to lift it to my mouth beside hold it there while I spoke. I returned it immediately. Eventually a microphone was provided some time later.

I also asked to have racks provided in the dressing room for contestants to hang their clothes rather than draping them over the many chairs in the room. In all my years in the dressing room I was unsuccessful in providing this convenience for the girls. I was soon to learn through the years that everyone in charge of the stage area would treat me with every courtesy, listen respectfully, but just didn't hear me. Our personal needs were low man on the totem pole. I developed a strong sense that we woman volunteers of the Pageant were a necessary but unimportant part of the Pageant to our male associates. Gradually I refused to accept that conclusion. We were important. Whatever differences of opinion arose with newer members of the Pageant family through the years, the origin of those differences in my belief was that only a few officials ever really listened to us. When I finished my years as chairman, I still believed that conclusion was true. Women didn't really count.

We had some interesting problems in the dressing room. Once the police found a man who had crawled through the large pipes of the air conditioning system to a vent in the wall near the ceiling where he could look into the dressing room and watch the girls dressing and undressing.

Obscene letters were sometimes sent to contestants in the Hall, some were really disgusting. One state chaperone asked me to withhold mail from her girl and give it to her for checking. Her contestant had been too upset.

One medical problem occurred which caused the Pageant nurse some concern. The girl laid on a cot in our medical corner as often as she could but seemed faint most of the time. Dr. Allman was called but found no health problem. After a couple of days, one of the contestants traveling with her said the girl had been dieting and hadn't eaten all week. That was soon remedied.

We were most fortunate in having in the dressing room two excellent wardrobe mistresses. Their main duty was to keep the clothes of the contestants in good repair; accidents do happen to some of the finest and most expensive clothes and evening gowns. Sometimes the rips or tears, loose zippers or buttons, created an emergency situation between the segments of the stage show. I was always surprised at the efficiency and rapidity with which repairs were made with superb skill. I have seen girls sewn into their clothes when necessary in an instant. It was kind of fun to watch the girls in evening gowns head to the ironing board when they arrived for the show. They would back up to the boards, have their full skirts lifted up over them while our wardrobe mistresses ironed out any wrinkles from their ride in the car.

Wearing fashion creations, there were times when some gowns with long lines of teeny weeny satin buttons required too long to open and close. Rather than declare the gowns unusable during competition, I issued a requirement that a zipper would have to be installed inconspicuously in such gowns.

After Yolande Betbeze's year, the dressing room was always a happy place, more like a sorority than competitors. The girls were friendly and helpful to each other and a joy to know. There were always birthdays to be celebrated, a cake to be cut and a happy period of congratulations and relaxation during rehearsal breaks. One day when a Hostess and I were moving a small table onto the stage apron for the large birthday cake, Captain Cade stopped me with humor and a grin and said, "You can't do that. Don't move that table." I asked why not. He said, "The union won't let you. When that table is moved a union man has to do it." So we stood around and waited for a union man to show up to move what I could have carried by myself the few feet necessary.

We never seemed to have a knife handy to cut the cake. This year Captain Cade came to our rescue. He reached in his pocket for a pocketknife. It was not the small knife men usually carry in their pockets, but one with a longer blade. He handed the knife to me open, handle first, but he didn't let go. He looked me straight in the eye and said very seriously, "This is a lethal weapon. Be very careful with it." I've never forgotten the solemnity with which he spoke. I also was scared at the possibilities of what could happen and my personal responsibility. I stood around keeping a sharp eye on that knife until I could thankfully return it to Captain Cade.

One of my early years backstage, I noticed that our firemen drivers always stood through the show in the open area near our dressing room. No one had thought to provide seats for them. I asked the production staff to provide seats on the apron of the stage not used for the shows. They did so to the immense satisfaction of the drivers. As a result, they gave me a very pretty artificial floral arrangement in a ceramic dish with their thanks. I kept the arrangement long past its usefulness because it's the only time I can ever remember anyone in the Pageant saying "thank you" to me. There were times when there was a bit of controversy over whether the girls were padding their bras. State sponsors complained occasionally, girls sometimes mentioned it, local people argued about it. Lenora had one answer. If the girls could get away with making themselves more attractive, so be it. I was once solidly berated by a local businessman for not checking every girl to see if she was padded. I had one answer for that. I was not going to thrust my hand down anyone's bosom. We have watched, though, some very interesting efforts in those years before built-in bras in swimsuits and evening gowns. Occasionally someone might use a whole box of Kleenex. Sometimes it shows to the experienced eye as they walk the runways. Sometimes it doesn't. "Beauty is in the eye of the beholder." Even a few Miss Americas have been undeveloped physically.

I always felt sorry for girls who had or thought they had a cosmetic problem. One lovely redhead had the pale, white skin of someone of that coloring. While most contestants have a bit of suntan, she was as white as if she never saw the sun. For the swimsuit competition, her pale legs stood out in the group. She wanted to wear stockings with her swimsuit. I don't know of any time when a girl has ever worn stockings during swimsuit competition. She was very upset when I told her stockings were not allowed. I suggested make-up on her legs. She was not being judged on the color of her legs but her overall beauty and physical fitness. I felt much concern for her. Lenora didn't like the swimsuit competition because of the image the Pageant projects as a bathing beauty contest. She always advocated that playsuits should replace swimsuits. There are many attractive playsuits that reveal the attributes of the girls just as much if not more attractively than swimsuits. Through the years the Pageant board, mostly composed of men, has been unwilling to make the change. Men like swimsuits.

One time I was incorrectly quoted in an Associated Press article as stating that the Pageant was going to eliminate the swimsuit competition. The mail I received was amazing. Men wrote to castigate me for taking away their "fun," their fantasies, their sexual emotions and other unrepeatable expressions. Letters came from everywhere. I am convinced the swimsuit competition is one of the reasons that some women continue to believe, mistakenly, that the Pageant exploits women.

I remember debating the issue with some students at Stockton College. I was representing the board of trustees on a college committee preparing for the college's first evaluation by Middle States Accreditation Association. The students could see nothing but exploitation. The chairman of the committee was one of the most popular and most likable professors in the college community. I invited him and his wife to attend the Pageant in my box. He agreed with me that the Pageant was a beautiful show without any exploitation. I heard less discussion by students afterward.

One of my interesting duties was instructing the newly crowned Miss America on the events following her crowning. Of first interest was the press conference the following morning. I explained what she should wear, where the conference would be held and the press who would be present. I noted some of the questions usually asked each year, some tricky ones, and ones about the issues of the day. I could usually tell right then which girls would be great Miss Americas' by the attention they gave and the questions asked.

I always escorted Miss America to her hotel. One year I remember with some humor. Our Queen was staying at the excellent Marlborough-Blenheim Hotel which had a new manager who was new to the town. A large crowd awaited our arrival. The manager seemed to think he was going to have the joy of rushing her into the hotel for he reached to grab her arm, politely trying to elbow me out of the way. He was wrong. Men do not escort our Queens. I was quicker than he was and escorted Miss America into the hotel. Soon, a huge bucket of champagne arrived in her room with the manager ready for a party. The champagne went back along with him. I suggested he take it to the state sponsors.

As I began changing the hostess committee from a chaperone service to one with important responsibilities, I also began changing the qualifications for membership, choosing for replacements women I knew had leadership abilities. These were women who were smart, organized and would successfully complete the duties I required of them. While social standing was valuable, it was not the main qualification I was seeking. Our 65 women became a close-knit, smoothly running operation, able and willing to perform their duties easily and well.

After the girls went on stage for rehearsals in the early mornings, our 25 hostesses caring for contestants met with me in a corner of the dressing room. Over coffee and a danish, we discussed whatever problems or difficulties had arisen the previous day. Hostesses in those days served from early morning all day straight through the evening shows. In that way, I knew who in the Pageant was doing what, where, when and why. In a reasonably short time, I was satisfied that I learned more factual information about what was happening in the Pageant than almost anyone. On the other hand, I became a conduit for information received from state sponsors, drivers, parents and the press who told me much in privacy, which remained secure with me unless action was required.

Chapter 21

One of my earliest problems, when I had become co-chairman of the hostess committee, was the early arrival of contestants in Atlantic City before Labor Day, the official opening of Pageant activities and registration. Our hotels were always full to overflowing the weekend before Labor Day. Contestants were given hospitality at the hotels only from Labor Day through the following week.

Whenever state pageant sponsors wanted to arrive a day or two early, personal arrangements had to be made with a hotel long in advance, with the expenses payable by the state sponsors for those before-Pageant days.

I was not only surprised but downright shocked to learn from a fireman driver a situation that never should have happened and which had had the potential of personal danger to the contestant as well as damage to the Pageant image. A contestant from a western state had arrived in Atlantic City on Friday before Labor Day. Her first mistake was that she was alone, unaccompanied by a state chaperone or state sponsor representative. She had no hotel reservation and was unable to secure a room in our hotels. In effect, she was stranded.

I'm not sure how the fireman driver met her, but my best guess is that he happened to meet her at one of the hotels and realized the seriousness of her problems. He told me that he took the contestant to his home in Brigantine where his wife and children had had the unusual pleasure of entertaining her until Labor Day.

I knew that our firemen drivers had been carefully selected by chairman William Peterson. I always had much respect for them, for our hostesses spoke highly of "their" drivers. I also knew that the fireman who had come forward to tell me his story, when he could have kept it to himself, was personally concerned that no other contestant be subjected to a similar situation. I was thankful that no harm had come to a fine contestant through the generosity and compassion of a fireman driver who cared enough about the safety and well-being of our contestant to take her into his own home.

I agreed with him that the situation had to be corrected. And it was. Lenora instructed state sponsors on their responsibilities concerning state chaperones and arrival times for registration. In polite words and in her best executive manners, she laid down the law in those years on procedures the states were required to follow in Atlantic City. In retrospect, it was the many incidents that needed correcting in the Pageant that led me to go beyond the escort/chaperone duties assigned to hostesses, creating a gradual transition into a more valuable committee management system for the improvement of Pageant operations as we hostesses saw and experienced them.

"There She is . . . Miss America" became the theme song in 1956. Bernie Wayne always claimed he had written his famous song for Miss America in just a short time. He had presented the song to the Pageant as a musical number when Miss America was crowned. He was led to believe the song would be sung after the crowning. Unfortunately, Bob Russell, the emcee, refused to sing it in favor of a song of his own which he had written. Wayne put the song away, disappointed.

One day at a social gathering he played the song. Pierson Mapes, in charge of Philco advertising, heard the song and enjoyed it. He asked Wayne why he hadn't heard it. Wayne asked why he should have, receiving the answer that Mapes represented the sponsor.

"There She is . . . Miss America" was first introduced by Johnny Desmond on a *Philco Playhouse* program when it was sung to Lee Ann Meriwether. It was first heard at the Pageant when Bert

Parks sang it to Sharon Kay Ritchie, Miss America 1956, making it beloved for many years.

Lee Ann Meriwether has had a prominent, long career on the stage, on television and in the movies. Once she met the Shah of Iran at a party and asked him to dance; he accepted. She met Juan Peron in South America on her birthday. He sent her roses and his helicopter for a tour of Buenos Aires. Lee Ann traveled with 11 suitcases and 50 gowns. Some years later Miss America carried only two suitcases of mostly permanent press clothing.

Lee Ann also was the first weather girl on Dave Garroway's *Today Show*. She was succeeded by Barbara Walters when Lee Ann moved to the West Coast for movie and television shows two years later.

⁂

One night, for the first and only time, I had a problem with a hostess that was difficult for me to handle. It was a long standing policy that hostesses were to be decorous at all times, including strict limitations on drinking before meeting contestants. This was never a problem. One night during rehearsals in Convention Hall, Lenora came to me with the sad news that one of our most popular hostesses was not only apparently under the influence, but one of our most important state sponsors requested her removal. I was shocked. I had never had to fire a hostess on duty before and didn't relish the necessity now. I took her aside to tell her to go home and not come back. Needless to say, she had a first class fit, was highly insulted, but she had the good sense to leave. The situation bothered me for quite a while. Although she had been a good hostess for a few years, she must have had a problem. She died several years later.

Dr. Theodore A. Distler, who had succeeded Dr. Guy E. Snavely as executive director of the American Association of American Colleges, was named national director of the scholarship foundation. The scholarship program across the country and in Atlantic

City had passed the $1,000,000 mark. In eleven years, $291,400 had been awarded to 354 state and key city winners at the national finals. State Pageants had awarded their winners and runners-up with $386,000 in scholarships. The approximately 2,500 local Pageants over the nation had awarded another $403,000 to their home-town girls.

Olive Rundstrom and I were able to handle the business of dealing with the problems of hostesses and contestants quite well. Dealing with the working press was more difficult. First, the rules and regulations of the hostess committee established in 1937 by Mrs. White were known only by word of mouth. Consequently, new members of the press each year were not necessarily aware of the extent of policy regulations. That created problems with hostesses which eventually reflected upon Olive and me.

Second, we didn't have West Hall, with its comfortable rooms for control center, press interviews and refreshments. There was just no place in that great Hall that was comfortable or convenient or even satisfactorily accessible to the press for their interviews. They worked as best they could near the runways and in the Hall during rehearsals. It was a highly inefficient system, but it was the only facility we had. We did allow representative press on stage during breaks.

I remember one night in particular in the early years when I was having difficulty coordinating all of the contestants on stage after the show along with all of their hostesses and the excess crowd of reporters and photographers. Some members of the press would wander into the corridor leading to the dressing room where they didn't belong and weren't permitted. The police had left to perform other duties in the Hall.

This night I was having much trouble trying to watch the stage and the wandering press. Two Canadian Mounted Police had been used in the shows. When I found one of them watching the after-the-show activities, I sought his services, outfitted in his red Royal Canadian Mounted Police uniform, and asked him to stand at the doorway leading back to the dressing room and prevent anyone but hostesses from coming or going through the doorway while I went back to remove the wandering press from forbidden territory. The Canadian accepted my request, was most helpful and apparently enjoyed his role. That, too, was a first for the Pageant and no doubt a rare event.

It was soon obvious to me that I needed a place where I could coordinate the myriad of details, papers, instructions, production information and miscellaneous information. I needed a make-shift desk, a private place and a telephone. The only place was a corner in the dressing room sometimes used by the Pageant nurse.

This small area became the first control information center of the Pageant, the first time such a center had been established. Today the control center, called anchor station, is a highly efficient operation in West Hall manned by a sizable committee which handles information and press relations very well.

The center I started was born out of sheer necessity and an overpowering need to bring order into the backstage Pageant operations. I operated it alone in the beginning. How simple it is today compared to yesterday. Large committees now perform the necessary duties so painfully organized in the 1950s and 1960s. The hostess committee has grown in size, power and prestige from 65 women to 148. I had felt constrained to limit the size of the committee because of budgetary restraints. Today, each sub-committee should be able to function almost independently, relieving the chairman of most of the hour-by-hour problems I had to face so long ago.

Elizabeth B. Alton

Chapter 22

hanges for improvement in the Pageant were always taking place. I had made my first real contribution in that direction when I put in writing the *Basic Rules of the Miss America Pageant.* Dissemination by word of mouth created too many unnecessary problems. I simply put in written form all the hostess committee rules originally established by Mrs. White when the committee was first organized and some of my own.

Lenora printed the *Basic Rules* in the 1957 working schedule which was available to all the working press. At least to the time of this writing, the *Rules* have appeared henceforth in the working schedule with necessary changes and additions. Much of the language has been kept as I worded it for some time.

Lenora had established the hostess committee as an important means of preventing scandalous activity on the part of contestants and controlling all their movements while in Atlantic City in order to preserve the good name and reputation of the Pageant. Mrs. White had accepted the chairmanship appointment by the board only on condition that she could (1) select the women for the committee, (2) be free from political pressure, since her husband was mayor, and (3) be free from pressure by members of the Pageant board. The committee was established as reasonably autonomous and has remained so through the years.

The first rule as printed then made it clear for everyone involved with the Pageant. "The Atlantic City hostess committee has complete charge of all activities, interviews, pictures, recordings, etc. of the contestants during Pageant week. The chairman of the hostess committee must approve all requests for interviews and pictures."

To eliminate the possibility of repeating the mistakes of the 1920s, the second rule stated, "Contestants are not permitted at any time to enter a cocktail lounge, night club, bar, inn, tavern or any place where liquor is served, while competing for the Miss America title. Violation of this rule will bring automatic elimination from further judging although they will not be advised of this action."

The third rule has perhaps been the most misunderstood and laughed at, at times, by the public, news media and TV. "Contestants are not permitted to speak to any man, including male members of their own families, unless a local hostess is present. They are not permitted to dine with a man at their hotels or elsewhere, nor are they permitted to receive a man in their rooms, their own families not excepted."

Many people, then and now, still think it's silly that a father can't visit his daughter in her hotel room. It may appear silly on the surface, but based upon past Pageant experiences, the rule is vitally important for the fine reputation of the girls and the Pageant. Many of the fathers have been young, fortyish, good looking to handsome men, men who could easily appear to be a date. Given all the frailties of human nature, hotel guests and others can be curious about that man going in and out of Miss State's room. That kind of curiosity leads to speculation. Speculation leads to rumors. Rumors have a way of being embellished to the point that they unexpectedly become an untrue, but maybe juicy, scandal. By keeping daddy and brother and sponsor and any other male out of the girls' rooms, speculative rumors cannot start. The hostess committee liked keeping it that way.

Rule number four said, "No interviews or pictures will be permitted unless a local hostess is present. If a contestant's personal hostess is not immediately available, any hostess will substitute temporarily, particularly in Convention Hall during the day and backstage after the show at night."

Rule five said, "No telephone interviews will be permitted at any time whether a hostess is present or not." Hostesses obviously could have no control over interviews by telephone.

Rule seven allowed, "Accredited publicity men and photographers covering contestants from their home states have automatic approval for interviews and pictures of their particular contestants, provided the necessary arrangements are made with the local hostesses to be present."

Rule eight, "Interviews and pictures are permitted in Convention Hall during rehearsal breaks; at hotels or elsewhere by appointment with hostesses."

Rule nine, "No one is allowed on stage during rehearsals except hostesses, police and stage personnel. During rehearsal breaks candid pictures may be made on stage only by special arrangements with the chairman of the hostess committee."

Rule ten, "No one is allowed backstage at any time, or in the corridor leading to the contestants' dressing room, except hostesses, police and stage personnel."

Rule eleven, "No one may enter the contestants' dressing room at any time except hostesses."

Rule twelve, "Following each night's competition, contestants will be held backstage for a short time for interviews and pictures. Only those contestants will be detained whose names are in the hands of the chairman by the time the curtain closes. Local hostesses will be on stage."

Rule fifteen, "Hostesses will discontinue any interview which causes distress to a contestant, reflects upon her family, her personal integrity, or moral conduct."

Rule sixteen, "No interviews or pictures are permitted at the coronation ball, either upon arrival of contestants at the hotel or during the ball."

Most of these rules I had originated between 1954 and 1956 from a desperate need to bring some form of organized order in what I considered to be chaos in dealing with the press. Pageant publicity was handled by Mall Dodson, head of Atlantic City's press bureau, and Jimmie McCullough, a local reporter and publicity expert who controlled in a very general way the publicity pictures and interviews after the shows at night in the Hall, if it could be called control.

With the working press all fighting for their opportunities to get their stories and pictures, there was scarcely room to move, let alone control, as a hostess chairman, what was happening with contestants.

When television arrived in 1954, portable TV cameras carried on the shoulders of TV reporters were not only large and bulky; they were obviously heavy. The length of time for interviews and pictures on stage after the shows went on and on and on. No one seemed in charge of saying when it was time to stop. It became midnight. It became 1:00 a.m. One night I was still struggling to get all contestants off stage after 1:00 a.m. As I was busy sending the last girls on their way home, I always remember a woman TV camera person carrying one of those really heavy TV cameras on her shoulder, complaining to me that she hadn't been able to complete her assignment. I felt a great sense of sympathy for her, but we'd already been far too long. Changes had to be made.

Before my second year as co-chairman arrived, I had begun asking questions. Who's in charge? To whom do I talk to bring some order out of this wild happening on stage at night? The system needed a drastic overhaul in my opinion. Not getting satisfactory answers, I began making my own plan for organizing what happened with the press in Convention Hall.

The first need was to control how the working press got on stage after the curtain went down. I'd received legitimate complaints from the largest newspaper representatives that the papers having the earliest deadlines should be allowed on stage first before those who could wait a little and the weekly papers. That made sense to me. I was successful in having Mall Dodson issue press badges according to the deadlines of their newspapers. Newsmen were allowed on stage in waves, one group at a time according to their badges.

The next step was controlling which contestants would be on stage. There was no need for every contestant to be present just in case she might be interviewed or pictured. Rule twelve, thus became necessary. The press was required to send backstage to me the names of the girls to be interviewed on stage before the curtain went down on the show. It was then more efficient to allow on stage only those girls and their hostesses. The other girls were free to leave for their hotels. The rule also specified a short time for the interviews.

Gradually, the wild rush, pandemonium, bedlam, and chaos of the after show press mania began being reduced to a more orderly, workable process. It wasn't completely controlled yet, but progress was being made little by little.

Shortly after Lenora had printed the rules established by the hostess committee in the working schedule, state pageants began adopting those rules. It wasn't long before all state pageants had conformed.

When Mildred Brick succeeded me as chairman, she changed the title "Rules" to "Precepts," a softer word, but the provisions were basically the same with whatever additions or corrections she deemed necessary.

One of the cute Pageant stories happened when Marion McKnight, Miss America 1957, was competing in talent. She did an excellent imitation of Marilyn Monroe, the popular star. Unknown to her at the time, Marilyn's former husband, Joe DiMaggio, a baseball star, was in the audience. Marion was considerably embarrassed when she discovered DiMaggio's presence. After their meeting she dated him for a while.

When she was crowned, her small home town of Manning, South Carolina, population 2,275, celebrated enthusiastically. Located on Route 30 to the Florida resorts, the entrance and exit of the town were blocked off by the fire department. All travelers were stopped, served refreshments, and invited to join the celebration. With community bells ringing, there was singing and dancing in the streets until sunrise.

Elizabeth B. Alton

Chapter 23

The national scholarship program was increased from $25,000 to $38,000. Six talent awards were made available for non-finalists. All preliminary or tie winners in any division of the competition were guaranteed $1,000.

The CBS Television Network was selected by the Philco Corporation to broadcast the 1957 finals and the crowning of Miss America. The Pepsi-Cola Company and the Sayco Doll Corporation, which was licensed to manufacture the Miss America Doll, replaced Camay and the Florida Citrus Commission as advertising sponsors. The Oldsmobile Division of General Motors replaced Nash Motors, also providing convertibles for the parade and transportation for hostesses and contestants during the week. In 1958, Oldsmobile would become a national advertising sponsor.

The outdated Miss America robe was redesigned by producer George Buzby, worn for the first time by reigning queen Marion McKnight. As millions watched the most exciting television show yet to be broadcast, a lovely debutante from Denver, Colorado, became Miss America in 1958. Marilyn Van Derbur, a talented University of Colorado junior, so captivated the hearts and imagination of the American public that renowned Edward R. Murrow featured her with her popular family on his *Person to Person* television program. After her year of public appearances in every state of our country and many foreign lands, she returned to graduate from her university with Phi Beta Kappa honors.

Thinking about Denver recalls to my mind an incident in Convention Hall that year. During rehearsals a beautifully-dressed, patrician, older woman with lovely jewelry, her hair recently coiffed, came to request that she be given unlimited access to Miss Colorado, Marilyn Van Derbur. This woman's personal elegance was matched only by her impeccable manners. Warning signals sounded. This was not an ordinary newspaper woman. She had to have some other position of authority. She said she represented a top newspaper in Denver as her badge showed. I never knew, but my impression was that she was either the wife of the owner or publisher, if not the owner herself. She spoke with dignity and courtesy in a modulated voice accustomed to authority.

In my speeches around the state as vice president of the Federation of Women's Clubs and various organizations, I had come in frequent contact with similar women of importance and stature. I knew how to talk to her in her own language style. What seriously bothered me, even pained me at the time, was the fact that I could not grant her request. What she wanted was to be free to talk with Marilyn without a hostess present whenever she pleased, to have her picture taken where and when she chose and to have her at locations not first approved or even known to anyone at that time. Her request was absolutely reasonable in her eyes. She knew she was trustworthy and would not harm the Pageant. Her standards were equally as high as ours. Her newspaper was one of the best in the West. And so on. With it all she was a lady. She just could not understand why I didn't approve and would not consent.

Used to dealing with women of all types and temperaments, I spent some very difficult minutes with all the skills I possess trying to assuage her pride, describing our rules and saying "no" as definitely and softly as I could. I'm sure she left me unconvinced. At least I'd maintained her respect for the Pageant even though she thought our rules were wrong. Life backstage was not always easy.

For some years Marilyn Van Derbur became one of the most popular representatives of the Pageant as Miss America 1958. Her talent presentation was playing an organ with the only two pieces she could play, "Tea for Two" and "Tenderly." Her personality was charismatic.

In those days, the five top finalists waited in our dressing room with me as they were called one by one to answer questions on the stage. All other girls were already there. I remember wondering which one would become the winner. The girls gave outward appearances of calm but internally were really nervously expectant. Finally, there was only one girl left to answer the questions posed to them, Marilyn. The decision was a popular choice.

Through the years Marilyn became one of the fine motivational speakers on the professional circuit, later developing her own motivational institute.

Olive Rundstrom and I often agreed in our decision-making with hostesses on allowable activities. We sometimes disagreed politely. But having two women with equal authority sometimes caused unnecessary problems. Smart hostesses soon learned that if one said "no," the other might say "yes" to whatever the request might be. This soon became a game which could not be permitted to continue.

The Pageant board has occasionally had co-chairmen of committees. It is an inefficient system and not really good management. *Robert's Rules of Order*, in its many revisions, creates only one person in charge of an office or committee. Parliamentary procedures as described by Roberts specify one person in authority, one president, one committee chairman in the organization. There is no provision for co-chairmen I could find. With care, Olive and I made our disapproval perfectly clear to the hostesses. The problem ended.

One of the simple matters Olive and I disagreed on was the matter of a photograph. The Pageant had for years two outstanding wardrobe mistresses in the dressing room. Mrs. Taliaferro was also a designer who made stage costumes when necessary. *Ebony* magazine had arranged to take publicity photographs of our two wardrobe mistresses in the dressing room before contestants would arrive. Olive and I agreed the picture could be taken when the room was empty. When we were invited to pose in advance with the wardrobe mistresses, I consented and arrived early for the picture. Olive declined.

Elizabeth B. Alton

Chapter 24

The year 1958–1959 was an important milestone in my public activities. I look back on those events as a step-by-step progression with one door of opportunity after another gradually opening for me.

In May 1958, I was elected president of the New Jersey State Federation of Women's Clubs. In September, I was elected the first woman member of the Pageant's board of directors, continuing as the only woman for eleven years. Lenora had finally achieved her ambition of having a woman on the board. Olive Rundstrom had previously resigned as co-chairman.

My new position as the leader of a statewide organization of 46,000 women, the largest in our state with 454 women's clubs, had given me sufficient stature to be acceptable to the board's distinguished members. My presidency also included membership on the board of directors of the General Federation of Women's Clubs, the largest organization of women in the United States with 800,000 members and sixteen million women in affiliated clubs in 46 countries of the world. Headquarters was located in a former embassy in Washington, D.C.

Having known some of the Pageant board members for a few years, I knew it was important for me to fit in comfortably with men of importance in the community. As the new state president, I couldn't help remembering the dream I had once had at the Amarcenth installation so many years ago of holding high office in a large organization. Without any effort or plan on my part, I could see a clear pattern in the leadership roles I had had, which brought me these new, exciting experiences.

One of my first public appearances as state president was representing the Federation at the installation of Dr. Mason Gross as president of Rutgers University. I don't know if these ceremonies are often held in this modern day, but in 1958, the Rutgers installation of a university president was certainly an outstanding and colorful one.

The university had provided me with a cap, gown and hood representing my lowly bachelor's degree in the humanities from Syracuse University, attested by the white trim around the neck of my hood. I was positioned with the guests near the head of the lengthy line containing the governor, elected officials, members of the board of governors and board of trustees of Rutgers, college and university presidents of prominent institutions of higher education, heads of large corporations, prestigious faculty, administrators and scholars. I was the lone woman in my range of vision which brought me courteous and friendly attention. The long line wound around the many curving lanes between buildings on campus as far as my eyes could see.

Intrigued with the display of academic splendor in the colorful caps, gowns and hoods all around me, I listened as those near me recognized the scarlet, gold and brightly colored academic robes in our view as representative of graduate degrees from European, Middle Eastern and Asian universities. I was fascinated with their ornate styles. The unusual tasseled caps, somewhat like berets, with their colorful robes could have come straight from a movie set.

As I watched the prominent guests around me, I discovered there was some small interest and curiosity about me, who I was, and in particular my hood which was a little shorter than the doctorate hoods being worn around me. They had apparently not been familiar with one like it. Mine was the usual black cap and gown commonly seen at graduations. Only the hood had been added. I supposed the hoods got comparatively longer as the degrees became more advanced. I don't think many bachelor of arts hoods are generally seen.

Anyway, I had a really good private laugh all to myself. Since they didn't know what my hood was, I was not about to tell them. I had never seen a bachelor of arts hood before either. I hadn't known they existed. I decided my academic credentials were best left undescribed in that large congregation of colorful doctoral degrees.

The ceremonial march, when it began, was to the tune of "Pomp and Circumstance" as we walked two by two toward the arena. I was seated with the most distinguished guests close to the platform. It was an impressive installation ceremony and for me a memorable day filled with interesting social events.

The important place I had been given in the line-up and seating had been a silent tribute to the importance of the Federation of Women's Clubs for their many valued contributions to the university through the years: their successful efforts to establish Douglass College; the building of buildings on the Douglass campus; the gifts of many thousands of dollars in scholarships each year and legislative support for the interests of Rutgers University. For many years prior to Rutgers becoming The State University, the presidents of the Federation had served consecutively on the boards of trustees. Our headquarters building is built on the Douglass College campus.

The state presidents of our Federation have always been sought by a variety of state organizations for membership on their boards of directors or boards of trustees. I was no exception. In addition, I served on governor's conferences on housing, education and aging, and was invited to speak at a congressional hearing on education. I was chosen to head two statewide campaigns as chairman of their women's divisions. The first was the Crusade for Freedom, then known as Radio Free Europe, which was involved in opposing the Berlin Wall at the time.

The second was a more prestigious organization, the U.S. Savings Bond campaign. I attended the dinner at the Spring Lake Country Club, attended by prominent corporation executives. Arriving early for dinner, I was starting through the empty dining room toward the outdoor activities when I was astonished to see Vice-President Richard Nixon approaching me with his secret service men as they were going in the opposite direction. I noticed that Mr. Nixon stopped to speak to a waitress or two, then came to shake hands and speak briefly to me before moving on.

As state chairman of the Women's Division, I was seated at the head table only the second chair from Mr. Nixon, who generously included me in table conversation. It became a memorable experience. Mr. Nixon had just returned from a highly publicized visit to Russia which has been described as "kitchen diplomacy" during the "cold war" period.

Only a few months after I became state president of the Federation, I had a surprising telephone call from my attorney, Elwood Kirkman. In our childhood years, he had been grocery delivery boy for our nearby grocer. He was few years older than me: I had known him all of my life. He had become the president of our town's largest bank, held presidencies in prestigious national banking organizations, and was close personal friends of long standing with South Jersey political leaders and elected officials. He was also, to my knowledge, the financial power behind the political powers of governments in and around Atlantic City.

The purpose of his call was one I could scarcely believe. He was asking me if I would accept the presidency of the Republican Women's Organization of the state. Not if I would run for the office. If I would accept.

I have never belonged to a political club nor participated in anything resembling politics. My quick personal assessment was that I had new stature as president of the Federation. My second thought was more politically astute. I think the elected officials of our area in the southern part of the state liked the possibility of having the kind of political power that women unobtrusively and quietly wield in the state, not only in their own jurisdiction, but in their, hopefully, control. Obviously I would need to be guided.

The Federation of Women's Clubs is a non-political organization. I knew I could not hold both positions at the same time.

I could not accept. If I had wanted public office in later years, the door was still open.

There have been many misconceptions through the years about what women's clubs do. We have been called tea drinkers, fashion plates, social gadflies and various other unflattering names. Nothing could be farther from the truth.

The influential General Federation of Women's Clubs had its origin in 1868 when a newspaper woman employed by a metropolitan paper wanted to attend a dinner given by the New York Press Club to honor Charles Dickens at the end of his second reading tour in the country. Jane Cunningham Croly, known as Jennie June Croly, and Sara Willis Parton, a well-known writer, were denied tickets. Only men were permitted.

Believing women should be able to enjoy the same cultural activities and common interests, Jennie June organized the Sorosis Club in New York. Other clubs had been gradually organizing in the country. On its twenty-first birthday, Sorosis issued a call to convention to 97 clubs through Jennie June's leadership. The convention was held in Madison Square Theater, New York, in 1889. Three New Jersey clubs attended. Thus was first planned a Federation of Clubs. Ratification of a constitution occurred in 1890. The first president of the Federation was a New Jersey woman, Charlotte Emerson Brown. The New Jersey Federation was organized in 1894.

At a district meeting of the New Jersey Federation in 1911 it was proposed that women be admitted to Rutgers College, an all-male institution, because Rutgers received substantial public money. Rutgers College was disenchanted. Women should not cross its threshold.

Mabel Smith Douglass, president of the College Club of Jersey City, undertook a statewide campaign to raise funds by a one-dollar subscription plan and other means to create a public college for women in the state. For eight years, Mabel Smith Douglass planned and lobbied as high as the White House with the strong support of the Federated Clubs throughout the state. The trustees of Rutgers continued unimpressed.

The histories I have read do not say so, but I like to think the New Jersey College for Women came into existence because there was a federal grant given to Rutgers College to establish a program in home economics in the sum of $25,000. Rather than turn the money down, the trustees finally agreed to establish a co-ordinate woman's college which opened in 1918.

I was once told that the reason there are two U-shaped campuses containing the first housing units was because the trustees believed the college would fail and the houses could be sold as private homes.

The New Jersey Federation built Federation Hall, the first science building, dedicated in 1922, by raising $25,000. Mabel Smith Douglass became the college's first Dean and women of the Federation served gratis in a variety of capacities.

By 1928, $100,000 had been raised to build the music building. Other substantial sums have been contributed for the student center building, furnishings for the library study center, and rooms for use by foreign students. In addition, Federation scholarships and many college projects have raised sums well over seven figures through the years.

The New Jersey Federation has a rich history of achievements equally comparable to the funding of Douglass College as it was re-named in 1956 for Mabel Smith Douglass.

When I became state president, it was carefully pointed out to me that it was inappropriate for the president of the New Jersey State Federation of Women's Clubs to be associated with "that Pageant." I should resign my position as chairman of the hostess committee and board membership.

I gave the situation a lot of thought, finally reaching a solution I believed would satisfy everyone. The Federation had been organized in 1894. Resolutions had been passed every one of the 64 years. I instructed the resolutions committee to review every resolution that had ever been passed for timeliness in order to bring our Federation policies up to date. Sure enough, when the report was presented at the convention, the Pageant resolution had been included in the historical file, thus removing it as an obstacle to my remaining as state president. The convention also adopted a new policy, that all active resolutions would be reviewed every two years for timeliness. The old resolution condemning the Pageant, passed in convention in 1927, had now become history, no longer effective. Lenora would be pleased to hear that news.

Due to the statewide prestige of the Federation, I quickly became involved in statewide activities. I was appointed a member of the governor's committee on employ the handicapped; the New Jersey roadside council; the advisory committee to the statewide survey for vocational education; the board of the New Jersey safety council; the honorary committee for national library week sponsored by the New Jersey Library Association.

I shared honors with Governor Robert B. Meyner at the opening of a historical building restored for use as a museum at the deserted village of Allaire at Allaire State Park, which the Federation was instrumental in establishing as a state park and recreation area, as well as funding the restoration of the museum.

A baseball field and a new modern kitchen were built with Federation funds at Boystown in Kearny by the evening membership department.

The civics and legislation department received awards for its "Get Out the Vote" campaign over the years from the New Jersey Citizenship Council and the American Heritage Foundation presented at the convention to the Federation which also cooperated with the New Jersey Broadcasters Association in a joint effort.

The Sears Roebuck Foundation invited me to speak at their forum for top executives of the Eastern region in New York on the community achievement contest sponsored jointly with the General Federation. All New Jersey Federation's 454 clubs had entered the contest for the first time with 100% participation, winning $500 as a top prize in the country. Every woman's club in our state was involved in a project to improve a particular community.

I was a platform guest at several conventions including the New Jersey Realtors Association where I presented the best realtor of the year award. I had been a judge for that contest. There was also the New Jersey Education Association, the League of Women Voters and the American Gold Star Mothers.

My date book was completely filled with speaking engagements and district and state conferences. One I particularly enjoyed was the Woman's Press Club of New York at a 71st anniversary banquet celebrating our organizations' common founder, Jenny June Croly, a newspaper woman in the 1860s.

The list of appearances at state and national organizations is far too lengthy to mention. The Federation was involved in programs and projects in the fields of art, conservation, American home, drama, education, garden, international relations, junior membership, music, public welfare, youth conservation, civics and legislation, and evening membership.

We strongly supported and opposed legislation statewide and nationally. We raised many thousands of dollars annually for scholarship programs, improvements at state institutions and agencies, and for building a library at Douglass College which the Federation had founded.

With our headquarters in Newark, I spent almost every day driving all over the state. My records show I drove 41,267 miles and burned 3,439 gallons of gasoline that year in ten months.

Yes, I poured tea at many tea tables innumerable times. Yes, I dressed in the latest couturier designs with my white gloves and designer hats, as badges of my office. Yes, I gave inspirational and motivational speeches over a couple of hundred times each year. More importantly, I heard the achievements of women all over the state who cared about making a difference in their communities and in our country. You may not read about them in your local papers, for women today have not yet achieved the full recognition for dedicated services they so richly deserve. Nevertheless, it is a basic fact that organized women are developing a stronger, more influential voice in local and public affairs nationally.

It was customary in those days to receive a handsome and colorful corsage everywhere I spoke. I had developed the habit of dressing in a simple but stylish outfit and wearing a somewhat fancy hat as the item of interest to those who had to see me as well as hear me. Feathered hats and pretty floral ones were among my favorites. Since I drove long distances almost daily, I carried a suitcase with necessities and change of wardrobe in case I decided to stop overnight or got caught in a snowstorm. Sometimes I would be invited to stay overnight with a state officer.

As an overnight guest one night, the husband of a friend presented me with an especially lovely orchid corsage. I had previously selected an orchid flowered hat in a simple cap shape. What disturbed me was that the colors clashed. There are many shades of orchid. I was uncomfortable in greeting several hundred women in a receiving line and speaking from their podium. After that I made it a habit to carry in the trunk of my car several hat boxes so that if the flowers clashed with my outfits, I could, and did, get another from my car more suitable to the color scheme of my corsages.

❦

Rutgers had succeeded in having a bond issue for higher education introduced in 1958 for the much needed expansion of the university and state colleges. The bond issue had been defeated at the polls. It was the era known as a crisis in education. There wasn't room for more students in our institutions of higher education. Students were not being accepted in other states because of their own state needs. Rutgers proposed that the state put another bond issue before the people at the November elections in 1959. They wanted the Federation's support, believing the first bond issue had not been properly presented to the people. I had met a key member of the board of governors of Rutgers and had had a politely disagreeing discussion with him about Atlantic City over luncheon at the college. He must have liked my refusal to agree with him. He also knew well the powers of the Federation.

One day, I had a call from Governor Robert B. Meyner's office that the governor wanted to see me. Believing he wanted to discuss some legislation which we strongly opposed, I gathered up all our research information and went to see the governor in his office. I was greatly surprised when he said he intended to appoint me as the only woman of nine men on the board of governors and to the board of trustees of Rutgers. Would I accept? I sure did.

He telephoned Senator Frank S. Farley, my local senator, in my hearing to inform him, for Senator Farley would be required to move my nomination for confirmation in the State Senate. After Farley's approval I was sent to meet with the commissioner of education. Howard Melvin told me later that he knew I was to be appointed to something, for the state police had been investigating me all over town. Horrors! I also learned that the senator had done his own checking.

Our Federation undertook an all-out campaign in our 454 clubs across the state. Women's clubs had speakers creating publicity. There's really no more powerful way of spreading the word than women talking to women, to family, to friends, to neighbors. The telephone lines sometimes get overworked. I'm sure our Federation had an impact on the passage of the 1959 bond issue for higher education. Rutgers and the state colleges all expanded their facilities substantially.

One other event of political influence in a state election took place unexpectedly during my presidency that year. Six hundred women attended our legislative luncheon in Trenton, preceded by a meeting in the morning and followed by tours of the capitol while the legislature was in session. I was introduced in the senate by Senator Farley and given the privilege of the floor to address the senate.

At the morning meeting, our legislation chairman always invited the major candidate for office in the state and nation. All had accepted as usual except one, a candidate of Governor Meyner's party for the United States Senate. Our chairman didn't take "no" for an answer. This one persisted. He refused because he said he had promised to take his mother-in-law to the seashore on that day in March. He had been invited four months in advance. He finally got quite nasty. He "wasn't going to meet with a bunch of women." After our legislative luncheon, our chairman told the story of this candidate who wanted to be a U.S. senator. Many press representatives were present. The next morning there were prominent and first page stories in major newspapers in New York, Philadelphia and large cities in our state. I was personally embarrassed. The governor had appointed me to a prestigious position and in return our organization was doing political harm to his party's candidate, and harm we did. The story went the rounds of our clubs like a juicy scandal would. A non-political organization, individual club women have a powerful clout when they work together. Our senatorial candidate was soundly defeated at the polls.

To make peace with Governor Robert B. Meyner, I wrote him a letter explaining how foolhardy I thought it had been for a candidate to ignore an organization of 46,000 women who vote. I invited him to be a speaker at our coming convention. He accepted my invitation and made a fine speech to our 1,200 women.

To us, this was a case of discrimination against women, for ours was not the only women's organization he had offended. Some men think women don't count and treat them as unimportant. Some men, like our U.S. senatorial candidate, find out differently.

One of my amusing days was meeting with a commissioner of institutions and agencies in his office on a bitter cold, snowy day in January. I had made the trip to Trenton on icy, dangerous roads because the Federation's interests in some of our institutions at that time were paramount.

When the lunch hour arrived at the close of our business, the commissioner graciously invited me to lunch at the nearby hotel. Since I was hungry and free for a while, I accepted. We were given a table for two in a prominent area of the dining room.

I had known the commissioner for a couple of years when the Federation had raised thousands of dollars to benefit our state's hospitals and institutions. It was a comfortable, chatty luncheon.

Perhaps I should say that I was dressed smartly but conservatively, women's club style, with an interesting chapeau. In a little while, I noticed that individual men were walking directly to our table to speak casually in greeting to the commissioner. He introduced me to each man, giving my name but not my title. I soon saw the humor in the situation. These men were obviously curious about whom the commissioner was entertaining over luncheon. The commissioner was not helping them. My name meant nothing. Who I was remained a mystery. I enjoyed that.

I had one other very satisfying event the first year of my presidency. Our state chairman of public welfare and her associates had been studying the penal institutions for women in the state. We had a brand new commissioner who had succeeded my luncheon companion in Trenton. He was new to New Jersey, having recently been a warden of a large prison in the Midwest. He had written a book of some prominence about jails which our state officer wanted to have available for study. She had written the new commissioner for a copy and had been refused. She had asked personally and been refused. The book was not yet available in our bookstores.

I attended a statewide meeting in the War Memorial Building in Trenton when I knew the new commissioner was a speaker. After the conference was over I waited at the exit door until the commissioner approached and spoke to him, giving my name and position with the Federation. I explained why we desired a copy of his book. He was short and to the point. "No." There are times when "no" is not an acceptable answer. Especially since his "no" had been said six inches from my face. I wondered if that was his tough intimidating method of speaking to prisoners.

Without moving a muscle or removing my face one inch from his, I informed him that our state Federation was a member of the national and international Federation of Women's Clubs with state organizations in every state. We had access to reports of what other states were doing in comparison to New Jersey's prison system.

He backed away and in conciliatory tones assured me a copy of the book would be available. As we went out the door together, he took my arm and walked me to my car parked two blocks away, opened the car door for me, and stood talking through the car window for several minutes.

I don't know if he made any inquiries about our organization, but I do know that he was most cooperative with our Federation, became a keynote speaker at state conferences, and welcomed our financial support for much needed programs and buildings. We had made a new friend in state government. There are times when women do count.

Elizabeth B. Alton

Chapter 25
1958

Lenora had inherited the original Pageant emphasis on feminine beauty which was the only hallmark of the Pageant from 1921–1935 when she was brought from the Florida Chamber of Commerce to manage the parade and assist Eddie Corcoran. As a woman, Lenora didn't like the beauty only emphasis; in fact, she never did like it during her years. She worked long and diligently to improve the Pageant from what was plainly more of a leg show than a Pageant.

She was the only woman's voice on a board of twenty plus men, the most distinguished civic leaders in the city. Her voice not only had to be strong and influential—it was. When it was necessary, she would really fight for her point of view. She didn't always win, but no one can ever say that she certainly didn't try.

One thing Lenora didn't like was the swimsuit competition. Men loved it then and love it now. Many women never liked it from the beginning and some women still dislike it today, giving rise to the accusations loudly heard around the country from time to time that the Pageant "exploits women." The Pageant doesn't. Swimsuits became an issue years ago.

What Lenora sought from the board members during my membership was having a playsuit rather than a swimsuit competition. Playsuits could be as short, interesting and sexily provocative as swimsuits, but the men of the board wouldn't buy the idea. In later years, Al Marks came close to the idea, but so many letters arrived from angry males that he gave up. As I write today, the accent is on physical fitness. If men and women have their way, the swimsuit will remain. Besides, times have changed considerably.

The Pageant scholarship program was strongly supported this year by new advertising sponsor Pepsi-Cola with its 556 bottlers. They offered a position to a former Miss Vermont, also a winner of Miss Congeniality with its $1,000 scholarship, Sandra Jean Simpson. A fine artist, she had been asked to illustrate the 1957 Pageant program book. She was chosen to tour the country soliciting $500 scholarship contributions from bottlers. With the parent company matching the sum, a $1,000 Pepsi-Cola scholarship would be awarded to state winners; state runners-up and talent winners would be included. By this year, the Pepsi-Cola scholarships totaled $250,000 at local and state pageants. The national Pageant increased its award to $10,000 for Miss America.

The Toni Division of the Gillette Company replaced Sayco Doll Company as sponsor.

The Tuesday morning panorama picture in swimsuit was no longer taken at the City Press Bureau. The picture had been taken in the pool area of Haddon Hall. Individual and group pictures had been taken in the hotel's private cabana area on the beach. This year, the panorama picture was taken at the Sheraton Ritz-Carlton Hotel with newsreel and television. The girls were taken on the beach for pictures near the ocean. Registration had changed from Haddon Hall to the Dennis Hotel on the Boardwalk.

Mary Ann Mobley, a senior at Ole' Miss, the University of Mississippi, a Chi Omega, was the first to become Miss America from Mississippi. One of the most loved and popular title holders, she had charmed the audience and judges with her routine as a singer, dancer and comedienne.

The ball this year was different in the fact that cadets from the United States Military Academy at West Point had been escorts for contestants. George Bruni, manager and vice president of the Claridge Hotel, had arranged for their presence. He'd also spent some time with me discussing details. My only critique was an unexpressed personal one. The girls had apparently been assigned according to matching their home states as far as possible. That was commendable. In a few cases, it was sort of humorous. Like the contestants, the cadets were not all the same size. One could see on the dance floor a very tall girl dancing with a cadet who was too short. My personal preference would have been to match the sizes more equally. However, everyone was obviously enjoying the relaxation and dance.

No contestants were permitted to leave the ball until all were released together for their hotels. This night, a hostess came to me to say there was trouble in the powder room. When I arrived, there was a contestant flat on the floor in her evening gown refusing to get up. I went to find our Pageant physician, Dr. Allman, and took him into the powder room to attend the disturbed girl. We discovered she was using this unusual action because she wanted to leave and return to her hotel. One of my instructions from Lenora had been to see that the contestants stayed in the ballroom until she said they could leave. When our contestant realized she wasn't going to leave for her hotel right then, she got up and went back to her cadet date.

One of Lenora's most difficult problems in developing new state pageants was fairly widespread in the 1950s throughout the South and Southwest states where the Catholic Church had a strong influence. The leaders of the church hierarchy had denounced beauty pageants in general as inappropriate for young Catholic women to enter. Their criticism was not aimed directly at the Miss America Pageant. Church disapproval had a strong impact on local and state pageants as well as the development of new state pageants. Lenora struggled in every way possible for years to overcome the situation but it was slow going. I believe church opposition gradually decreased as the scholarship program continued to grow and the Pageant became known for its excellence and high standards.

The south is known as the Bible Belt. Many contestants have deep religious convictions. Singers will sometimes start a song or gospel music in the dressing room, soon joined by others in a sing-along. Our prayer corner backstage was always well used.

❦

Joseph Wagenheim had been vice president of the Pageant when I became a hostess in 1945. He had given valuable services during the war years, including substantial financial assistance in raising much needed funds for survival. In 1958 he was honored on the completion of his term as vice president by being named honorary chairman of the board of directors. He held that title until 1966. I'm not sure if that's the year he died. He was certainly one of the outstanding business men of our community who was one of the Pageant's strongest supporters and advocates. Wagenheim has been the only board member to be elected an honorary chairman of the board, recognition well deserved.

I mention Wagenheim because I have a pleasant memory of him as a gracious host one year. He entertained the members of the board of directors at dinner in a special dining room at Haddon Hall Hotel, later Merv Griffin's Resort's Casino and Hotel. The room had been attractively decorated for the occasion. The table arrangements had been a work of art, tall candlesticks, beautiful floral arrangements, the hotel's best china, glassware and silverware all added to the conviviality of the occasion.

Wagenheim was a courtly gentleman of the old school, his manners impeccable, his courtesies as a fine host adding pleasure to the occasion. As the only woman present among 24 men, I was personally seated by Wagenheim in the center of the long table. He sat directly opposite me as the host.

The first thing I noticed about my place setting was the array of half a dozen wine glasses in front of me, graduating from large to small. Each glass had been selected for the special wine, liquor or liqueur for each individual course to be served. For a connoisseur of fine dining, this was state of the art. Perfectly planned.

My tummy developed a touch of nervous tension for I have been a life-long teetotaler, as I've mentioned before. I could not have managed what was going to fill those glasses. Even worse, the host sat opposite me, well able to notice my inability to partake of his gracious hospitality.

Sure enough, Wagenheim noticed when I didn't indulge in the first wine served with the first course. "You must try it," he said. "It's" and he mentioned some name and year of something I'd never heard of, apparently a fine wine.

I lifted the glass as though to try it and then put it back down. My companion on my right, knowing my predicament, took pity on me. When Wagenheim's attention was elsewhere he exchanged glasses with me all evening so that I was able to appear to be enjoying this unusually fine dinner and its liquid embellishments. The dinner itself had been superb and Wagenheim the perfect host. I thoroughly enjoyed his friendliness and the courtesies he extended to me. He was a fine gentleman. I might note there was always a board member willing to be seated next to me when liquor was served at social events.

I've always laughed about an occasion at the beachfront Dennis Hotel, one of our city's finest then. It was a cocktail party for the judges after the preliminary contest. The women were dressed in evening gowns, the men in tuxedos. The occasion was one of dignity as well as fun.

The waiters were formally attired and wearing white gloves as they served drinks by order. When the waiter asked me what I wanted to drink, I told him I'd like plain ginger ale. I had found that I could carry a glass of ginger ale around and no one would notice it was a soft drink. The waiter seemed surprised. He looked at me for a moment and then he said to my amusement, "You're kidding." "No, I'm not," I told him, "Just a plain ginger ale." He left me shaking his head.

I was surprised. This was the elegant Dennis Hotel. Waiters didn't respond or react in a class hotel. In a few minutes he came back with my drink. I didn't have to get it too near my nose to know I had a glass full of whiskey. I suppose I must have made a face, for President Howard Melvin came over to me, took the glass out of my hand for himself and went to get me my well-known ginger ale.

Elizabeth B. Alton

Chapter 26
1960

The Pageant had an unwritten policy that local businessmen could not invite the contestants to their establishments for publicity advantages. Marks had warned me not to permit it. The owner of the Wax Museum on the Boardwalk was insistent that I send contestants to his establishment. I explained the Pageant did not permit this contact. He wouldn't take "No" for an answer. He returned again with a handful of free tickets. The answer was still, "No." Finally I sent him to Al Marks on the runway after I had first talked with Marks. The owner still argued longer than necessary, but finally left unsatisfied.

One day, Marks sent me a letter from a prominent Jewish woman leader, voicing a complaint that there were no Jewish women on the hostess committee. We had kept the original committee. In selecting new women for the committee I had given no thought to their religious or cultural background. I tended to select new members from women I had worked with in a variety of organizations. I went over my list of names and agreed with her privately. I remedied that situation as soon as there was a vacancy.

Joe Grossman, United Press correspondent and a local resident, was named news director for the Pageant. He was busy planning the 1960 reunion of former contestants, a dream Lenora had had for several years. He also published an annual magazine.

A conference of governors all over the country was held in Atlantic City in June. The Pageant was asked to entertain the wives of the governors with a fashion show in the American Room of the Hotel Dennis. Selected professional models of

Marie McCullough's modeling agency displayed the fashions with Marie as commentator. I was asked to be a guest model, which I had done previously. She often used several local women with her professionals for local interest.

The theme of the show was "Fashions of Pageant Week." Everglaze clothing for every occasion was shown. The highlight of the show was a preview of Miss America's magnificent gown as well as gowns for the court of honor. Bert Parks was the emcee. The court of honor presented the entertainment and Miss America, Sharon Kay Ritchie, spoke of her travels all over the world.

I had been in a fashion show a couple of weeks previously at the Claridge Hotel. The lighting on the runway had been particularly bad with the spotlights aimed directly into the faces of models. For some stupid reason I had been blinded just at the end of the runway and walked off the end, a drop of two feet or so. I landed flat on my foot and did not fall, but was considerably embarrassed. I stepped back on the runway and returned as though the incident hadn't happened.

For the fashion show for the governors' wives, a hairdresser had been stationed in the dressing room to style the model's hair. She did mine in a high front pompadour, which changed my appearance considerably.

Al Marks was involved in the general planning of the runway. He gave me a wide grin when I walked as a model, for there, at the very end of the runway, which was four or five feet high off the ground, was a fairly thick row of plants as a precaution. I was quick to realize it was meant for me. We had a good laugh about it.

On July 18, Arthur Godfrey devoted his hour-long television show to the Pageant. There was a cute story about Mary Ann Mobley when she became Miss America 1959. Accompanied by two state troopers, she entered an elevator where there were two young boys. One said to the other, "Who is she?" The other boy answered, "I don't know, but she must be dangerous."

In order to provide more free time for contestants, a parents activities committee was organized. Contestants had too little time to have visits from their parents. In later years, I approved a tour of the back stage area so that parents could visualize what their daughters were experiencing.

Occasionally there were requests from the news media to view the dressing room. Tours back stage were also arranged for them. The press lined up each side of the runway during the shows at night. Reporters sat on one side and photographers on the other. A badge received from Mall Dodson entitled each to a free seat. The system in those years was badly abused. Wives accompanied husbands, sometimes children. In effect, the first press to arrive got squatter's rights. The unimportant got seats that should have been available to the important press.

Tom Kenny made an excellent contribution to improve press relations with the Pageant by preparing a separate press pamphlet describing the rules and regulations established by the hostess committee as printed in the working schedule. It became an effective way of helping to eliminate some unnecessary problems.

Hostesses were always willing to do the unexpected for their contestants. One year, Miss Florida's talent required bubble gum as part of her act. There wasn't time for her to chew the gum sufficiently before she went on stage. Eugenia Fischer, her hostess, valiantly chewed the gum to its proper consistency for her and had it ready backstage for her entrance.

Elizabeth B. Alton

Chapter 27

One of the most distressingly difficult experiences for me came over a problem with swimsuits. In Lenora's campaign to eliminate the swimsuit as a symbol of Miss America as a beauty queen, she had already mandated that she be crowned in an evening gown. Lenora wanted to take the next step and prevent swimsuit pictures of Miss America on the beach Sunday morning after her press conference. That year the press conference was held in the West Room and the outside deck of Haddon Hall. Lenora didn't usually come to the conference which was attended by the president and other Pageant officials.

When I arrived, Lenora was present but President Melvin was not. I sat with Lenora while pictures of Miss America in her chic outfit were taken. When the moment arrived that she would usually change into her swimsuit, Lenora told the press the pictures would not be taken. The few press representatives who were present were recognized leaders in their fields. They persuaded, they argued, they persisted. Finally, Lenora said to them that I was chairman of the hostess committee and I would make the decision. At that moment, I would gladly have been able to vanish on the spot. The most prestigious member of the press said, "What about it, Mrs. Alton?"

It would have been easy to say "no" for that was what Lenora expected me to say and I would have said it. Only, it wasn't that simple of a decision. Also present that morning was Al Marks representing President Howard Melvin. He was there for the express purpose of seeing that the swimsuit picture was taken. There I was, right smack in the middle between the two most powerful people in the Pageant. If I said "yes," I would have Lenora angry with me, for I owed her not only my position as chairman, but my election to the board—which she had tried so long to achieve for a hostess chairman. If I said "no," I would have President Melvin's strong disapproval. I owed him much for accepting my election to the board of directors and for his strong support of me as chairman of the hostess committee.

When I was asked, "What about it?" I stood up and walked out of hearing with the press speaker. I told him I felt unable to ruin the relationship between Lenora and me by deciding against her, for I would not be able to work comfortably with her again. He understood my problem.

Al Marks and I then talked. I was so angry that I tapped him on the chest with my finger while I told him that I would never be placed in this impossible position again and this would have to be the end of my association with the Pageant. Al Marks went to the telephone to call Melvin.

In the meantime, I talked with the press leaders again. I asked them to bypass the swimsuit for this year so that the board of directors would have time to determine a solution once and for all. If they would agree, I would allow them to take any other pictures they wanted at that time. They all finally agreed and went to their work. Al Marks returned to say that President Melvin agreed with my position. Once more, all had ended well. But being chairman of the hostess committee was a long way from being peaches and cream.

Later I suggested to President Melvin that it would be helpful and more efficient to have a member of the press in charge of the press and a photographer in charge of photographers, both of whom I could work with. It seemed best to me that professionals should be handling professionals, thus eliminating misunderstandings. He considered the matter for a while but nothing yet was done.

I had an interesting friendly disagreement with a couple of newspaper reporters over a story they had and wanted to print.

I wasn't sure it was the kind of publicity the Pageant wanted and had not approved it even though I thought it was a cute story. The reporters had learned that two of our contestants from different states were dating the same young college man. Contestants often represented either their own state or their college state which made this possible. Interviews had been requested with both girls. Customarily, hostesses do not allow personal questions about the girls' private lives or their families. The requests had been denied.

In a little while, Al Marks asked me to meet the two reporters with him. We laughed together and agreed the story was harmless. I asked the girls if they cared to be interviewed on the subject. Neither objected and it became an interesting Pageant story. The young man lost two dates.

One of the situations I found most troubling was telephone calls in the wee hours of the morning, sometimes after I'd just gone to bed. The calls were always from some drunk, with the sound of bar noise in the background, berating me because he couldn't get a date with Miss Someone. Highly abusive in language, unrespectable, he shouted in my ears before I could hang up, only to have him call back again. I never had enough sleep during Pageant week; my hours of service were pretty close to going almost around the clock. Interruptions of sleep were really difficult.

Elizabeth B. Alton

Chapter 28

enora realized that the growth and development of the Pageant into a first class contest depended upon establishing state organizations with which she could work and have the same high standards and goals of her national Pageant. Recognizing the fine achievement of the Junior Chamber of Commerce throughout the country she had worked to achieve their support as state sponsors. Her first Jaycees to join the Pageant family were the North Carolina Jaycees. She went there personally to help them run their contest and their show. It was so successful that she next secured the Texas and then the Georgia Jaycees organizations as sponsors.

I didn't quite realize the full importance of this beginning group of state sponsors when I became co-chairman of the hostess committee. I do remember very well the day Lenora cautioned me to take special care in helping "her Jaycees" when introducing me to the North Carolina "boys." I did watch over them as best I could. It took a few years for Lenora to take sponsorship out of the hands of commercial interests and finally develop civic organizations whose reputations and leadership in their communities were unquestioned. The success and high standards of the Pageant through the years have remained in the hands of fine local and state pageants, carefully selected, constantly observed and, if necessary, their franchises removed. The national Miss America Organization of today keeps a firm hand in control of all Pageant operations throughout the country.

One of the few really unpleasant experiences of being a hostess, aside from the long hours, was the coronation ball each year. An elegant affair in one of our finest hotels, it should have been enjoyable relaxation. It wasn't.

Hostesses were all seated together in a small room opening into the ballroom. Getting a waiter to wait on us was almost impossible. Most of us wanted some food at that hour and liquid refreshment of choice. We were all tired out, in need of some sustenance. Waiters wouldn't wait on us even when one or two of our hostesses went to ask for service. Sitting out the hours of the ball, unfed and ignored, curdled most of our dispositions.

After a couple of years of this insulting treatment, I went to see Lenora. She suggested I go talk with George Bruni a member of the board of directors and manager of the Claridge Hotel. I arrived in his office by appointment one sunny August afternoon. After describing our problem to him and assuring him he was losing income from 25 hostesses, I was shocked to learn why we were being so badly treated. He said it almost with pride. We were Freebies! We had no standing. Everybody bought tickets for the ball. We didn't. Therefore, we were Freebies, unentitled, according to the maître d', to service. The worst kind of discrimination. Bruni sent for the maître d' for quite a discussion. The maître d' didn't say so, but it didn't take a genius to know that the basic problem was tips. Many waiters think women are not good tippers, especially Freebies. Maybe that's why.

The matter was settled when Bruni instructed the maître d' to see that our hostesses were attended by waiters and properly served. The maître d' was so angry, he performed as I have seen only in the movies. He snapped his heels together in German army style, actually jumped off the floor in a military style salute, and went out of the room slamming the office door behind him. I laughed. When Bruni went to open the door for me as I started to leave, the door wouldn't open. We were locked in that room for a fair amount of time until a mechanic arrived to replace the broken door knob.

That was not the end of the story. At the ball that year, hostesses were seated in the ballroom at tables near our former room. The maître d' stood at attention directly in back of our table. Waiters brought us hot food and served us in proper style, all the while our friend stood behind us at rigid military attention. Finally, George Bruni came to see if we were being served. He took one look at our maître d' and exploded. "For God's sake," he said, "Go someplace else. You look like a house dick." The maître d' left us alone while all our hostesses also exploded with laughter. It was a very happy evening for us, at long last.

Elizabeth B. Alton

Chapter 29

My second year in 1959 as president of the Federation was equally as busy and demanding as the first. I crammed even more speaking engagements and personal appearances into my schedule. Many times I had to be in a northern section of the state two or three hours distant from Atlantic City for an early morning state or district conference by 10:00 a.m. Sometimes I would drive on to another city for an afternoon meeting and another city for an evening meeting, driving home on the parkway in the early morning hours.

I am not an early morning person, unable to rise comfortably in the dawn to reach North Jersey on time. My husband knew my early morning shortcomings. He would always leave home early on business. He developed a habit of rousing me out of bed at some ungodly hour and, while I dressed, he would start breakfast for me in the kitchen. He was no cook, but somewhere he had learned how to scramble eggs to perfection, fix coffee and toast. He would stand at the foot of the stairs and call up to me that breakfast was ready, knowing I would have left the house on my own without eating to save time. If I didn't come downstairs fast enough, he would call again and again, "Everything's ready. The coffee is hot. You know you don't like cold coffee. Hurry up."

When I was at last ready to leave the house, he would accompany me to the car and go down his check list. "Do you have your purse? Do you have your driver's license? Have you enough money? Do you know where you're going? Do you have your papers? When will you be home?" And finally, sticking his head through the open window, "Are you awake?"

We received many awards in this second year of my adminis-tration: Meals for Millions for the second year for some $10,000 in contributions; the New Jersey Division of the American Cancer Society for outstanding support for the cancer program; the New Jersey Society for Crippled Children and Adults for support of the Easter Seal Program. The State Department of Civil Defense and Disaster Control presented the highest civic award possible to the Federation for the fall-out shelter project which resulted in building fourteen fall-out shelters in the state during the Cold War Era with 30 more under way.

The fall-out shelter project was undertaken with donated labor and materials in all the counties of the state, winning national as well as state honors. The state chairman was invited to Massachu-setts to speak at a conference about the "New Jersey Plan," with expenses paid by the New Jersey Department of Civil Defense and Disaster Control. The plan was being considered nation-wide at a time when nuclear fall-out was a threat.

C.A.R.E. presented awards to clubs contributing 100%. The Junior Membership Department was highest in the country in contributions. The Sears Roebuck Foundation presented awards to the five top community improvement club projects in the state, the winning club having transportation paid to Washington to speak about the project.

The juvenile court program won national recognition for its program which interested club women in visiting juvenile courts. The chairman was invited to speak at the general Federation convention on New Jersey's project, considered the best in the country. Two Federation officers were invited to attend the White House conference on children and youth in Washington. Our American Art Week project placed first in the country for the participation of women in American art. The Veterans Adminis-tration presented an award for Federation's volunteer services at East Orange Veterans Administration Hospital.

College Day at Douglass College brought over 2,000 high school girls to the campus. The Citizenship Institute, held by the

Federation for 335 junior high school girls, offered programs on government, welfare and social agencies.

Over $100,000 was given in scholarships by our clubs that year. Our fellowship aided a Chinese-American girl to study medicine at New York University—Bellevue School of Medicine. A Pan American scholarship was awarded a student from Rio De Janeiro for study at Douglass College. Two art scholarships for painting and one for sculpture were awarded through a statewide contest.

The Vineland Research Project contributed funds to the Vineland Training School for research on mental retardation. The evening membership department contributed over $20,000 to build a psychiatric building at Vineland State School with matching funds from state and national governments.

State chairmen attended public hearings of the Youth Study Commission's budget hearings of the Rehabilitation Commission; Mental Health Commission; Public Medical Care Commission; the state budget and many legislative bills, some of which have been supported by the Federation. The Federation later worked strenuously to secure passage of the 1969 bond issue for higher education of $66 million which permitted the expansion of Rutgers University and our state college system.

Following an invited tour of Clinton's Prison for Women and the State Home for Girls in Trenton, a committee of Federation women was appointed to study the rehabilitative practices of our state's women's penal institutions in order to improve these institutions and their services. The junior membership department raised well over $25,000 to build a recreation field for the State Home for Girls in Trenton as a much needed rehabilitative measure. Women's clubs raised enough money to buy a small-size delivery table for the infirmary at Clinton Farms, suitable for delivering babies from eleven, twelve and thirteen-year-old girls too small for full-size delivery tables.

I added to my schedule serving on the White House conference on aging, as a member of the housing and shelter committee and as moderator of one of four workshops in the state. A few of the long list of the Federation's leadership representation include the following: national conferences on citizenship and civil defense in Washington; women's planning committee; Japan International Christian University foundation; nutrition council; State department of health; adult education association; national conference for social workers; New Jersey welfare council; State women's council on human relations; citizens advisory committee on migrant education of the migrant labor board; committee for the division of chronic illness; workshop for the chronically ill and arthritis workshop of the department of health; Greystone, Lyons and Marlboro State Hospitals; Penjerdel, a corporation for the development of metropolitan areas in Pennsylvania, New Jersey and Delaware; 87th annual forum of the national conference on social welfare and other fields of interest.

It can be truly said that the Federation exemplified well my administration theme that we can make our world better when we do "better" ourselves.

Chapter 30

or the first time every state in the country was represented in the Pageant in 1959. In our states and in the provinces of Canada, 3,500 local Pageants were staged. Work began in earnest on the Royal Reunion planned for 1960. Fifteen hundred former contestants were invited to return to Atlantic City. CBS Television broadcast a half-hour preview of the parade.

Lenora had been more than busy in her strenuous efforts to develop and improve the operation of state and local Pageants. She had decided to conduct a three-hour forum in Convention Hall for the 44 state pageant directors who attended the Pageant. Ways and means of improving local and state pageants were discussed. Many problems were solved and many new ideas introduced as the civic leaders met daily to exchange ideas and develop closer working relationships with the states and the Pageant.

Howard Melvin, an executive vice president of the Atlantic City Electric Company, had been president of the Pageant the year previously when I had been elected to the board for this year. I had developed not only a tremendous amount of respect for his executive abilities but a welcome rapport where my responsibilities were concerned. We saw eye to eye on many things. In our discussions, he told me that he had advised Lenora to take time away from the auditorium of the Hall to meet with all the state sponsors and perform other necessary business, leaving me in the Hall during her absence.

During these early years, it had been the practice of the *Atlantic City Press* to take swimsuit pictures of every contestant on the beach, placing upon each head the Miss America crown while holding a scepter. It was necessary to take this picture every year because *The Press* ran a full page picture of Miss America on the front page of the *Sunday Press* the morning after the Pageant. Since their deadline was midnight, and the Pageant ended at midnight, there wasn't time to prepare a picture and write-up for Sunday's paper otherwise.

Lenora had already decreed that Miss America would be crowned on stage in evening gown. A picture in swimsuit on the front page of the Sunday Press was anathema to her. She refused to permit *The Press* photographer to take the swimsuit pictures of girls posed as Miss America in their swimsuits. This created an uproar at *The Press*. The battle raged behind the scenes.

The hostess committee was always seated in their beautiful evening gowns in a row of boxes closest to the stage. Lenora and I sat in the first box nearest the stage for easy access to the dressing room. This night of *The Press* problem, Howard Melvin came to our box and asked me to come with him. He explained that he had arranged for *The Press* photographer to take pictures of every contestant in evening gown in a room on the balcony floor. I was to supervise. Each was to pose as Miss America.

The mechanics of getting the picture printed immediately after the crowning was a simple one. When word leaked out to *The Press* of the ten finalists during the day, *Press* reporters wrote a story about each of the finalists. When the winner's name was announced, presto, the picture and write-up were printed and Sunday papers were on the Boardwalk within the hour. *The Press* was thus able to be the first in the country with the news.

The Press also decided to oppose the hostess committee rule that interviews with contestants could not be held over the telephone. President Howard Melvin arranged a meeting in the Electric Company with Stanley Fink, editor of *The Press*, a couple of top newsmen and me. Before the meeting opened, he asked me to let him do the talking, an obviously wise decision. I was glad. My role was answering questions. Mr. Fink wanted to know why an interview couldn't be held over the phone.

My answers apparently satisfied him for no argument ensued. I explained that his reporters, unlike other reporters who came to Convention Hall and contestants' hotels, were not doing leg work, but simply using the telephone, or trying to, for their stories. That surprised Mr. Fink. Obviously he didn't approve and said so. He accepted the other reasons I gave and from then on *The Press* reporters were much in evidence.

This year I was listed in the working schedule as giving instructions to contestants regarding their participation in both television and the Boardwalk parade at a business meeting Labor Day night. The panorama picture in swimsuits was taken in the Marlborough-Blenheim Hotel Pool Club for beach and resort pictures. Girls always brought clothes to dress in Convention Hall for rehearsal. This year they were told to "bring hoops for rehearsal." Evening gowns in those days had voluminous skirts.

The Pool Club was private to everyone except the Pageant officials, hostesses and press. In past years there had been difficulty keeping the public out of the way, interfering unnecessarily when on the beach.

Before the parade Tuesday evening, contestants and hostesses had dinner at Hackney's famous restaurant. The beef for dinner had been provided by Miss Nebraska. For the first time, the Pageant parade was televised by CBS, sponsored by Maybelline. Some of the girls, as usual, had their own decorated floats provided by their states. All others rode in decorated Oldsmobile convertibles.

For the evening gown panorama picture on Wednesday night after the show, contestants were instructed to bring long white gloves. The girls still met with the judges at Haddon Hall for breakfast Thursday and Friday mornings. Movie star Grace Kelly, later to become Princess of Monaco, was a judge one year. A resident of the Philadelphia area, her family had an ocean-front home in nearby Ocean City. She could often be seen on the beach there in summer. After her marriage, she returned periodically with her husband, the Prince of Monaco. Grace was a gracious, warm, lovely woman who took her role as a judge seriously.

On Saturday, there was full dress rehearsal for the finals. This year I had established a new system for the dressing room for the final ten. Hostesses were required to transfer their girls' cosmetic belongings from their assigned dressing table places, and the clothes necessary for final competition, to an area where dressing tables had been set up together just for the final ten. Their own hostesses were instructed to assist each finalist during her competition. Each hostess was responsible to see that her girl was dressed, ready, and on stage at the right time.

Also, for the first time, hostesses to chaperones were required to find the parents of the top five and take them to Brad Frapart at the stage apron stairs so they could be taken on stage quickly.

The Coronation Ball had United States Air Force Academy cadets enjoying some very happy duty as escorts and dancing partners for the contestants.

Our registration had been held in the Founders Room of the Hotel Dennis for the second year. I had felt that better procedures for the process would eliminate the confusion I'd noticed the first year. I asked Mildred Brick, a hostess to chaperones, to take charge of organizing registration there. A highly efficient woman who eventually succeeded me as chairman of the hostess committee, she did an excellent job and all went well. That, too, was a kind of milestone for the Pageant. She was the first to hold a committee position within the hostess committee.

Nineteen fifty-nine was also a special year for Lenora who celebrated her 25th anniversary with the Pageant. The board held a dinner in her honor.

Chapter 31
The 1960s

Beginning in 1960, the basic rules in the working schedule were reorganized to place the rules for contestants in one category followed by the rules for reporters, photographers and other public relations representatives. The third category described rules for Convention Hall.

Among the rules for contestants, I had added Lenora's instructions that the girls could not smoke in public. Also, "Contestants are not permitted to speak to a judge at any time, nor to appear in the presence of a judge or a group of judges, except at regularly scheduled events."

Another new rule: "All contestants must attend the Coronation Ball with official escorts provided by the Pageant and must stay until curfew for contestants. They must go directly to the Ball from Convention Hall, while their personal belongings will be sent to their hotels. Following the Ball, local hostesses will accompany contestants to their hotel rooms. No dates are permitted after the Ball, or during the Ball. Also, all rules and regulations of the Pageant must be observed until Sunday noon. Hostesses will continue their duties and responsibilities until then, and will call for scholarship winners on Sunday morning to escort them for scholarship interviews."

Sometimes in those early years, girls wanted to leave Convention Hall and go to their hotels even before the show had ended on Saturday night. We posted hostesses at the stage entrance on Pacific Avenue for a while to keep all girls in the Hall. In later years we arranged with the production staff to have the girls not needed on stage to watch TV together on chairs in Room B across the Hall. Eventually it became desirable to use every girl in the finale, then throughout the show.

To the category for reporters we added the rule, "Interviews by long distance telephone will be permitted in Convention Hall when a local hostess is present."

Another rule stated, "A room in Convention Hall will be reserved for tape recording. Questions for tape recorded interviews must be approved in advance of recording."

Also, "Contestants are not permitted to have swimsuit pictures taken on the beach or Boardwalk. All swimsuit pictures must be taken on Tuesday at the regularly scheduled time. No special arrangements for any other time will be made."

Finally, the solution to that problem Lenora had, which placed me in the middle between President Melvin and Lenora. "No swimsuit pictures of the new Miss America will be permitted after she has been crowned."

Before the parade, contestants and hostesses had dinner again at Hackney's Restaurant. The Philco Corporation sponsored the parade on CBS Television.

It had been customary for the board of directors and judges to have dinner together on Wednesday night before the show. This year dinner was at Haddon Hall. Millie had been maître d' there for a long time, well known and very well-liked by everyone. After dinner, our driver was taking my husband and I to Convention Hall. I happened to notice that the center diamond was missing from my three-diamond ring. We drove back to the hotel immediately. At the entrance door I met Tony Rey, a member of the board of directors, vice president and general manager of the hotel. He telephoned the dining room we had used. By the time I reached the room, Millie had found my diamond on the floor under the table where I had been sitting. She knew exactly where I had been seated. I was deeply grateful to Millie, one of the finest of Haddon Hall's employees for many years.

Nineteen sixty was a special year for the Pageant. The Royal Reunion was held for former titleholders and hundreds of former contestants. They enjoyed the Boardwalk, attended beach parties, luncheons and banquets in their honor. Former Miss Americas strolled the runway to tremendous applause. Suzanne Bruni, Miss Atlantic City 1958, was Reunion coordinator.

George Buzby, who had produced the Pageant for some years, resigned to accept a position abroad. James Hatcher, a professor at the University of Alabama, was chosen to produce the 1960 stage show. The theme he chose was the Cinderella story, "The Cinderella Girl of the Cinderella Country," paying tribute to all former Miss Americas. A member of the New York City Ballet, Jacques d'Amboise, portrayed Prince Charming with Bert Parks as Master of Ceremonies.

If I were to select an outstanding show in my memory, it would be the Cinderella show. The scene of the golden carriage drawn by six of our resort's finest young men, traveling on a platform well above the stage from one side of the stage to the other was dramatically stunning. It was a beautiful show. It was also the first theme show.

Margaret Gorman, Miss America 1921, had been Grand Marshal of the parade. Marilyn Van Derbur, Miss America 1958, was official hostess of the two-hour broadcast of the finals on CBS.

The Naval Aviation Cadets from Pensacola, Florida, sang during the finals on Saturday night. An outstanding group of young men, handsome in their cadet uniforms, gentlemen in every respect, they became a real headache to me. Like all young men, some older ones too, they had a healthy interest in watching the contestants hurrying in and out of the dressing room. Our corridor was long and narrow. A large group of young men standing in the corridor obstructed the passageway needed for girls. I tried not to fuss about it to production, but finally asked for their help in solving the problem. The young men spent more time off stage upstairs in their own dressing room.

The Royal Reunion was conceived by Pageant news director, Josef Grossman, as he worked to carry out Lenora's dream. Both were made honorary members of Mu Alpha Sigma, the Miss America sorority.

On the final evening before the largest live television audience in history, lovely Nancy Anne Fleming, Miss Michigan, was named Miss America 1961. Former contestants joined the state Queens in a magnificent Coronation Ball. The Naval Academy Glee Club, which had performed each evening, were escorts for dancing.

❧

A change in the balloting procedures was instituted this year to give more points to talent than to swimsuit and evening gown competition. The greatest array of talent ever to perform on our stage had been presented by the 54 girls who had competed.

The new producer for the Reunion Pageant was James Hatcher. He had received his A. B. from Birmingham Southern College in 1943 and served in the United States Navy during World War II. After he received his Master of Arts degree in 1950, he returned to his Alma Mater as a faculty member, eventually becoming Professor of Speech at the University of Birmingham and Director of Town and Gown Civic Theater. He used the United States Naval Academy Glee Club in the show. As an added feature, Lenora walked on the runway in the Miss America march portion of the show. He had been associated with the Miss Alabama Pageant as producer-director for a number of years. Hatcher had been accustomed to producing plays at the University of Birmingham and at theaters in an atmosphere where he had been in control of all conditions during rehearsals, particularly noise. He found working in the vast open arena of Convention Hall extremely trying, difficult to concentrate, and psychologically upsetting for his difficult task of producing his outstanding show.

It takes a long time for the 23,000 or more seats to be put into place in the huge Hall. The noise at times is deafening.

Heavy machines run around bringing scaffolding for the elevated flooring, planks, and individual chairs which are all slammed down in place, echoing all over. There is banging and hammering and motors running and more. It is noise that cannot be controlled without stopping work entirely.

Mr. Hatcher had different ideas. He wanted quiet. Quiet he was going to have. It was up to me, he thought, to stop it. He instructed me to stop the noise, not once, but over and over. I couldn't. I did what I could. It wasn't enough. He ordered people usually needed on and off stage, off. He spoke to me repeatedly. I couldn't have ordered the work in the Hall to be stopped even if I had had the power. There had to be seats for the show that night.

When Hatcher ordered the police backstage to leave, my patience had become exhausted. Captain Cade told me, as he removed the police from the Hall, that he had been ordered out and he was leaving. Our drivers had disappeared. This still wasn't satisfactory. When Hatcher came yet again in a burst of complaints, I finally gave back as well as I had received. He, in a sense, was blaming me for the noise and the conditions in the Hall. I was expected to bring calm and quiet for him. I explained quite pointedly with appropriate gestures that we no longer had police protection for our contestants, no firemen watching the dangerous, high voltage electrical equipment backstage for our safety, no stage personnel available for his assistance. He had ordered them all to leave, not me. If he needed any of them now, that was his problem. Hatcher gave in. He asked the police and the others necessary to return. I produced them.

When everyone had left that night after the show, Hatcher asked to speak with me. In the presence of Captain Cade and one of the production staff, Hatcher voiced in no uncertain terms his solid disapproval of me. I didn't bother to reply. I was just as tired as he was and I knew he was simply letting off steam, a necessary release from the extreme tension and pressure of producing one of our fine shows. He deserved praise for that. Finally, Hatcher reached a point in his tirade, perhaps because I hadn't responded at all, that he said, "Mrs. Alton, you're a bitch." Captain Cade jumped in front of me as though I might jump up and physically attack Hatcher in any way I could. That was not my style. I understood Hatcher's reasoning and his opinion of me at that moment. In his eyes, everything he had painfully suffered had been my fault. He was unloading his emotions on me. That was a condition I was to face in future years from a couple of the young, newer members of the Pageant board of directors.

I often found that my decisions, when necessary for the care and protection of contestants, were expected to be subservient to the wishes and plans made by other pageant committees, without my knowledge, discussion, or any consultation with me. I occasionally found girls going places and doing things without approval that I knew nothing about. That caused friction. And it stopped.

Lenora had always insisted on upholding the basic principle upon which the hostess committee had been founded in 1937, as expressed in the basic rules of the pageant. Rule number one read, "The Atlantic City hostess committee has complete charge of all activities, interviews, pictures, recordings, etc. of the contestants during Pageant Week. Mrs. John M. Alton, chairman, has full authority to make decisions governing contacts with contestants." There were always a couple who wanted to make decisions for me. And they tried.

The transition of the hostess committee from a chaperone service to one of responsible management of contestants was a long time in the accomplishment. The opposition to the new role of our committee was subtle; to most people, unnoticeable; to a few, unacceptable. The form the opposition took, in a few instances, was opposition to me personally. I understood that, too.

When Hatcher returned to visit the pageant a couple of years later, he apologized to me in a friendly, respectful and contrite way. I accepted his apology in the good spirit with which he had expressed it.

Chapter 32

There were people outside the Pageant who had a differ-ent and better opinion of me. When my term as state president of the Federation had expired, the president of the General Federation of Women's Clubs appointed me to the important international affairs committee as chairman of arms control, an important issue in our country for years at that time.

The average public doesn't know it, but the GFWC had the respect of the United States Department of State which periodically briefed the GFWC international affairs committee. In turn, the committee briefed the Federations in every state and had contacts with Federations of 46 countries.

I can't describe the mixed emotions I felt as I sat with four other women being briefed on international affairs and problems in our world. I couldn't believe that I was sitting in the U.S. State Department Building listening to several top officials whose names were often in newspapers, whose voices were heard on the radio and who appeared now and then on television. Men who were in charge of the European Theater, the South American Theater and others.

I had known that GFWC presidents had been guests in the White House, had been summoned to meetings with military officials at the capitol during the most serious crises, so that women would understand what was happening in the world and why. I had known that senators and congressmen conferred with the GFWC presidents. Officials in Washington and in embassies who wanted support from women, or wanted their influence used for the common good, kept in touch. But I never dreamed that

I would one day be sitting, most of that special day, where I was at that moment, in the U.S. Department of State. Incredible! I had had tea with Mamie Eisenhower when the GFWC board of directors had been invited to the White House. That had been a fascinating event, but the State Department—Amazing!

A couple of years later, I had a letter from the State Department asking me to entertain a prominent educator from the Philippines who was a guest of the United States. The educator wanted to study the Catholic school systems in the United States. Atlantic City was on his list. I agreed, but not without difficulty. It was Pageant time. I was not home day or night. I had to house him in a hotel and arrange transportation. My second problem was that I am not a Catholic with entry into the church. School officials looked with suspicion upon a foreigner and a local woman who wanted to visit their private schools. I finally had to ask a prominent businessman to intercede with his priest. Our guest made his visit and study to his satisfaction.

Sometimes Lenora sent me to settle a problem situation which didn't add to my popularity. This time the stage manager had employed two young girls to take charge of the dressing room. As chairman, Lenora had put me in charge. She didn't want inexperienced girls in the dressing room or involved with contestants. I was sent to tell him the news. The stage manager at the time was talking with a recently new member of the board of directors. Neither man liked very much what I was saying, that the dressing room was under my jurisdiction. No one else but hostesses were allowed in the room. I've always believed that that particular board member's perennial disapproval of me began that day. First impressions are lasting.

It apparently antagonized him even more when he came to tell me to stop a hostess from interfering with the stage hands who had been snapping candid camera pictures of the girls in unguarded moments backstage, when they were relaxing or sleeping where they could. He thought these were personal pictures, therefore acceptable. I knew photographers at the Pageant tried every way possible to get candid shots like those any way they could. I learned from Sam Myers in later years that many Pageant swimsuit pictures taken on the runway end up in bars, parties and smokers frequented by men. He showed me some awful ones.

The woman that the board member wanted me to remove from backstage was Grace Yard Christian, an area resident all of her life, born in Atlantic City. She had been appointed by President Eisenhower to be head of Civil Defense and Disaster Control for all of the New England states and Puerto Rico. She had been state president of the Federation and a GFWC board member. During her vacation home, I had appointed her a hostess backstage. If she said the pictures taken by the stage hands were inappropriate, I had no hesitation whatsoever in accepting her judgment. The board member didn't. He argued. Grace was just another woman to him. I stood firm. I don't think he was convinced until another board member spoke to him, if then. In fact, he tried to have me removed I learned later.

It was the first time anyone had ordered a course of action for me. It was not the last. I have the ability and experience to work well with people on an equal basis. I just don't jump to an action against my better judgment. The role of a hostess chairman was by tradition to be free from pressure by board members.

In 1961, several changes took place. Contestants no longer met the panel of judges at breakfast conferences. Instead, one-third of the girls met with the judges in groups of three prior to their appearance that evening in formal gown competition. As a result, all contestants had an equal amount of time to talk with all eleven members of the panel. All judges had an equal opportunity to evaluate the personality of each contestant.

Cash scholarships for non-finalists were raised from $100 to $200. The Coronation Ball was discontinued. In its place an awards luncheon was inaugurated held on Sunday following the crowning. A new staging manual was published by Lenora to help all local and state contestants in their productions. Alexander E. Cantwell produced the show, "A Salute of the American Girl."

The finals were broadcast for two-and-a-half hours on CBS. Miss North Carolina, Maria Beale Fletcher, was crowned Miss America 1962. She had been sponsored by the North Carolina Junior Chamber of Commerce, the first Jaycees organization to join the Pageant program in 1944.

Chapter 33

In those early years, I was disturbed that so many people wandered around backstage. The Convention Hall had many maintenance workers who always had some reason to come backstage. I never knew who the others were. Members of the board of directors brought their wives and children before the shows.

Captain Cade had an excellent police detail covering all of the entrances to the stage and dressing room areas. Still too many unauthorized people wandered around. I had enough to do watching contestants without watching strange people. I decided to organize a security committee of hostesses. I chose very carefully new hostesses who had the intestinal fortitude to do exactly what I wanted without fail. My instructions to each of them each year were simple. "If you let anyone through your door who doesn't belong, you'll not be a member of the hostess committee." I placed hostesses at every entrance from the Hall into the backstage area. Police were usually close inside.

The improvement backstage was immediate. There were still men carrying a hammer or screwdriver and some tools, but most of them didn't belong there. I arranged with Hall management for badges to be given to those workers who had a right to be backstage.

The wisdom of the security system of the hostess special duties committee soon proved itself. Captain Cade distributed to all of us in the Pageant, backstage and around the Hall, an artist's drawing of a man named Stanley Berman who had developed a hobby of crashing parties and public events. He had managed to get into the President's private box after his inauguration and had appeared on national TV to present Bob Hope an award at the Academy Awards. His goal was to present the newly-crowned Miss America with an orchid on TV. Our police had learned of his plan to get on stage for the crowning.

I never knew how it happened that production had decided that Lenora would be on stage and I would be with her in those final moments of the crowning. In the late afternoon, to my surprise, I had been brought from the dressing room to rehearse with Lenora. There was no time to find a new evening gown. I quickly chose a white beaded gown I usually wore at special occasions in the Eastern Star.

Our impostor, as he was called, made his first effort to get backstage at our dressing room area. The hostess called me to the door. The impostor stood there with a well-dressed man and woman asking admittance, for whatever reason I don't remember. I refused him entrance and they left. I went immediately to the policeman outside our door and told him of the imposter's presence. Would he please go warn Captain Cade? He had been instructed not to leave his post and did not have a walkie-talkie. We had no telephone.

Pageant officials were on the far side of the stage, the best part of a city block away. I could not run that far and back in my high heels before the curtain went up. I was needed where I was. No other hostess was available.

During the portion of the show just prior to the crowning, the impostor made his move. While Lenora and I were on stage, he leaped over the shoulders of Jack Rowe and dashed out on stage. He was removed immediately. Most fortunately he had chosen a moment when a commercial was being aired and was not seen on TV. In that respect he had failed. And that's how I came to have the long asked for telephone backstage in the dressing room. For want of a phone to communicate with Pageant officials, an embarrassing situation had occurred.

Governor Hughes came up on stage that night after our show. His state police aides informed me that he would like to have his picture taken with the newly-crowned Miss America who was, at the moment, besieged with photographers after the curtain had closed. I went directly to the photographer in charge to request the governor's picture. He did his best, but as far as the photographers were concerned, the governor was unimportant at that moment, he would have to wait, and wait he did until they were ready for him. I was highly embarrassed, but that's the way it was. Miss America was the story, not the governor.

At the November 1961 board meeting, Albert A. Marks Jr. was elected president of the Miss America Pageant. Since 1955, when he had been elected to the board, a year after I had become chairman of the hostess committee, Marks had served as chairman of several committees: program book, contract, television and production; also as vice president and a member of the executive committee. Jack Rowe had joined the Pageant board of directors in 1960 along with Adrian Phillips.

Sometimes famous stars served as judges. Joan Crawford was one who also was Grand Marshal of the Boardwalk parade this year. She was married at the time to the president of Pepsi-Cola, one of our sponsors. She was more stunning in person than she was on the screen. She exuded warmth and charm, was easy to talk with, and enjoyable to know even briefly. She gave some real down-to-earth advice to our new Miss America, words of wisdom and beauty I was surprised to hear.

For the first time, two field directors joined the Miss America staff: Bill Muncrief, director of the Miss Arkansas Pageant; and George J. Cavalier, director of the Miss California Pageant. They would visit with each state Pageant committee and aid in organizing and producing state pageants, taking over and relieving Lenora of responsibilities she had found necessary to perform.

Joan Crawford had brought her two adopted daughters with her, who were nearly teenagers to the best of my memory. I believe it was one of them who wrote the unpleasant book *Mommie Dearest* about their lives with the famous star. I don't know if the girls had seats in the auditorium. I'm sure they must have, but they came backstage into the dressing room where they were not only in the way during the final competition, but seriously interfered with the hostesses and contestants by hovering over each girl every chance they could. Time is of the essence, without a moment to lose inefficiently, while girls were quickly changing and repairing cosmetics and hair-do. I asked the girls to step aside repeatedly where they could watch but not interfere. They had been brought backstage by a board member.

One thing that could have been written truthfully in that unpleasant book was the fact that these two daughters of a famous star were completely undisciplined on that night. They refused to get out of the way. It's a wonder hostesses managed to get near their girls long enough to hand them their clothes, shoes and accessories for the next competition.

Talent rehearsals were always long, tiring events that lasted almost to dinner time in those years. Each girl had been allotted three minutes for her competition. It was common for some girls to run over their time limit. That made it necessary for time to be used in cutting to the approved minutes. Some dramatic actresses had failed to secure copyright approval for their material. That created problems. Some girls, upon hearing other contestants sing their songs, changed their talent presentation. I've always remembered a fine contestant, Miss Canada, who had her talent changed so completely by her sponsor that she had to learn an entirely new routine on the spot. I always felt sorry for her.

Sometimes the girls had to stop rehearsing to let professional talent rehearse. As a result, the talent girls had to hang around doing nothing. I objected to the production staff often but no changes were made for several years. Contestants were tired, needed rest when they could find a few minutes. They would lie down wherever they could, sometimes in view of the stage hands in positions not particularly pleasant. To avoid the candid camera problem, Mildred Brick, a hostess to chaperones, who volunteered services backstage, came up with an idea. She found a way to provide some cots in a room upstairs above the dressing room and a couple of free hostesses to monitor the room. She and her co-workers called the room "Sleepy Hollow." I noticed that some girls liked to be alone in a corner behind the curtain on the stage to say a prayer before competing. We arranged a place and called it our "Prayer Corner." It was well used.

The reigning queen, Maria Beale Fletcher, made a whirlwind tour of the United States, Canada, England, France and Germany, including 31 army hospitals and servicemen's clubs. She had planned to open a dancing school with her scholarship money, but four former Miss Americas advised her to complete her education to prepare for her future. Maria enrolled at Vanderbilt University as a French major, winning a Vanderbilt scholarship to study six months in France. She graduated in 1966.

Television rights were sold to Philco, Pepsi-Cola and Toni Company. Pepsi-Cola was available backstage in large quantities everywhere during Pepsi's sponsorship. Along with Joseph Bancroft and Sons, the Oldsmobile Division of General Motors were national scholarship sponsors.

Alexander Cantwell produced the show, "The Magic of Miss America." Four immediate past Miss Americas returned to perform in the production and be hostesses for the broadcast. Bernie Wayne composed new song hits for this show as he had done previously. Miss America of 1963, Jacquelyn Mayer, formerly Miss Ohio, was unique in that she had 52-inch long hair. She attended Northwestern University.

I had added to Lenora's rule prohibiting girls from smoking in public that they also could not smoke on stage or in the dressing room. Other rules stated, "No parties or dates are permitted after the crowning of Miss America on Saturday night." The Ball had been discontinued. The next rule stated, "All rules and regulations of the Pageant must be observed until after the awards luncheon on Sunday. Hostesses must escort contestants to and from the awards luncheon."

One of my duties as chairman was to go back to the hotel with Miss America after the awards luncheon and prepare her for her trip to New York with Lenora and Brad that afternoon. It was necessary to choose the clothes to be packed and taken home by her state chaperone. She would need a minimum of outfits for New York. There the Bancroft Company would provide her with a new "Everglaze" wardrobe. There were always some clothes ready for immediate wear with only a minor adjustment if necessary.

I didn't really understand how this was possible, for the girls come in all sizes, shapes and heights. One day, a Bancroft representative told me how it was done. They had a composite figure of the dimensions of all former Miss Americas. They make outfits to fit the composite figure in a size ten. Adjustments could quickly be made by expert seamstresses to take in or let out a dress, shorten or lengthen it as its case required.

When everything had been packed and all was in readiness, then came the hard part for me, waiting until Lenora and Brad were free to arrive. Captain Cade paced the floor in the corridor outside while I sat watching the next hour, or more, go by in what seemed to me, in my exhausted state, an interminable wait. I had far too little sleep those past six days. I had lived through much nervous tension, many problems, unexpected difficult situations and some wonderfully happy ones. I was tired. I wanted to go home, rest and relax. As I waited, I sometimes stewed about how to improve this situation. Finally, it dawned on me. I asked Lenora to have Miss America's traveling companion come to the hotel after the awards luncheon and take over the duties which were better hers than mine. That worked great for me and Captain Cade.

Chapter 34

This year of 1962 was a milestone of sorts for the hostess committee. Adrian Phillips, a board member, had come to me the year before to ask me to select a vice-chairman of the committee. He grinned when he said it and was carefully insistent that I not think I was about to be replaced. A fine executive in several national hotel associations, he explained it was good management to have a successor in place. A good friend of long standing, I agreed with his management ideas, but I nevertheless had enough experience to know how easy it is to be here today and gone tomorrow.

I spent quite some time thinking about the leadership qualifications of the hostesses. I finally decided on Kathryn R. Morgan, principal of Friends School. She had the administrative abilities I wanted.

I also had decided that I should organize the hostess committee so that it could function more efficiently. For the first time in the committee's history, I organized particular committees within the hostess committee, the origin of the present-day committee operation (at least to the time of this writing). I appointed Mrs. Robert James Smith assistant vice-chairman, in charge of registration, and the following committees: dressing room, advisors to new hostesses, parade, press and TV, publicity, special photography, awards luncheon and personal assistant to me. We were making more business-like progress in achieving my goal of developing an organization of importance and value to the Pageant.

In 1963 the Philco Corporation became a subsidiary of the Ford Motor Company and was no longer able to participate in our scholarship program. Bancroft and Toni Company volunteered to provide a $500 wardrobe award to each state queen. Oldsmobile volunteered to provide cars for state queens during the year of their reign. Pepsi-Cola continued their scholarships at local and state pageants.

Our hostesses often used to comment on the difference in wardrobes the contestants had. Some states provided lavish ball gowns and expensive outfits. Some provided a minimum of less expensive clothing. Some girls had simply provided their own wardrobes. We used to marvel at the number of large suitcases accompanying some girls, ten to twelve or more. Sometimes they got lost on the way which gave us some pretty good headaches. Bringing 50 outfits and many pairs of shoes was not uncommon.

Clothes didn't always make Miss America. Personality had a way of giving each contestant that little something extra to catch the judges' eyes and hearts. I remember several Miss Americas who arrived with reasonably simple wardrobes who could have won if they'd worn a house dress, their charisma was that outstanding. The $500 clothing awards, in later years raised to $1,000, would help girls who came from smaller pageants.

The national broadcast of the finals by CBS was heard live in all time zones of the country for the first time with a two-hour show. Three former Miss Americas served as on-air hostesses: Marilyn Van Derbur, BeBe Shopp and Jacque Mercer. Cash scholarships were raised to $300 for each finalist. A beautiful and talented University of Arkansas senior, Donna Axum, had spent three years in the climb to Miss America 1964. She was second runner-up in the 1960 Miss Arkansas Pageant. She was not successful in her local preliminary in 1961. She spent 1962 improving her talents and developing her personality and self-confidence. In 1963 she returned to capture the Miss Arkansas title at Hot Springs, leading to the Miss America crown.

During her year as Miss America, Donna Axum, had a frighteningly dangerous experience in the Roosevelt Hotel in Jacksonville, Florida, when the hotel became engulfed in flames and 21 people died in the fire. Donna was able to drag her unconscious traveling companion where there was still some air until help arrived. They both suffered from chemical burns of the throat and bronchial tubes from the heavy smoke.

❧

The early 1960s were busy ones for me. The nine-member board of governors, which governs Rutgers, The State University, met monthly. Its committees also met monthly. Possibly because I had more free time, I was on several committees requiring my presence in New Brunswick almost every week. I was on the building and grounds committees, which was involved with architects, planners and recommending builders for the extensive expansion of the University as a result of the 1959 bond issue. Construction was taking place not only in New Brunswick, but in Newark, at Douglass College, and Rutgers College of South Jersey in Camden.

I was also on the bicentennial committee planning to celebrate the two-hundredth anniversary of the University and the honorary degrees committee. At meetings of this committee I stated once that the faculty had recommended prominent men, no women. This gave me the impression that the University didn't consider a single woman in the entire country eligible for an honorary degree. As a result, Lillian Hellman, the author, was honored.

The board of trustees of Rutgers holds title to investments and real property. I was on the trustees committees for Douglass College, the Newark College of Nursing and the College of South Jersey in Camden. The trustees met quarterly, but the committees, regularly.

As a result of my Rutgers and Federation activities, I was included in *Who's Who in America*, *Who's Who of American Women*, and *Who's Who in the East*.

I noted with interest the difference in treatment by *The Press of Atlantic City* between men and women in the news, a subtle form of discrimination where women were concerned. A local man listed in *Who's Who* was given a nice write-up. With three listings I was not news.

Chapter 35

There were many happy relationships with Pageant board members, national and state sponsors. One of the most pleasant was the formal family dinner held mid-winter each year in one of our top beachfront hotels. Lenora had organized the dinner for board members and national sponsors. It was an opportunity to socialize and enjoy the companionship and friendship of people most involved with the successes of the Pageant. Top representatives of national sponsors were always present during Pageant week, easy to know, and friendly. They truly became members of our pageant family. They also brought gifts at the dinner that I have treasured through the years. Each board member went home with a goodie bag at times containing Lenox china, Waterford crystal or other fine keepsakes.

The hotel provided royal treatment. The Shelburne Hotel once hosted an unforgettable dinner. The private dining room was beautifully decorated with floral arrangements. As we entered the room our eyes first beheld a huge lighted ice sculpture. Dinner was served in the most elegant style at two long tables, the food a creation of delicious entrees to delight the eyes as well as the palate. Waiters in their colorful red jackets and white gloves were each serving only four people. The attention was so continuous I almost felt as though I might be helped to lift my fork or raise my glass. Dessert was the "pièce de résistance." Two top chefs, I could tell by the height of their hats, rolled in two tables and created before our eyes our sumptuous crêpes suzette. A teetotaler, I was fascinated with the number of various bottles of liquor being tipped alternately into their crêpes pan before being flamed. I enjoy a number of dishes prepared with liquor flambé. When I went home I was glad I'd chosen a special evening gown. It had suited its occasion.

Max Malamut, owner of the Shelburne, was always a gracious host. I remember another Pageant informal dinner at his hotel where he couldn't remain seated at our dinner tables. In his eyes, the service was not quite what he demanded. He got up and proceeded to take over the responsibilities of the maître d' to the latter's consternation. It was kind of fun to watch. Malamut was a board member for a number of years.

Other family dinners I especially remember were at the Marlborough-Blenheim and Haddon Hall, where I once ate thick filet mignon so tender I was able to cut it with a fork. Always the hotels provided china and silverware saved only for V.I.P.s and special occasions.

Bess Myerson returned after several previous broadcasts to be hostess for this year's telecast. She had been the first Miss America to receive a scholarship in 1945.

Bess often used to come voluntarily into the dressing room to visit with the girls and encourage them. One day a contestant asked about the publicized $250,000 diamond necklace. To everyone's surprise she unfastened the neck of her jacket and revealed the gorgeous necklace. Everyone gathered around to admire with oohs and aahs. Having brought the necklace for her TV appearances, she said she wore it day and night invisibly under her clothing.

The presence of such valuable jewelry gave me pause for thought. I remembered Captain Cade had warned me one time about jewelry being worn and kept in the dressing room. "Be careful, Mrs. Alton," he had said. While I hadn't really thought about it, the police had been watching more than our dressing room doors. I began thinking about our general security in a new, more knowledgeable way. We needed the best protection possible for any contingency or emergency. I believed a board member should have the responsibility to coordinate with the police for every possible eventuality. I added one more contribution to the

Pageant then, for a board member was appointed. There has been a board chairman of security for many years now.

I'm sure the police had many a laugh, and perhaps rightfully so, at some of our hostess security committees. On Saturday we often had police in civilian or work clothes we didn't recognize as police. They would always be stopped when in or near the stage area. I myself stopped what looked like a workman on the stage apron one Saturday night. He smiled broadly at me, slipped his hand in his pants pocket, and removed his hand just far enough for me to see cupped in his fingers a police badge. I enjoyed his grin with a matching grin.

Carol Fiore and William Cowart were elected to the board in 1963. Fiore was associated with Fiore, Keppel and Quigley, an accounting firm. He had been past president of the Pageant and a continuous member of the board until today. Cowart was a vice president of the Electric Company.

Nineteen sixty-four was an eventful year in New Jersey. Our state celebrated its 300th Anniversary. The Democratic National Convention was held in Atlantic City's Convention Hall, where President Lyndon Johnson was nominated, and, at long last, Convention Hall was air conditioned. Sometimes the dressing room and Hall had been oppressively hot. The State of New Jersey celebrated its anniversary with the theme "Happy Birthday – Garden State." Alexander Cantwell continued producing the show and Bert Parks served as master of ceremonies for his tenth year.

The 3,500 state and local pageants had disbursed more than five million dollars in scholarships. Our national Pageant had provided $675,975. Of the 342 national finalists, their $1,000 to $10,000 awards had been used to attend 212 different colleges and universities.

A record was achieved when Vonda Kay Van Dyke became the first and only Miss America to become Miss Congeniality with its $1,000 award.

The Pageant lost two important supporters. John Hollinger, who had by sheer determination been the mastermind behind a board operation that had provided the foundation for the first successful Pageant beginning in 1935, died. So did Hugh Wathen, Pageant president during the war years and originator of the TV program. I had a special interest in Wathen for he had appointed me chairman of the hostess committee.

The bylaws increased board membership from 18 to 21. A representative from the District of Columbia competed for the last time, having been sponsored by radio station WWDC for a number of years. Going forward, only fifty states were allowed sponsorship. Cities were entirely eliminated. The general audiences in Convention Hall were really happy that year for the hot, muggy atmosphere had at last been improved with air conditioning for the Democratic convention.

There were stage escorts for contestants in the shows representing the Colonial Guard of Rutgers University. These young men were selected from the members of the Army and Air Force Reserve Officers Training Corps at Rutgers. They wore the uniforms of the Colonial Color Guard patterned after those worn by the famous "Jersey Blues" militia during the Pre Revolutionary period. Their presence was in honor of New Jersey's 300th Anniversary.

Girls wore longer, more natural hair with gowns not as bouffant with hoops as previous years. Some wore beaded or handsome sheaths with short sleeves and sometimes drapery on the hips.

Fine honors came to our executive director, Lenora Slaughter, the first of many, when she was named "Woman of the Year" by the Atlantic City Models Guild and "Saleswoman of the Year" by the sales and marketing executives of Philadelphia.

The year was also unique in that four board members were elected to the office of vice president. Usually the board has two, occasionally three.

Some additional press rules were included in the basic rules to meet situations as they arose. In 1965, the first committees of the hostess committee were increased to include the executive committee, advisory council and registration. Mildred Brick took over registration, organizing it with a state map signed by each contestant, table decorations, and in other ways which had not been done before. She also became chairman of our special duties committee, a fancy name for our hostess security system. This committee later became the first control center. Today it is the anchor station and information center.

A new event as hostess chairman was to invite sponsors and parents to tour backstage and in the dressing room when contestants were not present. This provided a better understanding for them of Pageant operation behind the scenes. At the request of the press, a similar tour was arranged for them.

One new talent presentation was presented in 1966. Jayne Jayroe, who became Miss America, conducted the Pageant orchestra as part of her musical talent. I don't know if the orchestra was following her lead or the conductor, but it came out evenly.

Jayne Jayroe was the only Miss America in my experience who exhibited a lot of cold feet after her crowning. Many girls take a sober look at a year away from home, family, college, and friends. The opportunities provided are more important, though, at the time. Jayne had strong misgivings about becoming Miss America for a short time. In her room before I left her, she voiced those misgivings in such a way that I began to believe she was possibly considering giving up the crown. I spent some time talking with her about what her future as Miss America could mean to her, the prominent appearances she would make, and her financial future.

I was concerned enough about her that I alerted Al Marks to the situation. I'm sure Marks was able to allay her concerns. She went on to become a fine Miss America, gained much personal success, eventually becoming an anchor woman on TV as well as other achievements.

My contacts with Jayne introduced me to Visine, the product advertised "to get the red out." Adrian Phillips had asked me to have Jayne present for a photographer at 8:00 a.m. on Sunday morning before her press conference. I confess to having some feelings of objection for both of us. I had left Jayne early in the morning after the ball. The appointed hour meant only three or four hours of sleep to give me time to get to Jayne's hotel. I remember telling Adrian that Jayne would have blood-shot eyes for a color photo. Adrian was not deterred. "I'll bring some Visine," he said. "That will take the red out." He did, and it did. I bought myself some Visine later.

Jack Rowe was president of the Pageant. He did one thing for hostesses they all enjoyed. He presented a charm to each of us with Pageant insignia on it each year. I always hoped one charm would be in a crown shape, but I was no longer associated with the Pageant when an attractive crown charm was given. I have always been disappointed.

Jessie Wilcox, a local girl who became Miss Atlantic City, went to New York to become a model for Harry Conover of the Conover Cover Girl fame. She changed her name to Candy Jones, appearing on countless magazine covers. She became quite famous as a model and her "Candy Jones Career School for Girls." She has written books on charm and personality, becoming a columnist.

Shirley Jones, the popular actress, entered several contests in her area, becoming Miss Pittsburgh in the Miss Pennsylvania Pageant. While she didn't make it to Atlantic City, talent scouts recognized her unusual voice and talent. She has been well remembered as the star of Richard Rogers and Oscar Hammerstein's famous musical "Oklahoma," among many others and many popular television shows.

Once in my personal Pageant experience we had a very difficult and potentially dangerous situation all during the Pageant. Al Marks, president, and Captain William Cade took me aside to tell me that some serious death threats had been received against Miss Mississippi. It was the era when the civil rights unrest in the South was at its height. The police considered the threat valid. Precautions were to be taken.

Marks instructed me to go with Captain Cade to the Traymore Hotel, where Miss Mississippi was staying, to talk to the manager about safety precautions in the hotel. I was surprised to find the manager was the same maître d' of the Claridge Hotel a few years previously who had slammed the door, imprisoning me with George Bruni temporarily in his office.

Miss Mississippi's room was changed to a beachfront room high in the hotel, inaccessible from any outside entrance. A policeman was stationed outside her door in the hall whenever she was in her room, day and all night. A number of other precautions were arranged.

Her enclosed convertible and driver were escorted by police cars in front and in the rear of her car. When she left Convention Hall, a policeman walked in front of me, I walked in front of Miss Mississippi and a policeman followed her the several feet from the Pacific Avenue stage entrance to the car. She was under extra close supervision in the Hall. No incident occurred. I'm sure we all breathed some sighs of relief when she left town.

Elizabeth B. Alton

Chapter 36

There have been some wonderfully happy memories of my Pageant years. Warm relationships with unforgettable people, our executive officers, national sponsors, state pageant directors, members of the board and some very special hostesses. Being chairman of the hostess committee had many personal and private rewards. I cherish the letters, in particular those, from top representatives of the press. We often disagreed, but they respected our accomplishments.

There were, of course, incidents and experiences that were so painfully difficult that they were headaches for quite some time. An unpleasant situation with Convention Hall guards had been developing. One day several hostesses told me that the guard sitting on the stairway landing leading from the dressing room to the powder room on the balcony floor was sound asleep in the middle of the day. His duty was to keep anyone from the balcony getting down to the dressing room. Why he had been placed in a chair on the landing so close to the girls I didn't know. He should rightfully have been placed at the top of the stairs. Anyway, he was on the landing sleeping in the chair.

I didn't go look. I told Al Marks on the runway who did go. As a result, the guard was fired. He had been drinking. I also pointed out to Marks, so he could see for himself, where the maintenance workers who built the seating had stashed liquor bottles under the seat scaffolding. If Marks wanted, he could see workers having their nips from the bottle. He did.

I was sorry the guard had been fired, but that was not my responsibility. Apparently, Convention Hall guards thought I was at fault. I became target number one, harassed in every way possible.

On the first night of the show, a couple of hostesses came backstage to tell me there were no seats for the hostesses. When I went out in the Hall to see, there were fifty hostesses beautifully dressed in fine evening gowns and a Hall guard with them. Apparently, the Convention Hall ticket office had not reserved the boxes always used by the hostesses and had sold the tickets to the public. On Wednesday night there were always lots of seats available. I asked the guard to seat the women in available seats. He refused. The women had no tickets, they would have to stand. And he was quite nasty about it. I wondered later if the fiasco had been planned. I tend to believe so. I tried to tell the guard to seat the women in as pleasant and reasonable a tone as possible, that they had to be seated somewhere. He turned on me in full, furious anger that could only have developed for quite a while. He almost shouted at me, "You're under arrest!"

Anyone who has not been told in no uncertain terms by a red-faced guard that he or she is under arrest cannot possibly understand the shock to the physical system such words create. I told him in as forceful manner as I could develop then that I was going backstage for Al Marks. It's a long hike in high heels from the middle of Convention Hall to the stage, across the backstage to where Marks was in Room B. I was moving at full speed, my blood pressure probably rising to the bursting point. When we returned to the guard, Marks ordered him to seat the women in the seats already available. He meekly did so, which ended the confrontation. I returned to the dressing room and then to the powder room for a few minutes of privacy to recover my equilibrium.

Unfortunately, the guard kept coming backstage the next days where I knew he had no business to be, allowed in because of his uniform, and continued to get in my way with whatever tactics he could manage, simply as harassment. Eventually a board member noticed his presence and ordered him to leave and not return.

After the Pageant was over I asked myself many times why I put up with these experiences. I had considered resigning several times through the years. While I had good personal rapport with board members, some of whom had been personal friends for a long time, I know that there were two, who eventually would become president, who not only strongly disapproved of me but occasionally let me know it without saying so.

As I thought about resigning, I reviewed in my mind the good changes in Pageant procedures which I had been able to achieve at some cost to my personal popularity in a few instances. Which was more important? Doing what needed to be done or my personal feelings? The balance always came down on using my best efforts to improve the Pageant procedures related to the well-being of contestants, based upon my knowledge and experience. I felt I had something worthwhile to contribute to the Pageant until one or the other of my two disapproving board members thought otherwise when he became president. I would stay until the door was finally closed on my services and achievements. I was strong enough to face what had to be faced if necessary.

Several years later I changed my mind about resigning. One of my two disapproving board members, who had become president, went with another board member to ask Kathryn Morgan to become chairman of the hostess committee. I had appointed her vice-chairman where she had served well and was both qualified and trained to succeed me. Kathryn declined the invitation. It wasn't long before the rumors that percolated from the executive committee became common knowledge and I was told, but not by Kathryn, who continued as vice-chairman.

When I heard, I called Marks on the phone and resigned as chairman. He wouldn't accept my resignation. It became a couple of weeks before the Pageant and I still resigned. Apparently, a successor had not been appointed. Rather than leave the Pageant without adequate hostess leadership, I agreed to stay for that Pageant only, which became a few more at Marks' request.

❦

The current hostess committee management system as it is so efficiently and smoothly operating today had its beginning in 1960. While each committee at the time of this writing has a large number of hostesses performing duties, the early committees were small, beginning with two members and then building as the duties of the committee progressed.

In the first committee system of 1960 there were hostesses for the Ball, four charming, interesting wives of prominent board members. Kathryn Morgan, vice-chairman, was in charge of the dressing room with another hostess. Two were appointed as liaison with the press as press assistants; two were parade assistants. In addition the hostess committee had its own publicity assistant in Betsy Barker who provided publicity for the hostess committee as liaison with the *Atlantic City Press*.

Through the years, Mildred Brick became a valued worker and friend. She was hostess to visiting chaperones but used her days helping backstage. I had appointed her chairman of the special duties committee, later known as control center. There her executive abilities were used in full measure, proposing suggestions and performing duties for improving both the Pageant and our operation.

One of her duties was controlling the badge system. Aside from the several hundred badges Mall Dodson gave to anyone and everyone, there were also too many associates of national sponsors, some of whom arrived for Saturday only. Many of these people congregated in the Hall close to our dressing room, overfilling the space where they stood. Some of them managed to get backstage with a sponsor badge.

Mildred and I decided to eliminate the unnecessary confusion in our area that we were forced to monitor so carefully. After some discussion, I approved a special badge to be prepared for Saturday night especially for this area. Mildred designed the badge, prepared it, and handled its distribution. I expected the shocked surprise it received. For some time, I held my breath that all would be well. Eventually it was. A somewhat delicate situation was ended.

I noted that the Pageant board usually had two vice-presidents, in years past up to four. I added Mildred as vice-chairman of our committee with Kathryn Morgan, each with individual responsibilities. Mildred became chairman of control operations, registration and parade problems. Control operations now numbered 15 hostesses. Additional committees were press room and TV aides, social news and special photography. Hostesses were not responsible for providing food in the dressing room area as they are today.

Hostess chairmen are appointees of the Pageant president. Since I had appointed Kathryn and Mildred as vice-chairmen, I was surprised to learn that the president considered the right to appoint vice-chairmen his for one-year appointments. To my disappointment, the new Pageant president told me that he would not appoint Kathryn vice-chairman again. I was shocked. Kathryn had served with considerable efficiency for six years. There had been no problems. She was well liked. I was told that the president had had an unpleasant family problem with their children at Friends school where Kathryn was principal. For personal reasons the president would not reappoint her. I was left with the embarrassing problem of having to tell Kathryn.

I invited her to lunch with Mildred Brick where I broke the sad news. She was considerably upset. I was equally upset, knowing that she had declined to replace me as chairman. It was a most difficult hour and one I deeply regretted. Even today it is a sore point.

I was determined that Mildred should not suffer the same casualty while I was still chairman. At a board meeting the following year with a new president presiding, I made a motion that Mildred be appointed vice-chairman of the hostess committee. The motion was seconded and carried. Al Marks, sitting across the table, raised his eyebrows and grinned. He knew exactly what I was doing and why. I raised my eyebrows too, and grinned back, enjoying the situation with him.

It is a matter of record that Mildred Brick is the only hostess vice-chairman and probably the only other vice-chairman of any committee, to be elected to that position by the board of directors rather than appointed by the president.

❧

A somewhat humorous event happened one night. Our esteemed Dr. David B. Allman, past president of the American Medical Society and Pageant physician, had made his usual courtesy call backstage to inquire about any health problems. Our security hostess had denied him entrance to our area. When I heard about it, I went personally out into the auditorium to assuage any hurt feelings and escort him personally backstage with my sincere apology.

On my way to find Dr. Allman's box I passed some personal friends in their box. I was dressed as all hostesses in full evening gown, my mink stole still draped around my shoulders. As I stopped for a minute to say "Hello," Allen said to me with a brief whistle, "By golly, Libby, who's keeping you?" Without missing a beat, I replied in full voice, overheard by those in several boxes nearby, "Why didn't you know, Allen, I have a married man keeping me." As I passed by I was somewhat chagrined to observe some amused chuckles on the faces of those nearby.

The governor of our state used to attend the finals on Saturday night. This year, Governor Richard J. Hughes visited Convention Hall with his state police guards while Pepsi was a sponsor. There were always large quantities of Pepsi available backstage. Governor Hughes decided he wanted a Pepsi break during the show.

I had selected some carefully chosen women to serve on our special duties committee. Our women had been instructed to allow no one backstage without the special badge which I had approved for the finals and which Mildred Brick had carefully made out of obsolete tapes. No one meant NO ONE, if anyone wanted to be a hostess in the future.

Governor Hughes did not have the special badge. Our hostess at his door, Anita Krenn, obeyed her instructions and politely but firmly denied the governor entrance backstage. She arranged for a Pepsi to be taken to him, but backstage he could not come. The governor good-naturedly departed.

The press nearby and everyone else in the vicinity were hilarious. I knew about the incident as fast as someone could come tell me. It was a good story that went the rounds for a while. This story is an example of the effectiveness of our hostess security watch system over those who wore official badges, including board members. Our eyes were everywhere and reports were kept.

We had an incident in the dressing room one night which had a serious impact on the talent portion during the final competition on Saturday night. Up to this time the stage show had had no professional acts between each segment of competition. The girls simply had to run in their high heels, holding their evening gowns up off the floor, down a flight of stairs from the stage, down its long, too long corridor to the dressing room. A lightning quick change was necessary for the first girl next due on stage.

I had watched this mad rush off stage for several years, my heart in my mouth, deeply worried that one of those girls was going to be hurt with possible serious injuries. I spoke to the director of the show, to the producer, to the assistant producer, to the stage personnel. Everyone gave me polite attention, but no one really listened. Nothing was done.

On this final competition night, Miss Washington State was the first due on stage for talent. She raced backstage and tore off her evening gown. Her hostess held her leotards for her to put her feet in. In her haste, and before she could be stopped, she thrust her foot with high heeled shoes on into the leg of the leotard. The results became a real problem. The mesh of her leotards was firmly tangled on the high heel of her shoe. The hostess tried to untangle the mesh. Other hostesses stood by to help. A minute passed, another minute passed. Al Castagnola on the production staff was shouting outside the door. "Mrs. Alton," he cried. "Mrs. Alton," yelling louder each second.

No one had time to talk to him. We had a decision to make and we made it. Was it better to tear the leotards, dress the contestant and get her on stage with a large hole showing in her leotards for the vast television audience to laugh about? Or was it better to take the time necessary to remove the shoe without damaging the leotards? We took the time while Al Castagnola almost had heart failure outside our door.

Meanwhile, in the footlights on stage there is a red light which indicates something is not ready—curtains, scenery, girls—and a green light for the show to proceed. This night, for the first time, Bert Parks missed the red light. In his entertaining way he announced Miss Washington and her talent. Miss Washington wasn't anywhere near ready and she wasn't there.

When we finally sent her on her way to present her talent, her hair was disheveled, and she was perspiring. A singer, she had to run down that long corridor, up a flight of stairs onto the stage and begin to sing. If anyone was improperly prepared to perform that night, she was, especially as a singer.

When I finally met Al Castagnola at the door I was so angry I pounded on his chest and said, "That is the most unfair competition I have ever seen and if anyone asks me I'll say so. NBC can have the greatest show on television, but if we can't get a girl on stage on time, there goes the show."

There were good results. Miss Washington proved to be a great performer. She became first runner-up to Miss America. But more important to the Pageant, now NBC and the production staff listened for the first time with understanding of what I had been saying for several years. In a small way NBC paid attention to me. They invited me into their TV trailers to see how the show was televised, explaining the seven cameras active at once and how the instant decision for the broadcasting camera was made. They supplied me with the television scripts and other information to make my supervision of the dressing room easier. A TV monitor came to our dressing room for the first time.

I had made another meaningful contribution to the improvement of the Pageant. From then on professional talent has been provided in between the three competitions each night. No longer did the girls have to run at top speed to and from the dressing room. This time somebody had really listened to me at last. It was an unpleasant way to get their full attention, as well as to show the importance that the hostess committee has to production. We weren't just women acting as escorts any more. Our opinions should be heard. The services we were providing were an important part of the Pageant operation. At last someone else thought so too.

Elizabeth B. Alton

Chapter 37

Women of all ages seek to make themselves as attractive as possible by having a stylish hairdo suitable to the contours of their head and face. Many find the look they want at a beauty parlor, possibly with permanent waves periodically applied and shaped cutting of the hair, long or short. Many use curlers and curling products at home after their shampoos.

I can remember as a child when being attractive was just as important as it is today, only the means were different. Women had long hair stylishly pinned on top of the head. Some used what was commonly called "rats" to puff out a pompadour and the sides of the hair when the hairdo was overly full and large. These matching hair rats could be purchased or made from one's own hair.

Watching my mother curl her hair was a fascinating event for me as a child. The curling iron was the instrument of choice in those days. The iron was heated by being held over the gaslight in her bedroom, before electricity. Extreme care was necessary to have the iron clamping the hair in a curl not too hot, or one's hair simply burned off and fell to the floor. Mother didn't use individual curlers also in use. Some of these curlers were also made of material often called rags.

It was a happy day when the Marcel wave came into use after the First World War, named for the French beautician inventor. This was a long flat iron about an inch or so wide, heated over an alcohol burner, which created beautiful, symmetrical waves over naturally head-hugging hair. Women's crowning glory became a mass of waves after waves. The effect was most attractive. Once again care had to be given that the curling iron not become too hot.

There were many good beauty parlors in town. Mother used to frequent one popular with her friends. With the many formal dances and social events prior to television, Mother's hair was frequently done. Before long the beautician made house calls for Mother's convenience. I used to watch the proceedings with interest. Mother always looked lovely.

During my Pageant years, hair styles have changed many times, some of them requiring careful styling. Time to visit a beauty parlor was always important for some. Early in the Pageant, I was faced with beautician problems. All of the main hotels had beauty parlors within their buildings or close nearby. With contestants who went with the chaperones directly to a beauty parlor, there was no problem. The timing of rehearsals made appointment times difficult.

Some state sponsors had found excellent beauticians who annually serviced their contestants in their own hotel rooms at odd hours. When they were women, there was no problem. But Atlantic City had some fine beauticians who were men. They could not, by Pageant rules, enter a girl's room. It thus became necessary for the state chaperones to get my approval to have their contestant's hair done in a public room of the hotel in her presence. The difficulty was finding a public room not too public because it would draw a crowd. When the choice absolutely had to be that particular male beautician, permission was granted when the room had been approved.

Beginning with Elizabeth Arden, beauticians have from time to time been stationed in the dressing room for cosmetic advice. Some years NBC had its own cosmetologist check on and advise contestants, usually emphasizing the "natural look." No one wanted a painted doll.

Occasionally, girls would complain to their hostesses about the judging. For several years Vincent Price, a famous character actor in films, served as a judge. He had a deep and powerful voice. He also had a habit of making unpleasant comments about an occasional contestant during her time of competition on the runway. The girls could plainly hear him, causing both distress and anger as well as difficult problems for their hostesses to overcome.

I relayed this information periodically to the chairman of the judges committee but nothing was done about curbing Mr. Price's voice to a level out of hearing for the girls. They were sometimes well aware of the judges' apparent disinterest in them from their lack of attention during their competition.

One year the state chaperone sharing the room with her contestant complained to me that they could hear some of the deliberations of the judges who were using the hotel room right next door. Apparently the discussions were argumentative, their voices raised loudly enough to be overheard.

I went to their hotel room at the appropriate time to hear for myself. Yes, there was no doubt. I could hear some of the discussions, too. I spoke again to the board chairman of the judges, asking that a different room be assigned to the judges' deliberations. He simply didn't believe me. "Impossible," he said and again nothing was done. I suggested he come listened for himself, but he didn't. The situation continued. One of the problems in being a hostess chairman in those early years was the simple fact that most often the people who should have listened with understanding didn't or wouldn't. I often wondered if it was because I was an unimportant woman. As a result I tried even more persistently for necessary improvements.

In 1960, state chaperones were expected by the Pageant to have specific responsibilities in relation to their contestants. In its early years sometimes state chaperones were mothers or members of the girls' families. Sometimes the wives or relatives of state sponsors came to the Pageant as chaperones and sometimes a press representative or public relations woman of the state pageant did a dual job of covering the girls for newspapers back home and chaperoning. I remember how proud Lenora was one year when two women deans of large western universities arrived as chaperones.

There were always social events held by the states, during rehearsal times and after the shows at night, which chaperones attended.

Several important responsibilities were finally delegated to state chaperones. First and most important was the requirement to be in charge of their contestants when hostesses were not present. They were to be present when girls were in their rooms, eating in the dining room, and accompanying the girls whenever they were free. Secondly, they were to have clothes and personal effects ready for the girls to dress according to the events, to care for their every personal need efficiently. They were to watch over the well-being of the girls as they would their own daughters, encouraging and supporting them psychologically as well as physically.

Most chaperones did an excellent job. A few occasionally became problems. Some liked to party either too well or too long, not being in their rooms when the hostesses returned the girls, or helping them as they should to save time and energy. Some serving in a dual capacity as a reporter were too busy to be a chaperone at the same time. It was clear that the system needed upgrading.

One night, just before the show opened, a contestant came to me to say that her chaperone had been abusing her when she returned from afternoon cocktail parties under the influence. This night she had struck the girl. I took her from the dressing room across the backstage to the Room B area and had her tell her story directly to Al Marks. He sent a Pageant official immediately to the girl's hotel, had her belongings transferred to another room, and arranged for the state sponsor to produce a new chaperone.

After I had a difficult personal experience with a chaperone serving in a dual capacity as a reporter from her state, it was clear that changes needed to be made and more specific general regulations adopted.

Contestants signed a contract with the Pageant in advance. After they were crowned Miss America the contract was in effect. A reporter/chaperone did not have the authority to arrange engagements that pour in over the telephone at this late hour in the early morning. This particular chaperone declined to accept my advice and let the new Miss America get some sleep, since she would have to be up and dressed for a press conference in about four hours. She continued long phone conversations, even placing Miss America on the telephone discussing arrangements that I knew could not be kept.

After that encounter, I prepared information for Lenora which was approved and sent to state sponsors spelling out the requirements for chaperones in Atlantic City. During regional conferences, I spoke at meetings with state sponsors about the kind of chaperones needed. Improvements were being made as a result.

⁂

In 1964 when the Democratic Party had held its convention in our Convention Hall there had been many parties and social events. One day a Pageant hostess and a friend had called me to say that there had been a large party in Ventnor where lobsters had been served. She had a few live lobsters left, would I like some?

I took an extra large soup pot to her house where she gave me two huge lobsters which must have weighed close to five pounds each. I never saw such big ones. Each claw alone would have fed a small family. After boiling the lobsters I proceeded to crack the shells to take out all the meat. The shells were as hard as concrete. No average lobster-cracker would make a dent. I finally reached for a hammer and pounded away with all my strength until I succeeded in breaking the claws open.

Of course my efforts were disastrous to my kitchen. I should have gone outside. I had the liquid from the lobsters all over everywhere: the ceiling, the windows, the sink, the floor. What a mess. It took a long time to clean the kitchen and me. But I ended with the tastiest, most enjoyable lobster I've ever eaten. I fixed it in several different ways for the next couple of days. What a feast for my family.

Lenora's early decision to interest the young men of the Jaycees in undertaking sponsorship of state pageants had proved to be a successful endeavor in her constant goal to improve the quality of both local and state contests and the young women who competed in the nationals. Gradually, civic organizations commanding respect in their communities had replaced the commercial interests seeking additional promotion primarily for their financial gains.

When the national president of the Jaycees was invited to become a judge at the finals, I wondered why organizations of women were not also being involved. It was the women of our country who were claiming the Pageant exploited our young women. Women who disapproved of various factors of the competition. Women who had strong feelings of disapproval about the swimsuit competition. Women who saw the Pageant as a beauty contest without many, if any, redeeming factors.

I had been a member of the board of directors of the General Federation of Women's Clubs, the largest organization of women in our country, claiming a membership of 800,000 at that time in the United States, and 16 million women in 46 countries of the world. I believed that a strong and influential organization of women should be having a voice in the Pageant as equally important as the national Jaycees.

I talked with Al Marks who had become chairman of the board and chief executive officer after Lenora's retirement. I pointed out that both the Alabama and Virginia Federations of Women's Clubs had been state sponsors. Marks agreed with my point of view. Three national presidents of the General Federation of Women's Clubs were selected as national judges in the next several years. The message about the Pageant's value in the form of scholarships and career opportunities was gradually being told and, I think, more generally known among women leaders in the country.

Unfortunately we lived in a decade where women were not considered of any particular importance by the male fraternity in business and civic activities. Few and far between were the women leaders who were accepted as such in the community.

The General Federation of Women's Clubs was first represented by Mrs. Dexter Otis Arnold as a judge. The theme for the Pageant shows was "Hail Alma Mater" as produced by Alexander Cantwell. There were eight stage escorts for the girls representing the universities of Northwestern, Harvard, Columbia, Yale, Pennsylvania, Rutgers, Johns Hopkins and Indiana. Al Marks' son, Albert A. Marks III, represented Rutgers University. Bernie Wayne wrote the music and lyrics.

Elizabeth B. Alton

Chapter 38

One of the earliest responsibilities that Lenora had assigned to me was parade duty. After the girls were in their cars at the head of the parade on Garden Pier, my duty was to go to the end of the parade and check on each girl as her car left the Boardwalk at Albany Avenue to return to her hotel. There a couple of firemen would remove each contestant from her special seat on top of the convertible and seat her safely in the car for the return ride. I checked each girl for problems, usually health problems. I also noticed that the parade committee made excellent plans to begin the parade but almost nothing was done about the parade's end. It was not surprising to me when I was faced occasionally with a grand marshal who had no transportation when leaving his or her float. I had to solve those extra problems that should have been arranged in advance.

Soon the firemen assured me it was more convenient to move contestants' cars onto Atlantic Avenue to seat the girls in the cars properly than at the ramp on Albany Avenue. That made some sense, but not much. It also created a problem. I couldn't be in two places at one time, which I suspected was a main reason for the change. For far around the corner on Atlantic Avenue where the cars stopped was a popular bar whose patrons liked to leave the bar to watch and talk to the girls who were thus being subjected to more than I could accept graciously.

More drivers for the Oldsmobile cars were needed for the parade than the 25 firemen drivers we had regularly. The Pageant office arranged for extra drivers, usually young men around town. One year I watched a non-fireman driver stop his car at Pacific

Avenue while a couple of his friends jumped into the car with the girl as the driver proceeded up Pacific Avenue.

Gradually I developed a growing sense of anxiety. Albany Avenue was the main exit out of town in this part of the city. I had a mental picture of some young man just taking off with a contestant across the boulevard. I struggled with this fear for a couple of years. Finally I talked with Al Marks about my concern and asked that he allow each girl's hostess to ride in the front seat. He agreed with me and gave his consent for the coming year. The chairman of the parade committee, William Cowart, strongly disagreed. He didn't want a hostess to ride because it would detract from the contestant. My argument had been that it showed the public how carefully we protect our girls. Marks overruled Cowart, which eventually was one of the reasons that led to our parting of the ways a few years later when Cowart became president.

One other incident happened in those years which had been potentially dangerous to a contestant. Pacific Avenue was a narrow street filled with heavy, slow traffic after the parade. The smart way normally would be to drive up Arctic Avenue. This was not an approved route for parade drivers because it passed through areas, particularly near bars, where trouble often occurred.

This year a fireman driver headed up Arctic Avenue to avoid traffic. When he reached New York Avenue's bar section, two black men were having a fist fight in the middle of the street. The driver jumped out of the car leaving the contestant alone and unguarded while he tried to separate the two men. By the time the contestant reached her hotel she was in a state of hysteria, which took a while to calm. I saw to it that a police order went out to the parade drivers: in the future Arctic Avenue was off limits and the police would stop cars going that way.

Sometimes situations happened out of our control. I had a call one night after the show from a hostess who, herself, was not too far from hysteria. She had taken her contestant to her large side-avenue hotel. The two had entered the elevator operated by a young man. As the elevator went up the operator stopped between floors and began making sexual advances to the women so persistently and so long that he created serious emotional distress. The women finally made it to their floor without harm, both in a state of shock.

I spent the next hour, late as it was, on the telephone calling the pageant chairman of hotels, a board member owner of a beachfront hotel, and also reaching the manager of the hotel involved. The hotel manager was grateful that we could identify the elevator operator. Apparently he had been doing the same thing with other hotel guests. He was promptly fired. The police watched the hotel until after the Pageant was over in case the operator returned to do bodily harm.

For several years the Rotary Club invited Pageant officials and sponsors to luncheon during the Pageant. Every board member received an invitation each year except me. My being the only woman board member apparently made a difference, I assumed, although other women attended. When I was at last invited, I was seated at the entrance door in the back of the room as far away from the podium as possible while my fellow board members had choice tables in front. I couldn't help feeling a form of discrimination for being a woman, always a painful experience, especially so in the Pageant. My status as a board member was equal to that of any other board member, or should have been. My being a woman seemed to have been the problem, not unusual in those years.

I had one other unpleasant problem during those years. I had not extended the annual telephone invitation to one particular hostess because I had been displeased with her conduct. She was careless about observing Pageant rules, engaged in long telephone conversations with friends on our private hostess phone to the point where she'd make me wait to conduct necessary business. She exuded such an attitude of personal importance that I found her presence unsatisfactory.

One day in late August, shortly before Labor Day, I had a call from Al Marks asking me to return my uninvited hostess to the committee for one more year. It appeared that she and her husband had created an important problem for him and the Pageant. The hostess' husband was employed at the Atlantic City Electric Company. He and his family were all not only friends, but apparently the best of friends with the chief executive officers of the Electric Company.

The Pageant depended heavily on some special equipment the Electric Company loaned each year, and was greatly needed for use by the Boardwalk parade. The Pageant couldn't secure or replace that equipment in the few days before the parade. Marks asked me to reappoint this hostess for the current year only until other plans could be made. He was apologetic about it, for he knew as well as I did that the hostess committee had been founded on the premises that no political or Pageant influence should be made on the selection of hostesses.

I knew I could decline, but I am basically a reasonable person. I agreed to suffer one more year with the hostess. Howard Melvin, also a top-ranking official of the Electric Company, told me later that I should not have agreed. I called the hostess to invite her to join the committee, only to be told she couldn't talk to me, she was in the process of getting dressed to go out to luncheon. I would have to call her back. So much for me. To say that her conduct as hostess that year was insufferable is an understatement. I might have been taking orders from her. Untouchable was her attitude.

She found out differently the following year. Al Marks was always as good as his word. I told him I would not appoint her again. He agreed and when the pressures began mounting on him, he referred everyone to me. That didn't bother me. I simply refused to give reasons or answers. Finally there came a tearful phone call from the husband. His wife was devastated. The Pageant was her life. She could think of nothing else. She wouldn't eat. He was afraid of a breakdown. Would I please reappoint her. My heart was not touched. My answer was, "No."

Sometimes there were happy incidents. I began receiving invitations from state sponsors to judge several state pageants. I talked to Lenora about the first invitations. Her answer was one I already knew was right. It could be interpreted as a conflict of interest. But it was nice to have been asked.

Our seashore is subject to hurricanes in the early Fall. One September a hurricane was coming up the coast from the South, expected to arrive during the Pageant. The resultant wind, rain and high tides caused difficult flooding in vulnerable areas of our island. The worst part of the storm was expected to arrive one night at Pageant time. Contestants were able to reach Convention Hall, but hostesses were having difficulty, especially those Downbeach from Atlantic City or on the Mainland across the meadows. Telephone calls began coming in from hostesses saying they could make it to the Hall but couldn't get home later with the high tides after the show. Several wouldn't even try.

We needed these women in Convention Hall. In order to persuade as many as possible to arrive, I promised that my husband would see that they got home safely. How he would be able to do this only the Good Lord knew. I certainly didn't. Most fortunately the worst of the storm held off long enough for our women all to get home safely. Also fortunately, my long-suffering husband didn't know how generously I had been volunteering his services for he was an early-to-bed, early-to-rise man. Unfortunately, we can't control the weather.

Elizabeth B. Alton

Chapter 39

One day during a rehearsal break when the press was allowed access to the girls on stage, veteran newsmen Sam Myers came to me in a state of outrage that *Life Magazine* had been allowed to take a contestant, highly rated by the press as the next Miss America, to the beach for pictures. I couldn't believe him at first. This was not only against our press rules, but could actually interfere with the rehearsal in progress. I telephoned Haddon Hall. The judges were on the beach!

Captain Cade produced a police car and driver who took me quickly to Haddon Hall. I rushed down on the beach and there was the *Life* photographer with his tripod set up and aimed very nicely at a picture that would have made quite a headline story, untrue in every aspect of it, but as had been said, "pictures don't lie." This had the making of the most unfavorable publicity for our Pageant that we had faced since before 1935.

Some of the judges were seated in Haddon Hall's private cabanas on the beach; among them screen actress Kitty Carlisle and Bennet Cerf, president of Random House Publishing Company. Not with them, but angled a short distance away as though the judges were contemplating her, was Miss Massachusetts. All would appear in the pictures together. I could mentally see headlines about unfair and fixed competition. Fortunately no pictures had yet been taken. Miss Massachusetts returned to rehearsal with me at once. Judges are not allowed to view or meet girls privately.

I had had my critics of our hostess committee press rules, but I thanked my God that day that we were as strict and as careful of the Pageant's good name as we were. That was the reason for our existence as a committee in the first place. I thanked Sam Myers sincerely, for he had been our guardian angel that day, angry as he had been. I never knew whether the reporters and photographers who wore *Life* badges issued by Mall Dodson were freelancers or not. I never observed any activity I could define as a particular assignment.

The event of removing a contestant from a rehearsal in progress for an unapproved picture was known in short order throughout Convention Hall by the news media with considerable displeasure. I was kept informed after that by members of the press whenever anyone wearing a *Life* badge was present. I felt the warmth of their obvious interest in protecting the Pageant.

A year or two later a new situation arose: a woman wearing a *Life* badge for the first time in my experience. I wondered if she thought she would be admitted in areas prohibited to men. She wandered off stage one night and went back into the dressing room after the show. I saw her go and followed her immediately. When I asked her to leave she refused. She was going to interview girls in the dressing room where they had not ever been interviewed. The dressing room was off limits to the press. It was not until I went to bring a policeman backstage that she left.

For some years General Motors had an exhibit of their cars on Steel Pier. Thomas Kenny, director of the exhibit, was a board member. Not long after he became board chairman of publicity he had been influenced by Mall Dodson to change the location of the Tuesday morning swimsuit pictures to the President Hotel Annex across Albany Avenue from the main hotel. He had asked me what I thought of the arrangements which had been already made. I had a one word answer. Miserable. They had in fact removed the privacy of those photography opportunities, opening the girls to interference and contact once again with the general public. Something we'd worked years to prevent.

When my driver and I drove down Albany Avenue to the hotel I knew instantly that all was not well with Tom Kenny. His agitation was visible a whole block away as he paced the street.

I couldn't help laughing. When I met him he poured out his dissatisfaction with the arrangements. We all suffered through the hours devoted to the press. Police Captain Cade assured me he couldn't remove hotel guests who were allowed there. The public filtered between girls and photographers, in the way most of the time. It was unpleasant confusion. Everyone was glad when it was over. Tom Kenny was content, I think, to return to our more private locations in the future.

A couple of years previously I had suggested to President Howard Melvin that it would be more efficient to have a newsman in charge of reporters and a photographer in charge of photographers. Professionals with whom I could deal, supervising professionals.

One day Lenora invited me to luncheon at Haddon Hall for a meeting. When I arrived I found Adrian Phillips, Tom Kenny, Mall Dodson and Lenora. The purpose of the meeting was to inform me that Sam Myers, a highly respected local photographer, and Sam Schor, equally well regarded by newsmen, had been selected to be in charge of the press. Discussion followed. I had the feeling that most of those present thought the fait accompli was a surprise to me and there was some concern about my reaction. Actually I was quite happy with the arrangement, although I was as outwardly noncommittal as possible.

Adrian Phillips was a man of many talents and a few surprising skills. One was his ability to read the reactions of people by their body language. He used to amuse me on occasion with stories of his experience proposing courses of action to corporation leaders. He could always tell by how they moved their hands or body in certain ways whether the proposal was being considered favorably or unfavorably. I've always remembered that body language is plainly understandable to those who can discern it, especially Adrian.

I carefully willed my hands to stay still, my body motions immobile, my relaxation visible, for Adrian was sitting next to me. I allowed no reaction of pleasure or displeasure to show, manifested no dissent. The system worked better than I had hoped, relieving me of many problems that should never have been mine. I had long before appointed two hostesses as liaison with the press. Marie Meyers and Betty Frisch were two women of considerable personal charm, well liked by the press. They cooperated with Sam Myers and Sam Schor, making an efficient publicity team for the Pageant. They all came to me when necessary.

The moment of the greatest personal satisfaction I ever had in the Pageant arrived the day the two Sams came to me and said they had never realized the problems I had been having. Even they found members of the press unreasonable. They were facing what I had endured so long. What a happy day!

In the early years it was not unusual for an occasional member of the press to try to maneuver contestants into locations where he had the only access to contestants for a period of time. On one of the first days available for photography at the beginning of the Pageant, an enterprising photographer was able to lure most of the contestants to a private, secluded area of the Traymore Hotel. It wasn't long before some of the press were unhappy. A hostess called me on the telephone to tell me what was happening.

I sent Kathryn Morgan, our vice-chairman, to have every contestant returned to our registration area at Haddon Hall, available to every press representative. To my surprise I received praise, genuine praise, for my action from some grateful press. To show their appreciation they insisted on taking my picture with contestants, something rarely done. These pictures were printed prominently in the next day's *Press of Atlantic City*, somewhat to my embarrassment.

I had gradually developed a fine rapport with the leading members of the Associated Press, United Press, representatives of the large newspapers in our country and fine magazines. Since I had once asked for their help in distinguishing between the good and not-so-good among the press, they had taken the time now and then to talk to me about certain individuals or publications. I always listened well. Mall Dodson had told me one year that he'd issued badges to nearly 600 people. That was a lot of press to watch over, to deal with and be concerned about.

One other occasion occurred in my personal experience where a photographer tried to get an exclusive picture of Miss America. Lenora had disapproved publicity pictures at the Ball after crowning. I had included in the basic rules, according to her decision, a rule which stated, "No interviews or pictures will be permitted at the Coronation Ball, either upon arrival or departure of contestants, or during the Ball, except certain authorized pictures by the official Pageant photographer."

The press always abided by this rule, having finished their assignment after the crowning. One year when I arrived with Miss America at the Claridge Hotel, there was a *Sports Illustrated* photographer in the lobby set up to take an exclusive picture of Miss America as she walked up a beautiful circular staircase. I interfered with his picture taking by blocking Miss America from his camera. He tried. I blocked until I reached the upper floor. It was a decision I found necessary but difficult to make, especially unpleasant.

I informed Lenora immediately. She approved. Favoritism in press relations was one thing I had always tried to avoid. Everyone was afforded, as far as I could manage, an equal opportunity. I didn't want to be accused by those members of the press who had trusted me of favoritism with *Sports Illustrated*.

❧

My personal life had developed new interest while I was on the Rutgers University boards. Our new state president of the Federation had set as her goal for her administration the construction of a state headquarters building for the organization.

Many of our clubs have their own large club houses. Our president was thinking in terms of what they had cost. From my experience with contracts for construction in New Brunswick I knew she was off base. I asked Philip Levin, a wealthy lawyer/

contractor, who was a member of the board of governors, to meet informally with the president and vice-president during a board luncheon break for advice and information. He brought with him some architectural plans and pictures similar to my description of our needs and told the women it would cost $150,000. They were shocked but undaunted.

I spoke to Dr. Mason Gross, president of Rutgers, about the possibility of building on the campus of Douglass College which we had founded. He was enthusiastic, and later pointed out a site in an excellent location which the Federation approved.

I was able to shepherd through the board of governors and board of trustees a long-term lease of the land. The next decision was how to finance the construction. A state officer suggested that club women collect green stamps. Books were redeemable for two dollars each. Forty-six thousand women can collect a lot of green stamps. That project was undertaken throughout the state.

I was also on the committee which hired the architect and selected the builder. At a meeting with the builder I was concerned about the quality of construction. On the Rutgers buildings and grounds committee I remembered construction of a high-rise dormitory where every shower stall in the building leaked to the floor below when students moved in. It cost over $100,000 to repair. Our builder grinned from ear to ear and gave us an answer that satisfied everyone. He said, "My wife is a member of a woman's club. I already have orders to build it right or else."

The red brick Federation headquarters building is an imposing architectural structure on a large lot. It is unique also in the fact that it was built for $160,000 in 1965 by the collection and redemption of trading stamps. It received national honors. The women of our Federation, nationally and state-wide, can accomplish anything they set out to do by whatever means are available, however long it takes. The Good Book says, "If you have faith . . . nothing shall be impossible." We believe it.

As I looked back over some interesting, exciting and memorable experiences in my life, I have come to realize more and more that there has been a Master Planner in my life: many doors of opportunity have opened and closed, leading me step-by-step in the directions in which I have gone. I can see each one clearly. When one door closed there was always another one ready to open if I saw it, or already open.

Although I didn't recognize it at the time, my membership in the Eastern Star at eighteen, and other women's Masonic organizations, began indoctrinating me in teachings and stories of the Bible which I had not learned or understood fully. My parents had started me in Sunday school at the neighborhood Baptist church before I was seven. The minister was Dr. Thomas Cross, a "hell, fire and damnation" preacher. He almost knocked me over one Sunday when he rushed a boy out the front door of the church by the back of the neck, pushed him to curb, and said, "Spit!" My schoolmate had been guilty of chewing gum in church.

One Sunday as my father handed me my nickel for collection he said, "Don't spend this on candy." The thought had never crossed my mind, but that was an interesting thought. I promptly went across the street from the church to a candy store and spent my nickel. Young as I was, the candy didn't taste that good somehow, and I felt more than guilty as I sat in the church without my nickel for collection. The experience was not repeated.

As I grew older I was allowed to sing with the choir seated in a loft above the pulpit. One day one of my good friends was baptized. From the choir loft I saw some boards in the floor in back of the pulpit removed where there was a tank of water. My friend was dunked in the water as she was baptized, emerging dripping wet, her long hair plastered to her head. I spent a long time thinking about Deborah and her baptism. I was surprised completely by my first witnessing of such an unusual, to me, event.

My teen years were spent at the nearby Presbyterian church, lured there by school friends enjoying social programs at the church. Since I played the violin in the high school orchestra, I played in a small musical group at the church for a while. At

Syracuse University, chapel was not a requirement. My attendance was sporadic.

It was not until my Eastern Star days that I began to understand the sound Biblical teachings I had heard in church. I became an officer in a variety of offices, with lengthy Biblical lectures to recite, many containing direct quotations from the Bible. For fifty years I either recited these teachings or listened when I was recording secretary or treasurer. I learned as much about the Bible and faith as I had in church. That was my first open door.

The people in the Masonic organizations became friends who managed to involve me in a variety of civic events. Becoming president of the Woman's Research Club opened half a dozen new doors of opportunity.

The most important was becoming an officer of the New Jersey State Federation of Women's Clubs and then state president, a position that had led to my being appointed to the board of governors and board of trustees of Rutgers, the State University, a really big door. For after I left Rutgers, I became a member of the Citizens Committee for Higher Education, a group of 100 of the most prestigious and influential men, both statewide and nationally, who were corporation presidents and CEOs. This door of opportunity gave me knowledge of the state's plan to build two new state colleges, one in North Jersey and one in South Jersey. I knew well the key people involved in college planning.

My Federation years of experience had led to the Miss America Pageant Board which had been another open door, for I was associated closely with men who were able to support the biggest project of my life, trying to bring the planned South Jersey state college to our Atlantic County area. With my Rutgers University and Pageant contacts, I had the knowledge, experience and training necessary for a successful endeavor. My Master Planner not only opened this door wide, but he gave me a gentle shove. It happened this way.

Tom Kenny, chairman of the press for the Pageant board, who had arranged with Mall Dodson the "miserable" swimsuit publicity picture at the President Hotel Annex, was a member of the Kiwanis Club. He telephoned one day to invite me to speak at the Ladies Day Luncheon of the Kiwanis Club. My topic was to be the 200th Anniversary of Rutgers University.

I had read a small news item in *The Press* that a site committee was studying sites for the new state college in South Jersey. I told Kenny I had more interesting things to say about the possibility of our securing the college. The Kiwanis Club had not had a woman speaker before. He was taking no chances on me. Rutgers it was to be.

I have found in my lifetime that our Master Planner also changes the conditions in our lives so that we can go through that next open door if we so desire. My widowed mother had been living with me during her last years of declining health. I found her in her final sleep one morning a couple of weeks before Kenny had called me. I was now free of personal family responsibilities.

I spoke at the Kiwanis luncheon on Rutgers' rich history, but I couldn't resist tossing in a few comments about our opportunity for a state college so sorely needed in our area. I asked these prominent men to use their influence to secure the college. No one did.

The years I had spent in public service as an officer of the State Federation and other organizations had been an important learning experience in dealing with governmental agencies, political leaders and important officials of business, industry and education. One of the most difficult problems to overcome in those days was the role of women in our society who so frequently were not taken very seriously. We had only had the right to vote for a little over thirty years then.

I soon realized that to make the voices of women heard in high places on issues of real importance in our daily world, it was necessary to develop woman power as well as people power. In my experience women were qualified and capable of achieving a more active role in our society. We had been faced with subtle gender discrimination for decades that I often had found difficult to accept. The Citizens Committee for Higher Education was headed by Dr. Robert Goheen, president of Princeton University, and James Hayward, president of the Atlantic City Electric Company, vice-chairman. Among the key leaders was Tracy Voorhees, an alumni governor of Rutgers. The committee was composed of 100 of the state's most powerful corporate presidents. CEOs and prominent educators. Most of the committee names were nationally recognized.

The purpose of the committee was to promote the creation of a new state board of higher education and a new department headed by a chancellor. The era was a time of crisis in higher education with far too few college and university facilities available to meet the growing demands for college education in our state.

In retrospect, the Federation, the boards of Rutgers University, the Pageant board of directors, the Citizens Committee for Higher Education had been one very necessary door of opportunity before I was gently nudged through this really big one almost against my will: the founding of The Richard Stockton College of New Jersey, formerly named Richard Stockton State College.

The day following my Kiwanis speech there was a generous two-column article by Frank Prendergast announcing the possibility of a new state college in the area. When nothing was being done, another reporter wrote "Plea for Resort Effort to Get College Unheeded." Those two write-ups opened another special door.

Seymore Kravitz, a local radio personality, called to ask me to speak on his "Pinky's Corner" program. I was somewhat hesitant to be subjected to call-in questions, but he assured me his purpose was to promote the college. When he asked me on the radio what people should do, I suggested that letters be sent to George Smith, an easily remembered name, chairman of the State Board of Education in Trenton, so that as many people as possible could express their opinions to public officials. As a result, the office of the Commissioner of the State Department of Education was flooded with some 4,000 letters in three weeks.

Up to this point I had had no intention of undertaking a college campaign. I still expected community leaders to take the necessary steps. They didn't. I believe my Divine Guidance already had a plan for me. There is a biblical verse that is pertinent. "For I know the plans I have for you. Plans for you to prosper and not to harm you. Plans for you to have hope and a future." Jeremiah 29:11.

Two days later, on March 16, 1966, Rabbi Aaron Krauss, whom I had not met, came to see me. I knew of him as Rabbi of an important Atlantic City Synagogue, founder and president of Atlantic Human Resources, an organization serving the poor and underprivileged in Atlantic and Cape May Counties. Straightforward and to the point, he asked how "we" could get started and what "we" should do. As I listened to him, I knew I had the answers from long years of experience. The point really was, as I saw it, would I be willing to put into practice what I had been preaching so many years to women's clubs or would I simply let the challenge die.

I wondered if I had the courage or desire to undertake leadership of a public campaign, not as a woman talking to women with common interests, but as a woman in a man's world having to face the "slings and arrows" of the sometimes cruel and biased criticism that descends upon those who serve in public causes.

Rabbi Krauss was saying in his gentle, kindly way, let's get moving. Let's do something. My heart heard his message. My intellect said, "You have the training, you know the techniques. The challenge had to be accepted or refused. Not willing to say "Yes" or "No," I compromised.

My Master Planner had already opened another unexpected door. I had arranged to drive some women to a women's conference in the state house the following day, March 17, 1966. I told Rabbi Krauss I would telephone Commissioner Raubinger and ask if he would see me. If he would, I would inquire about the chances of locating the proposed southeastern college in Atlantic County.

When I did telephone the Commissioner on my arrival about 10 a.m. in Trenton, I was surprised to hear him say "come right over" to his office in the Education Building. One doesn't often get an immediate audience with a cabinet officer, although I knew him from meetings of the Rutgers board of governors.

When asked directly about a possible new college location, he indicated that the Toms River area was under consideration but our county would certainly be considered. He asked if I would like to appear before the State Board of Education at the coming meeting on April 6th to speak on behalf of Atlantic County. I readily accepted. And there I suddenly was, of no real volition on my part. I had walked hesitantly to a door named college, not sure whether I had wanted to open it or not. I had knocked gently on that door and to my surprise found it had opened wide. Before I knew it I was taking the first steps along a road that looked attractive at its beginning. I couldn't see the giant roadblocks that lay ahead.

As I look back I have a firm conviction of the unseen forces that propelled me into the role that became mine in 1966. I didn't choose them but I am certain in my mind that there was a master plan that had fashioned events in an orderly sequence and continued to do so throughout the entire three-year campaign. Doors opened in ways that were more than coincidental when the roadblocks were strongest.

The strangest combination of events in my mind was that a Jewish Rabbi had motivated a Protestant woman to see an important education commissioner on March 17th, a day in honor of Catholic St. Patrick. I've often thought my Divine Guidance may have been chuckling as he nudged me into the path I was to take, but his intentions for me were unmistakable.

I tell the long story of how The Richard Stockton College of New Jersey was secured for our area over the strongest possible state governmental opposition because the Pageant really got me involved in the first place. If Tom Kenny, my Pageant associate, had not invited me to be the first woman speaker of the Kiwanis Club, I am firmly convinced that Stockton would not exist where it is today. No one else in the community lifted a finger to implement the campaign. It was the resultant publicity from that speech which started me on the long, difficult, frustrating effort for state college opportunities for young people of our area. I believe the Pageant deserves credit for its indirect support of higher education in this area.

The campaign itself, fought strenuously over a three-year period in our three-county South Jersey area, is one of the most unique and publicly supported efforts, unparalleled in the history of our state. Led by two housewives, supported by every governmental body and political leader, educational official and association, civic, service, and religious organizations and a couple hundred clubs in three counties, the campaign became a North Jersey against South Jersey campaign, arousing the ire of those of us who live south of Trenton, so often overlooked.

My association as a member of the Pageant board of directors brought me into personal contact with men who had a great deal of political influence, their voices heard with respect in Trenton. These were invaluable contacts I probably would not have had otherwise. They knew me as a responsible person. They were the first to provide me with the kind of advice, information and contacts that were needed.

After meeting with Commissioner Raubinger the first thing I needed to do was prepare for my appearance before the State Board of Education in three weeks. The commissioner had suggested to me that I talk with William Cowart about a project he was heading to bring an Institute of Aerospace Science and Technology to the Naval Aviation Federal Experimental Center, NAFEC, now known as the Federal Administration Technology Center, FAA. He said that Cowart's group was too narrow in their planning for the post-graduate degrees they needed to be implemented, necessitating association with a four-year college. It was the commissioner's belief that if Cowart's group joined the proposed four-year college effort, both would have a better chance of being approved by the state.

I called Cowart on the telephone relaying the advice I had been given and suggesting a meeting. Cowart was vice-president of the Pageant board. He wasn't interested. He said his group expected to join with a prominent college and would be privately funded. No matter how courteous he had been, I felt brushed off. I also thought it was unwise not to at least listen to a state commissioner's idea.

I was not really surprised that Cowart wouldn't meet with me. He had been chairman of the parade committee for three years. There were problems experienced by contestants in and after that parade that needed solving. I had sought to speak to him about them, but he was never available. In one very serious situation I asked Lenora to arrange a meeting for both of us with him. She was not successful. My only means of communicating with any of the parade committee was through Ben Brick who became the liaison with the hostess committee.

I sent out letters to major business, industrial and utility companies seeking information on the educational needs of South Jersey. I went also to the Chamber of Commerce office on Central Pier to secure a list of organizations and their presidents. Al Owens, Chamber secretary, told me that in order to succeed I needed the support of Senator Farley. I already knew that.

Al Marks had been the first person to call me offering support. He had asked if I would like him to arrange a meeting with Senator Farley for the two of us. I had readily agreed. Marks called me back in a day or two to say regretfully that he had been unable to arrange a meeting. I was surprised. Marks was one of the most influential businessmen in town. It also seemed strange that the senator would be uninterested in a state college in his county. It didn't take me long to find out why.

As I crossed the Boardwalk after my meeting with Al Owens, I determined to find a way to secure the senator's attention. My Federation presidency had taught me how successful the power of women could be in influencing the passage of legislation in our state. That became my chief strategy. People power when used constructively is unbeatable. I would attempt to develop so much pressure on the senator and all other elected representatives, through people power, that they would have to carry our campaign into the legislature and fight for us.

The first important goal, and the most successful, had been established. I spoke at a Ventnor City town meeting on March 25, 1966. Mildred and Ben Brick came after the meeting to offer what proved to be invaluable support and assistance. Mildred became a co-worker, volunteer leader, speaker, confidant and partner. She produced on her office equipment thousands of resolutions, research information and printed material for distribution everywhere possible in Atlantic, Cape May and Cumberland Counties.

In preparation for my presentation at the State Board of Education meeting on April 6, 1966, I received at my request a copious amount of information on economic conditions and future plans for South Jersey from banks, utilities, boards of freeholders, chambers of commerce, Atlantic City Expressway, Delaware River Port Authority, Southern New Jersey Development Council, Cape May Ferry, large corporations and industry. I also received from the Atlantic City Electric Company a three-foot-tall map containing colored pins representing the locations of every college in the state. North and Central Jersey were almost covered with pins. South Jersey had only two. The map became the most valuable asset to our campaign. A smaller version was carried everywhere I spoke.

I wrote and Mildred printed a factual, interesting report on South Jersey with emphasis in our area. On April 6, 1966, I spoke for a half hour before the State Board of Education without notes while Mildred distributed our brochures. I was surprised with applause from the public and press present.

I soon learned why Senator Farley and William Cowart had been unwilling to talk with me. Al Owens had written me, "I would strongly suggest that you ask Senator Farley's knowledge of the attempts for a scientific college that he has refrained from revealing even to us in detail. Colonel Harrison, recently replaced as head of NAFEC has told us of the efforts in that direction and it is certain that knowledge of their plan would serve you well."

A fine editorial in *The Press of Atlantic City* supporting a state college had appeared on the morning I had spoken before the State Board of Education. It was followed one week later by an editorial and a fine write-up about the proposed Institute of Aerospace Science and Technology. Suddenly it was clear to me that I was either competing, or thought to be competing, with these influential men seeking their Institute. I was just a housewife and an unimportant woman.

A few days later Raymond G. Wood, head of the Southern New Jersey Development Council, sent me a letter saying "I would suggest your discussing with Dan DeBrier the matters pertaining to the Institute of Space and Science, as he is serving as chairman of the committee coordinating with NAFEC in handling this matter." I later learned the original idea had started with General DeBrier.

A social event of much local interest was held, a testimonial dinner in honor of Robert Leeds, one of the owners of Chalfonte-Haddon Hall, and his wife, Daphne. They were leaving Atlantic City to retire on an island off the coast of South America. Leeds was a Pageant board member.

During the cocktail hour, an opportunity arose to speak to the leaders involved with the Institute. Brigadier General Daniel DeBrier told me at some length about his optimistic plans. William Cowart in his affable way made some pleasant but noncommittal comments. Both wished me success but they obviously had no interest in sharing plans. There are times when being ignored, as I frequently was in the Pageant, is a good thing. In this instance I felt brushed off, no matter how pleasantly done. Frustration tends to arouse the fighting instinct in me when I believe the cause is right. I made a second decision that night. If the NAFEC group didn't want to work with me, so be it, but I decided I would join them by including NAFEC's Institute in my speeches, presentations, publicity and efforts. This I did well and often with Mildred Brick's help.

Several Board of Education meetings later George Smith indicated to me in a general, informal way that the site committee was looking favorably upon our request. "Not so," said the legislators from Bergen County, four senators and five assemblymen from the governor's party. The next new state college would be in Bergen County, not Atlantic County. In order to sidetrack and defeat our efforts, the Bergen County legislators, most powerful in the legislature, hurriedly introduced S-434 in the Senate on May 27, 1966, to create a new State Board of Higher Education and State Department of Higher Education to govern all colleges and universities in the state. Our campaign, so successful to date, came to a screeching halt. No new college decisions could be made until after the bill was passed by the new board.

Mildred and I had continued our campaign anyway. Too much popular support had been generated to give up. My date books show many continuing speeches before organizations with much favorable resultant publicity throughout our three counties. Radio broadcasts were especially helpful.

One of our earliest, strongest supporters had been Howard Hansman, treasurer of the Miss America Pageant and soon to be president. He was also director of the Atlantic County Board of Freeholders, chairman of the Atlantic County Republican Organization and the right hand of Senator Frank S. Farley. He had offered full county support.

One day Dr. Leon Schuck, director of the Cape May County Board of Freeholders telephoned me to say that Cape May County wanted to join our efforts. A county organization was quietly set up with Mayor Waldman of Ocean City and Mayor Guy Muziani of Wildwood, later elected to the New Jersey Senate, as Chairman. The Cape May County Chamber of Commerce became valued workers and supporters. An active campaign in that county resulted.

S-434 was passed by the legislature in November 1966, and signed by the governor on December 14, 1966. Mildred and I were present. We still didn't give up but renewed our efforts. We'd simply have to tell our story all over again to the new board which eventually had a couple of members from the first Board of Education.

By June 17, 1967, the governor appointed the members of the new Board of Higher Education to take office on July 1, 1967; the new chancellor, Ralph Dungan, on August 1, 1967. I was prepared to speak on the long neglect of South Jersey in the field of higher education at the first meeting of the Higher Education Board on September 15, 1967. Our politically powerful Legislative opponents in Bergen County decided to prevent me from being present so they could make their own presentation.

One morning two marshals came to my door to present me with a subpoena for jury duty, an unusual procedure at the beginning of a new jury term. I had received no preliminary questionnaire. When I appeared in Mays Landing there was an over supply of jurors, some of whom were excused. Obviously there had been no reason to subpoena me. When I asked to be excused for a later jury session, the two judges, whom I had known from high school days, said with a smile, "Elizabeth, just serve for a little while." Several days later Bergen County made their strong pitch for the new college while I sat in the Court House in Mays Landing. I was excused several days later.

The Press of Atlantic City, local newspapers and radio stations had taken up the educational battle with constant publicity. Thousands of petitions were being signed. Business, professional, corporate and civic leaders were deluging our area senators and assemblymen with their support. Service and civic clubs and educational boards and associations were adopting resolutions. Mildred and I had a real live active campaign under way.

Chapter 40

nother important event happened in 1967. Lenora Slaughter Frapart resigned as Executive Director of the Pageant to enjoy her new leisure and home in Scottsdale, Arizona, with her husband. The board held a family dinner in her honor. Large impressive write-ups in the newspaper included a fine editorial in the *The Atlantic City Press*, "A Fond Farewell."

The Miami Herald called her the "Real Miss America. No one is more deserving or has worked harder to deserve that title. For thirty-three years she was the Miss America Pageant, struggling with much difficulty to promote the growth and development of the fledgling beauty contest into one commanding national respect, admiration and acclaim. She succeeded almost single-handedly. Those who knew her could not forget her."

She has been honored by many organizations and has received prestigious awards including Woman of the Year from the South Jersey Development Council and the Shell award for having spread the name and fame of Atlantic City more than any other individual during her tenure.

Lenora described her retirement as "a dream come true. I've been dreaming of this opportunity the past few years. I had hoped to retire at the end of thirty years of service, but I felt that until we had members of the young generation on our staff it was my obligation to stay on the job."

Evaluating her 33 years with the organization she said, "I devoted my life to the Pageant. Some people paint great pictures, others are great musicians, still others are writers and they all have left their marks on the sands of time. I, too, wanted to leave my mark and it seemed my talents as an organizer of a civic event of merit to the youth of the country would be my way of leaving that mark. I've justified my existence to some small extent and it has been my privilege to live in a country like America."

In speaking of her scholarship program she said, "I feel the Pageant has helped these girls. It has taught them to crystallize a career, to know what they want to do, and to work toward accomplishing it."

I found it surprising that the Atlantic City Hall of Fame has continued to overlook the selection of a woman whose promotional activities on behalf of Atlantic City have been unmatched by any recipients named in that era.

At the dinner in her honor, Adrian Phillips, newly succeeding Jack Rowe as president, was the presiding officer and Robert Nesbitt Jr., past president, was master of ceremonies. During the dinner Al Marks, who succeeded Lenora as chief executive officer, praised Lenora's achievements calling her "a legend in her own time. With imagination, daring, persistence, and above all good taste, she molded a meandering and virtually defunct beauty contest into what is now known internationally as the Miss America Pageant.

"This great lady has been a paramount factor in the development and fruition of what is unquestionably a major segment of the contemporary scene. From coast to coast and border to border, Lenora Slaughter Frapart is and always will be known as the grande dame of pageantry, but more important her name and prowess will always be linked with the future progress of multitudes of young Americans, past and future."

Chief executives of our national sponsors, Pepsi-Cola, Oldsmobile, Toni and the Joseph Bancroft company presented gifts to Lenora with many words of much deserved praise. She was also given a crown similar to that worn by Miss America.

In an extensive write-up, the *The Press* stated that Lenora "brought more favorable publicity to this city than any other single event in resort history. She inaugurated the prestigious scholarship program while traveling 50,000 miles annually to promote the Miss America Pageant and help local and state pageants build and improve as preliminaries for Atlantic City competition.

"The Pageant board named Lenora Executive Director Emeritus, a fitting tribute: No one who has ever been associated with Lenora will fail to remember the dynamic energy, the determination to succeed, the wisdom, good taste and happy personality that were her such important characteristics during her Pageant years."

Lenora had always dreamed of going to college, which may be one reason the scholarship program was so important to her personally as well as to Pageant contestants. In her youth she had saved $453 to go to William and Mary College. Unfortunately the Great Depression, following the 1929 crash of the stock market, affected her family's fortunes and the money she'd saved had to go for groceries. She continued to regret her lack of college education, although Dr. Snavely, president of the American College Association, told her often that "she has the right to say she is as well educated as anyone." Lenora has turned down honorary degrees from colleges.

She has a valued file of a great many personal letters from former winners and contestants saying how much the Pageant has done for them in their careers and their lives. Miss Americas still stop in to see her for a visit in her Scottsdale, Arizona, home.

Lenora always told contestants every year that the most important event in the girls' lives would be that special moment when they walked down the aisle as a bride in their own wedding. A romantic at heart, Lenora had reached 40 when she married.

She also confessed in later years that the Pageant caused her many sleepless nights. Great were the serious problems moneywise and otherwise in her early years that she had to face and solve, often causing her to pound her pillow in frustration. A remarkable woman Lenora was, and is today.

While honoring Lenora with a dinner on her retirement, the Pageant also did the greatest possible disservice to her and her financial future. In recognition of her 33 years of illustrious service, the Pageant board provided her with an annual pension. As a condition of that pension she was forbidden to write a book. As a board member I thought this most unfair. No one would have done more to promote the Pageant than Lenora. She could no more have written anything derogatory of the Pageant than she could have stopped breathing.

Bennett Cerf, president of Random House Publishing Company, and a judge shortly before her retirement, had offered Lenora $50,000 in 1967 to write a book. With Bennett Cerf's backing and Random House's promotion, I firmly believe Lenora could have written a best seller, far more widely read than any of the books recently published. Cerf must have thought so, too.

Lenora's book would have given the American public an entirely new and different perspective of the Pageant, a new understanding of its purposes and goals, its opportunities for career advancement and its scholarship program. In all the years of her retirement she has not to my knowledge breathed a word of criticism or disapproval of the Pageant even to those of us who knew her in her active years and retirement.

Lenora Slaughter Frapart is still at heart the Pageant's greatest promoter and will continue to be as long as she lives. *The Miami Herald* said it best for us all. She is in every sense of the words the "Real Miss America."

I remember a dinner held for the judges by board members in later years. I was sitting at a table with the president of the General Federation of Women's Clubs when William Cowart joined us. About to become Pageant president, he was interested in the GFWC president. "What does the Federation do?" he asked. It was a natural question, but I had difficulty sitting still. I wondered how she would answer. She couldn't even get started on telling in a few sentences what fifty state organizations and some 46 affiliated countries in the world do.

I wondered if she'd tell about meetings with the President, members of Congress, the United Nations, the Department of

Defense, various embassies, trips to foreign countries to meet with rulers of those countries, of entertaining foreign dignitaries in their large headquarters in Washington. I wondered how she could possibly speak about what the Federation does in broad terms in less than a couple of hours. Each state publishes a year book of achievements more or less in excess of two inches thick.

To her credit she really didn't answer Cowart directly. I supposed she had been asked that question many times by men who knew little or nothing of what women really achieve or didn't really care.

At any rate, no GFWC president has been a judge since that year. What that really means is that the Pageant had no interest in promoting public relations with the largest organization of women in the country for their interest and support of the Pageant's programs.

⁂

"There She Is, Miss America," Bernie Wayne's song, was not only loved when it was sung at the crowning of Miss America, it was also used at state pageants. While the Pageant always stated officially that the song was discontinued at the national level because of disagreements over financial details in the contract, there was an additional reason. Wayne traveled to almost every state as either a judge or musical director. He charged the states $100 to use his famous song. As he became more prominent in the states there was the perception that his activities were becoming a money-making venture, whether that perception was correct or not. It is also clear that a personality conflict arose with Pageant officials. It was decided to end the relationship.

In 1968 after popular demand, Al Marks bought the rights to the song for 15 years at $17,500. The Pageant had used the song from 1955 without payment. The annual rights were also leased to the states for $100 each state. The copyright was renewed to the year 2010.

Bernie Wayne also composed other songs for the Pageant including the popular "Miss America Sisters," and was musical director for a few years prior to Glenn Osser. The most popular song played for the early Miss Americas had been "A Pretty Girl is Like a Melody."

Wayne had been musical director at the Paramount Studios in Hollywood, composing music for many movies. Best known were his popular Hit Parade songs, "Laughing on the Outside," "You Walk By," "Blue Velvet," and many others. He was also musical director at Coral Records and ABC Paramount Records where he conducted instrumental hits.

The Miss Atlantic City Pageant had been discontinued in 1961. Local young women were eligible to enter the Atlantic County pageant as a first step toward the crown.

❧

Albert Marks became president this year. Just after the 1967 Pageant, *The Press* was ready to do battle for the new state college with the written word and the sword of publicity. A two-column editorial was printed on the front page of the *Sunday Press* entitled "Why Ignore Us." The chancellor had been quoted as saying a week previously that he had given no consideration to a four-year college in Atlantic County but had been meeting frequently with groups from Bergen County. He stated that Bergen County had been given top priority for a four-year college when funds became available. *The Press* listed more than 25,000 petitions sent to Trenton from South Jersey.

The article also stated, "Can it be a mere coincidence that Bergen County is represented in the legislature by four Democratic senators and five Democratic assemblymen? Such influence with a Democratic administration is undoubtedly a factor even though Dungan downgrades it in giving Bergen County priority. This area has been the educational stepchild for much too long."

310

The next morning a front page write-up was prominently featured in *The Press*. "Governor Blamed in College Issue." The write-up stated that the governor, the recipient of so much pressure from our three counties, was at fault for not informing the chancellor of our needs. Governor Hughes at a news conference had said he "hopes to see a college in Bergen County before his present term is up in 1968."

The Press also reported that "every municipality, chamber of commerce, board of education, superintendent and principal and more than 200 organizations endorsed Mrs. Alton's actions along with county freeholders." Mildred Brick and I had already determined that a full-scale campaign would have to be done all over again with the new Board of Higher Education.

These write-ups received the governor's and chancellor's full attention. I had a telephone call from Chancellor Dungan intimating that my college efforts were the result of my desire to cause the governor difficulty and embarrassment. Unimportant me, with no political background and no axe to grind.

Reluctantly he gave me an appointment for October 19, 1967. Mildred and I took our large map and the supporting research. He liked our map, prepared by the engineers of the Electric Company, saying it was better than any he had. His casual comment that he was thinking about combining Rutgers College of South Jersey and Glassboro State College into a university for South Jersey, caused us to change the name of our committee to Citizens Committee for a State College-University.

A week or so later *The Press* had another front-page editorial entitled "An Open Letter to Mr. Dungan." The occasion was October 27, 1967, when both Governor Hughes and Chancellor Dungan were speakers at an educational convention in Atlantic City. The letter is a gem, too long for quoting entirely. It exercised the theme that we're "tired of being neglected, tired of seeing their best youngsters being forced to go elsewhere for their education and their life's work, tired of having industries located elsewhere because higher educational facilities are lacking here. They're tired of not being represented on key boards that determine educational policy for the state. They're tired of being behind as the state grows and develops. In short, Chancellor Dungan, they are fed up and they are determined to make their needs known." The editorial concluded with the notice that letters should be sent to Chancellor Dungan and Edward E. Booher, Chairman of the Board of Higher Education, to their address in Trenton.

Walter Clark, vice-president of the public relations and marketing department of the Guarantee Bank and Trust Company, sent me a letter saying that the bank was sending our reprints of the editorial "Our Open Letter to Mr. Dungan" to 14,000 bank depositors with space at the bottom for the signature and address of each person, asking it to be sent to Trenton. All the major newspapers in South Jersey and the *Philadelphia Inquirer* carried stories regularly of our campaign. The radio stations broadcast regularly and I found myself occasionally on TV.

Since Mildred and I had generated so much publicity and people power support, Cape May County's request to join our campaign was augmented by the political support of Cumberland County. I was invited to speak at the installation dinner of the Committee of 50 of Vineland. Mildred and I took our maps showing college locations. The large room in the restaurant was filled with men. Mayor Henry Garton introduced the guests who were present, the Who's Who of Cumberland County. They included the local senator and assemblymen, the mayors of cities, freeholders, councilmen, a representative of Congressman Sandman, the president of Cumberland County College, superintendents of public schools, owner of the radio station and top-level businessmen.

I couldn't help wondering why I had been invited to such a prestigious installation. My instinct told me that I understood why. The men were especially interested in where the college would be located. While the mayor opened the door for me politically and provided much needed assistance through his secretary—much support was given, including raising funds for advertising—I was aware of their interest in building the college in the Vineland area. Mildred and I had been shown a suitable location.

Howard Berger of radio station WFPG in Atlantic City was a constant source of radio publicity, invaluable throughout the campaign. I often heard myself in supermarkets and stores making spot announcements or asking the public to make some specific contacts with legislators according to the crisis of the moment.

Leonard Horn wrote me from his law firm, "I want you to feel free to call upon me for any legal work which may be necessary in connection with your endeavors."

I discovered what other kind of difficult competition we had when the local paper ran an editorial about plans at NAFEC saying, "Initially the institute will be a graduate school offering two years of advanced study in the field of aero and space technology. Later on provisions will be made to include facilities for college studies at the junior and senior levels. The Atlantic Community College soon to start functioning will offer two year study courses. Together they will provide full higher educational opportunities for studies leading to college degrees and post-graduate courses." That would make a state college unnecessary.

Mildred and I refused to give up. I wrote Senator Farley asking him to ask the Atlantic County League of Municipalities to endorse the state college movement when he was the main speaker at their dinner meeting. To my surprise he did so. *The Press* reported, "After a strong pitch to support a proposed four-year liberal arts college in this area, the Atlantic County League of Municipalities endorsed the project. The appeal was made by Senator Frank S. Farley, principal speaker at the meeting. Farley said the proposed college . . . being pressed by Mrs. John Alton, area civic leader, . . . is a vital necessity for the continued growth of this area. The senator asked for unanimity of action from every city, borough and township in Atlantic County." I had already invited every mayor to be an honorary member of our committee. They had accepted. In the publicity Farley had also said, "For the past four years, unbeknown to the general public, members of the freeholders board and various city officials have been quietly but effectively working on this science university. The proposed university would not be in conflict with the liberal arts college."

I realized that before my entrance onto the scene Farley had been committed by word and action to the institute project, and to the men involved. However, he did respond to my request for action from time to time. Our campaign was kept strictly nonpolitical. There was a difference in philosophy between the two college efforts. The institute leaders depended totally upon the political powers of Senator Farley which were awesome. Mildred and I depended upon people power applied in large numbers to assist our three county senators and assemblymen in passing a bill through the legislature for the college.

I was surprised to learn that the DeBrier-Cowart group had tried in every way possible to secure association with Rutgers University for the institution's post-graduate degrees. I had been a member of the board of governors during those four years as Cowart knew. Senator Farley's talks were with president Mason Gross. No formal or informal request on their behalf had ever come to the board whose decision was necessary.

The first I knew that an Atlantic County college was being considered was when Dr. Gross told the board that the extensive expansion to the University on four campuses made it impossible to discuss additional plans for an Atlantic County college. I was surprised. Not one of the institute leaders would ever in their wildest moment have asked little, unimportant me to intercede for them. I was just a woman. Farley was all-powerful, yet I could have used the powers of persuasion God had given me, when necessary, to attempt to achieve difficult goals. I could have spoken individually to board members on the educational neglect in South Jersey. I could at least have tried my best. I didn't have the chance.

Senator Farley was successful eventually in getting his bill through the legislature establishing the Institute of Aerospace Science and Technology at NAFEC in Pomona. The institute exists today on paper. The legislature has simply refused to fund it.

In April of that year I was summoned to a meeting with Governor Richard J. Hughes in his Trenton office. I presented him with our college report while photographers snapped pictures. I didn't know what the governor would say, but in my imagination I could not have guessed that I was as important to his plans at that moment as he was to our realization of a college dream.

The only other two people in the room, in addition to the governor and myself, were a reporter from the Associated Press and the governor's legal counsel, who sat directly across the room facing me, assessing my reactions. Governor Hughes spent 45 minutes making known the institutional needs of the state, which I knew from the Federation as well as he did; he spoke for the benefit of the press. I heard nothing I didn't already know.

The reason the governor was attempting to impress me with institutional needs was the fact that he was trying to get the sales tax bill passed. Senator Farley had not approved the tax as yet. In order to get the college I was supposed to win Senator Farley's support for the sales tax by using the thousands of people who supported the college movement. The governor needed Farley's vote to get the sales tax passed. He made it perfectly clear that the defeat of the sales tax meant no new college.

The governor graciously allowed me five minutes to reply. I explained that the college effort was non-partisan, supported by both political parties. I could not use the public trust placed in me for a political purpose for any reason. In all, the governor gave me 55 minutes of his valuable time. Neither of us won, but I wondered if our dream college was lost. I had just been a useful tool to apply a little pressure to the senator.

After I returned home I went to the home of a friend married to a local district court judge and told him the story, knowing he would tell Senator Farley. An *Atlantic City Press* reporter awaited my return for an interview. I had struggled with the words I would say on my ride home, fearing the wrong publicity. Fortunately the write-up was well done. No compromise was made on the campaign.

❦

An unusually unpleasant situation arose not long after Lenora's retirement. I began receiving complaints from hostesses about two reporters each wearing a *Life* badge. Good-looking men, each six-foot-four or so, built like football players, were walking directly into the hostesses, knocking them aside or off-balance. Apparently they were trying to intimidate the women.

My turn came on Saturday night, right after Miss America had been crowned and the press and photographers were on stage taking pictures and doing interviews. This year Miss New York had a sister who had been in the Miss Universe Pageant and who had been present during the Pageant. Miss New York had not made the final ten. She had some resentfully unpleasant things to say about our Pageant in comparison with the Miss Universe Pageant in her anger in not placing.

It was Pageant practice to have all contestants leave the stage after congratulations to the new Queen and leave Convention Hall for the ball. All contestants had done so and were leaving. Only Miss America and her runners-up were still on stage.

The hostess to Miss New York came to tell me that her contestant had been summoned back on stage. She had her in the hallway, was it O.K. to come on stage? I told her "no" immediately. "Leave for the ball. She's not to come on stage."

The photographers wearing a *Life* badge had managed to get Miss New York's sister on stage where they were going to photograph the two sisters together with Miss America and her runners-up in the background. It was apparently planned to be an exposé interview condemning the Pageant in no uncertain terms. When the man wearing the *Life* badge heard me send Miss New York away, he ran across the stage and physically tackled me around the waist, his head on my hip, almost tossing me down the flight of stairs off the stage where I was standing. Only the guard at the top of the stairs prevented my fall.

In my strong singer's voice I yelled, "Take your hands off me!" Al Marks and Police Captain Cade, standing nearby, had seen the incident as did other Pageant officials, hostesses and press reporters. Marks and Captain Cade came over to me and asked if I wanted to press charges. I thought about it for a moment, but only fleetingly. My attacker deserved the publicity, but it was all just one more Pageant harassment I could do without. I declined.

Once more the Pageant had been spared from contrived publicity damaging to the Pageant's image. I was most thankful when I fell at last into the comfort of my bed for a much-needed rest. My guardian angel had intervened once again.

Elizabeth B. Alton

Chapter 41

The growing importance of the hostess committee to the Pageant was evident in the new opportunities Al Marks began assigning me after he succeeded Lenora to become chairman of the board and chief executive officer in 1967. He had arranged for me to attend my first state pageant. For this occasion, Adrian and Emmaline Phillips drove me to Hershey, Pennsylvania, to join Al and Elizabeth Marks for the Miss Pennsylvania Pageant. It was a learning experience as well as an opportunity to discuss national Pageant operations. I assisted with such advice to hostesses as was necessary. Lenora had required for some time that all state pageants abide by national standards and regulations, particularly in judging.

I remember sitting with Marks while he discussed with the black president of nearby Cheyney College the opportunities inherent in his establishment of a local pageant which could enter the Miss Pennsylvania Pageant. His interest in securing scholarships for his young people was clearly evident. Marks, on the other hand, spent a considerable amount of time encouraging the president to sponsor a local pageant and explaining in detail the procedures.

The following year Marks sent me as the lone Pageant representative to the Miss Massachusetts Pageant. My travel arrangements and motel reservation had been made by our Pageant office. I was told that arrangements had been made for a state pageant official to meet me when I landed at the Hartford Airport in Connecticut. He would drive me to the town in Massachusetts where the state pageant would be held, some fifteen miles away.

I spent an unpleasant, unnecessary amount of time when I landed at the airport, waiting, expecting, then searching for the driver who was supposed to meet me. No one was there. I had to arrange for a taxi to drive me to my motel. If I had known what the next five days were going to be like, I would have taken the next plane home. The motel was on the outskirts of the town, a pretty good distance from the high school where the pageant was being held. No driver had been provided to escort me to and from the competition. In fact, no pageant arrangements had been made for me at all.

By chance at the motel I met Joe Lewis and his group representing Toni Division of Gillette, a national sponsor. He volunteered to drive me every morning and at show times, since there was no other transportation available. I spent the days watching rehearsals and occasionally talking with hostesses. I knew that our two field directors were also staying at the motel, but I didn't see them anywhere: They knew I was present.

Observing the lack of attention paid me, Joe Lewis spent some time with me, had photographers take my picture with a couple of girls, and arranged NBC interviews. At the lunch break he would find me a sandwich.

Getting back to the motel from the school was something else. No one offered me a ride. If and when I wanted to leave, I would have to call a taxi, which wasn't that easy. One day I decided to sit by the exit door and wait to see if anyone would offer a ride. One hour went by, a second passed, with people leaving all the time. Finally a woman who had passed me several times, coming and going, obviously curious, stopped to talk. When she realized I was waiting for a ride, she produced a driver after a while.

Aside from the fact that someone quickly handed me tickets for the shows, I was either completely ignored or simply forgotten. I don't know why. I wondered if it was thought that I had invited myself to their program instead of being the official Miss America Pageant representative. Was it because I was a woman of unimportance, lacking sufficient stature as hostess chairman?

I was not invited to a single social or civic event always held by pageants in the community. I knew of them because Joe Lewis told me about them when he attended. Our national field representatives finally decided to recognize my presence on Saturday night after the finals by inviting me to a small gathering in their motel room just a short way down the building from mine. They offered to take me with them on the taxi ride to the Hartford Airport in the morning. When I checked with the motel desk to see that all financial arrangements had been made, the manager had some uncomplimentary things to tell me about activities in the motel during the week, which had been filled with Pageant people.

I learned the two field directors had already left in a taxi without me, so he called a taxi for me and I made the solitary fifteen-mile ride back to Hartford. I remember reporting to George Cavalier, our producer, that the state queen chosen had been an excellent one. She was. She became First Runner-Up to the Miss America.

When the following year arrived Marks sent me, again as the lone pageant representative, to the Miss Tennessee Pageant. I was tempted to decline at first, but he must have remembered my report to the board of directors after I had been to the Massachusetts pageant. The Tennessee Pageant was known for its hospitality and fine organization. I soon found its reputation was well deserved.

My travel and hotel reservations arranged by the Pageant office again went smoothly. I was met at the airport, had a driver everywhere I went, usually the state sponsor himself. I was invited to all the social events, luncheons, dinners, parties after shows. I was on the go constantly. I was the main speaker at the Sunday morning breakfast after the crowning. Later I was driven 90 miles to an airport different from my travel plan because connections were easy and better. Much can be said for Southern hospitality and an excellent pageant organization. My bruised and badly battered ego of the previous year had been rejuvenated.

One year George Cavalier took me with him on a trip to the Miss Iowa Pageant producer and sponsor. It was not pageant time. The purpose was to help plan the various ways in which their shows could be improved. George had asked me to accompany him to fill in the information he thought necessary. We spent a couple of interesting days with excellent discussions and warm hospitality. I remember that it was mid-winter, for the farmlands were beautifully covered by snow as I had seen them from the plane.

In my memories, George Cavalier was unique in his several positions of importance with the Miss America Pageant. Lenora had first met him in Santa Cruz where he was selling real estate and was the director of the Miss California Pageant, a well organized event.

When it became necessary, from the standpoint of time, for Lenora to be relieved from traveling some 50,000 miles each year in order to promote the Pageant, meet with civic and service organizations, universities and colleges, corporations and others, it took two people to perform her duties. She chose George Cavalier as field director for Western states and Bill Muncrief, director of the Miss Arkansas Pageant, as director of Eastern states. These two men served well for some years.

In 1966 Lenora recommended that George Cavalier be selected as producer of the Miss America Pageant. He was so successful that a couple of years later he was given the titles of producer, director and writer of the shows. His creative ability was so well recognized that he served in that capacity until he died in 1986. By then he had added the new title, director of national and field producer. His talents had been extended to helping state pageants with their productions as well.

Cavalier made many changes in preparation and presentation of the talent competition. He established procedures first of all to shorten and, if possible, eliminate many of the unnecessary delays and problems happening each year during rehearsals. Girls had to arrive with a three-minute, accurately timed talent presentation.

To insure this result, he began requiring every contestant to deliver well in advance of the Pageant a tape recording of her talent presentation.

If she sang, that was her song to sing. If another contestant chose the same song, she was advised to make a different selection in time to send a new tape. If she danced, the sound of her dancing shoes had to be recorded. If she played an instrument, or was an actress performing to a musical background, that tape had to be recorded and copyright approval given. The end result was the dictum that three minutes was three minutes. Rehearsal could be more efficiently managed.

There was one other result that was valuable to Cavalier's production planning. He was able to divide the talent of 50 girls over three nightly shows, distributing their talent as evenly as possible for balanced shows. He was able to avoid having all the best talent showcased at once, giving every contestant a more equal opportunity for securing as many talent points as possible. Cavalier was not just a producer, director or writer. He became a valued member of the Pageant family, admired, respected and loved.

He and Al Marks made a remarkable team. Between them they had complete and total control over production of all stage operations from the writing of the TV script to the shows as viewed by the television audience. Marks and television network officials sometimes argued and fought, but in the end Marks usually had his way.

❧

State sponsors are selected and approved by pageant officials on a franchise agreement, the terms and conditions of which are determined by the Pageant board. Lenora had been empowered to change franchises from cities and commercial interests to state organizations such as the Jaycees, the Kiwanis, other service clubs and chambers of commerce during the early years of growth and development. Occasionally a franchise has been reviewed and changed when it was in the best interest of all concerned. Meanwhile, the organization of state pageants is a strong, healthy association of value to the Pageant and its individual members.

Meetings during the national Pageant and during the year are important ways for state pageants to keep well informed on ways and means to improve their operations, maintain friendships and be of general help to each other. For the first time state chaperones were invited backstage for a briefing on the requirements expected in Atlantic City on the care and assistance needed to help contestants prepare for their competition. General information about Pageant operations was given, a brief tour was then led backstage, followed by refreshments. Oldsmobile made a car available to every state winner for use at public appearances during her year. The Toni Company presented a $500.00 fashion award to every state winner. The Frigidaire Division of General Motors and the Toni Company originated the Toni-Frigidaire award of $1,000.00 for a state winner.

The judges were instructed to study the quality of the talent being performed during the competitions, the feeling, the technical skills, the discipline required, the levels of achievement, the stage presence, facial expressions, costuming and choreography.

I remember in some of my early experiences the bitter and angry protests that parents would aim at the quality of the judges. One mother in particular thought only skilled musicians or musical experts were required to judge her daughter's "exceptional" voice. The judges have always been chosen to have a diversity of talents. Sometimes Marks would ask me to make written statements pertaining to the problems of the moment.

Some 200 women from New York, calling themselves the Women's Liberation Front, decided to picket the Pageant for what they called the exploitation of women during Pageant competition.

They chanted slogans. They tossed bras, undies, girdles, make up, hair curlers and other articles into what they called freedom trash cans on the Boardwalk. Their conduct was anything but exemplary.

While contestants were busy with talent rehearsals one afternoon I decided to walk the 635 feet to the Boardwalk to see their activity. Police Captain Cade stopped me when I told him where I was going. "Don't go, Mrs. Alton," he said. "It is a disgusting show out there and not worth your time to see." I decided to accept his judgment. If a police captain, who sees everything in his official duties, said this Women's Liberation's activities were disgusting I certainly had better things to do with my time. I didn't go.

During the broadcast of the show on the final night some of the women had infiltrated the police who were stationed to prevent their entry into the Hall. In an attempt to disrupt the show, and shouting "You're being exploited," they tossed a stink bomb into the audience. The police promptly threw them out of the Hall.

The Women's Liberation Front returned to the Pageant the following year in 1969, but the police were ready for them and no incident occurred. The police had called Women's Liberation headquarters to inquire which charter bus company was bringing pickets to the Pageant. Shortly before time to leave New York, all the buses broke down at once. Marks obtained an injunction that left Women's Lib almost powerless. *The New York Post* reported that Police Chief Mario Floriani threatened to arrest pickets carrying placards featuring *Playboy* nippled fold-outs, a poster which Floriani decided was obscene. As far as he was concerned I'm sure he felt that if he said it was obscene, it was.

During the Women's Liberation demonstration the protesters exhibited a live sheep with a huge bow on its tail and crowned it Miss America. They compared the judging of contestants walking on the runway with the 4-H county fair where the best animal "specimens" receive the blue ribbon. In a similar way, they lectured that women in our society had to compete daily for male approval, enslaved by beauty standards women are conditioned to take seriously.

The basic purpose of Women's Lib in our city was to secure every ounce of publicity for their cause, no matter how "disgusting," dirty and unclean their language, along with their actions. Eventually the leadership of Women's Lib changed their tactics and became more conducive to better taste in their public utterances. They eventually became what we recognize today as the National Organization of Women.

Chapter 42

he college campaign Mildred and I had been conducting for nearly two years now had created massive publicity in many newspapers, on radio and TV. My husband never did adjust to seeing our name in the papers. He suffered the agonies of worrying about what I would say. When I was interviewed on the phone, he would wigwag his arms, shake his head violently and sometimes grunt. He would worry into the night. Next morning at the crack of dawn he'd drive all the way up to the Atlantic City Bus Terminal to buy the morning paper at the newsstand, unable to wait for our paper to be delivered. When he came home I could tell by the way he came upstairs if the news was okay. If he was upset I'd hear him all the way up the stairs. He paid me one compliment, though, that I've often enjoyed remembering. He said, "It's kind of fun being married to you. I never know what you're going to do next."

In September a write-up in the *The Press* stated that a master plan for higher education, including new colleges, would be released in March or April. We still had time to work. Being included in the master plan was a must. The Robert Heller Associates were preparing the master plan.

At least I knew the direction to take. The Heller Association had done much planning for Rutgers University. I had their reports. I also knew how to contact them. I wrote a letter to Tracy Voorhees who had been involved with the key people planning the new State Department of Higher Education asking for help. He invited me to visit him in his Washington, D.C., law office.

Mildred and I spent several hours over luncheon at the Navy Club being told who was making the final decisions on colleges, how and when. He promised to put us in touch with everyone we needed to know. He was as good as his word. He knew the officers of Heller Associates and said he would arrange to have us meet with one of their representatives in Atlantic City.

A month or so later, H. Baird Tenney of Robert Heller Associates Inc. met with us at the Ambassador Hotel, now the Tropicana Casino. Ned Gerber, our Atlantic City Electric Company official liaison, asked if he and William Cowart could be present to speak for the NAFEC institute. I readily agreed, feeling that speaking for two institutions was more powerful than one.

We three met Tenney at 9 a.m., but Cowart wasn't there. As a thorough researcher Mr. Tenney's questions were designed to clarify his thinking and ours. We had explored fully all the agreements and statistics which had been the strongest part of our presentation. Mildred and I were satisfied we had been treated seriously and had said everything necessary.

Gerber excused himself and went to telephone Cowart. In a little while Cowart arrived. The discussion then centered on NAFEC and the science institute. Tenney listened carefully, making notes.

I had made a serious effort to tie a four-year college with the graduate center planned for NAFEC, believing strongly that the chances for both institutions improved considerably when their goals were united. Cowart finally was almost forced to agree that this was so, but he admitted those fateful words: "that he had never agreed with Mrs. Alton on anything." Mr. Tenney ended the meeting by saying that a serious study would be made. He asked for additional research studies on graduate education. Tracy Voorhees also arranged for a meeting with Theodore Streibert, Executive Secretary of the New Jersey Citizens Committee for Higher Education. Mildred and I invited him to lunch at the Strand Restaurant which was our unofficial meeting place with business leaders. Streibert gave us a full briefing on what was being done in Trenton and gave us some excellent advice.

Believing that we needed a nucleus of prominent men to be associated with us, Mildred and I organized an advisory council.

We went to see Elwood Kirkman, president of the Boardwalk National Bank, who agreed to become vice-chairman of our committee; James Hayward, president of the Atlantic City Electric Company, vice-chairman; and William Gemmell, vice-chairman. Members of the advisory council were Dr. David B. Allman, past president of the American Medical Society; Joseph Bradway Sr., president of the Guarantee Bank and Trust Company; Dr. John Falzetta, superintendent, Greater Egg Harbor School District; Ned Gerber, vice-president, Atlantic City Electric Company, and a group member seeking the Institute of Aerospace Science and Technology; Rabbi Aaron Krauss, president of Atlantic Human Resources, rabbi of Community Synagogue; Karlos LaSane, plant staff supervisor, Southern New Jersey Bell Telephone Company; Albert A. Marks Jr., president and partner of Newburger and Company; Anthony Rey, executive vice president and general manager, Chalfonte-Haddon Hall; Charles Reynolds, editor of the *The Atlantic City Press*; Jack Webb, director, National Aviation Facilities Experimental Center (NAFEC), now known as the FAA Tech Center, also a member of the Institute of Aerospace Science and technology group; Joseph Curtin, district manager, New Jersey Bell Telephone; Albion Hart, superintendent of Atlantic City Schools; John Helmbold, superintendent of Atlantic County Schools; Leonard Horn, legal counsel for the Miss America Pageant, partner of Lloyd, Megargee, Steedle, Weinstein and Horn.

Mildred and I had begun completing this excellent research on the needs of graduate education in South Jersey. Ned Gerber had distributed questionnaires throughout the Electric Company and to utilities, and businesses and industry throughout our three southern counties. Mildred had handled the project with school administrators and superintendents. Civic clubs, professional organizations and government officials had also participated. We had covered as many people as possible and received in return thousands of questionnaires. Mildred and I were surprised to learn that the need for graduate education was almost as great as for undergraduates. Even much greater today I'm sure.

The graduate survey report we sent to Heller Associates was instrumental in their final decision to recommend a new college in our area. However, we could not have achieved inclusion in the master plan without the strong support and cooperation we had received from the men associated with the proposed Institute of Aerospace Science and Technology, who had helped us in spite of Cowart's opposition.

Three of them had joined in our advisory council including the director of NAFEC. Mr. Tenney responded enthusiastically to our report that the NAFEC graduate education needs made a convincing argument when combining with the needs for a four-year college. Periodically, through the influence of Tracy Voorhees, we were approached by leaders with inside knowledge of planning in the chancellor's office. Tracy had been one of those instrumental in the selection of Ralph Dungan as chancellor. For a while we were being strongly pressured to consider a junior college with a junior and senior class level to complement the first two years of Atlantic Community College.

Mildred and I just as strongly declined, holding out for a four-year college. Even Senator Farley had voiced public interest in a two-year additional college. Our advisory council had suggested that the chancellor, who had been supporting a new college in Bergen County rather than Atlantic, be invited to dinner to hear our story first hand. It took a while but the chancellor finally agreed. The news media and radio stations promoted the dinner almost daily.

On February 20, 1968, there were 400 prestigious political, educational and business leaders present in Haddon Hall. Anthony Rey, executive vice-president and general manager of the hotel, undertook personally all dinner and table arranging including decor. Albert A. Marks Jr. was the master of ceremonies. Senators, assemblymen, freeholders, mayor and council of Atlantic City and the political, business, educational and professional who's who of our three counties were present.

Nothing could have influenced the chancellor more or had a greater impact on him that night than unexpectedly meeting the principal of Wildwood Catholic High School who had once been his teacher at Holy Cross in the Mount Airy section of Philadelphia. She had been a strong supporter of our college effort. Their chance meeting had added something we never could have guessed or planned, important beyond measure. Maybe more of the Divine help we sorely had needed had been given. Following Senator Farley's main speech, the chancellor spoke glowingly of his former teacher and the tremendous support that had been generated so painstakingly for "our college."

Mildred and I had a feeling that at long last the college had a strong possibility of becoming a reality. However, there was still a long, long way to go. When the Heller report was finally presented to the State Board of Higher Education, it recommended that two new state colleges be built, one in the northwestern part of the state and one in the southeastern, exactly what the original Department of Education had been planning. A second big boost came when a report of the governor's commission on capital needs made the same recommendation. Bergen County is in the northeastern part of the state not northwestern.

On May 13, 1968, the chancellor telephoned that the Board of Higher Education had sent a report to the legislature recommending two new state colleges. On May 17, 1968, he telephoned again to say that the appropriations committee was meeting and the week of May 20–24 was a crucial week, for final recommendations would be made for the governor's budget before presentation to the legislature. The chancellor wanted as many letters and telegrams sent to the appropriations committee as possible voicing our need for a college.

Once more we had to reactivate, by as much publicity as possible, the thousands of people on our mailing lists, alert the news media, *The Atlantic City Press*, which had done yeoman service in publicizing our college needs, and the radio stations which had supported us. Howard Berger, of WFPG, had my spot announcements on the air constantly day and night, every hour on the hour, and then some. The Southern New Jersey Development

Council urged its members to "write, wire or contact personally the chairman of the appropriations committee," as did other civic and service organizations. WFPG sent tapes to other radio stations to be broadcast throughout the entire network in South Jersey. The response was excellent.

On June 17, 1968, the next to last hurdle was eliminated. The front-page headline story of *The Press* was, "Assembly Okays Bill for South Jersey College 64–0." Two new colleges had been locked into the proposed bond issues. This success had not been achieved lightly. An article appeared in *The Press* on October 5, which had told the full story: "State Senator Frank S. Farley of Atlantic County threw his full political endorsement behind the $990 million state bond issues and said that with the enactment of the bond program a four-year college could be in operation in South Jersey in three years. He . . . successfully 'locked' the college into the proposed bond proposal with a rough and tumble argument to fellow legislators at a Republican majority policy session earlier this year. Republicans, agreeing on a compromise with Democrats to support the $990 million bond issues, originally proposed to include $15 million to construct only one new state college in Bergen County, North Jersey.

"Assemblymen Albert S. Smith of Northfield and Samuel Curcio of Hammonton, along with Farley rose in objection and Farley launched a fight for a South Jersey College." Smith, recalling the two-hour policy session held in New Brunswick, said, "Senator Farley got up and raised an awful howl, as did Assemblyman Curcio and myself." He added, "The senator made quite a battle."

Farley also had declared that "under no circumstances could we support a bond issue without a South Jersey college included." As the powerful Atlantic County senator's argument took effect, a poll of the Republican legislators was taken. Instead of answering "yes" to inclusion of the Southern Jersey college in the bond issues, the legislators instead answered "Farley's college."

Curcio, assessing Farley's fight, remarked, "It was a masterful job."

When I read that account of Farley's fight for our college I had many mixed emotions. I remembered the determination I had had those first few days after I became involved by Rabbi Krauss in "doing something." When Farley wouldn't meet with Marks and me, I had determined to secure his full attention and persuade him to work for our college in the legislature by arousing so much public support that a college would become a political necessity. Mildred Brick and I had done just that. Our success could be measured by the fact that Farley, our other South Jersey senators, and all the assemblymen could not really come home without a college for our people. When "push came to shove" they had to fight the good fight and they did. There was still a big hurdle before our area. The huge $990 million dollar bond issue had to be passed or no college for us. We reactivated once again our news media, radio and TV supporters, spoke at clubs and organizations asking them to work for the bond issue passage as many others in the state were willing to do. South Jersey was solidly favorable in the vote.

The long struggle for a college at last had been successfully completed. What happened next was in the hands of the Board of Higher Education and the chancellor. Mildred and I could do no more. The year 1968 had ended on a happy note. My mind recalled the title of one of my speeches at women's clubs and organizations throughout the state and its biblical teaching, "If you have faith—nothing shall be impossible."

Two housewives of no particular standing or prestige in the community had been able to achieve by pressure exerted on our legislators, through people power, what the governor, the chancellor and the most important political legislators in the state had so strongly opposed in favor of Bergen County for three years. My Federation experience had taught me well what people power can accomplish when used constructively.

In early January 1969 I was surprised to have a telephone call from Chancellor Dungan inviting me to be a trustee of "our" college. I had not considered such an appointment as even remotely possible. I had been as outspoken as my sense of good taste would permit. My persistence had been aggravating to the political hierarchy in the state. Messages had come to me which made me realize that I had walked too long on tender toes. But I had known long before I started that personal popularity and achievement do not always go hand in hand. I preferred achievement.

At the dinner planned in his honor here, the chancellor had said to me, "You will let the professionals plan the college." It was a promise I intended, had always intended, to keep. "I will let the professionals plan the college," I replied. I was delighted that the chancellor had also selected the two men who had done the most, and whose influences and assistance had been the greatest help behind the scenes and with publicity. Among the real founders of The Richard Stockton College of New Jersey were James Hayward, vice-chairman of the Citizens Committee for Higher Education, president of the Atlantic City Electric Company; and Charles Reynolds, editor of *The Press of Atlantic City*.

Stockton College has never officially recognized that it owes its existence today to Senator Frank S. Farley, James Hayward, Charles Reynolds, Mildred Brick and the myriad of political, educational, professional, business leaders and thousands of people who struggled so long for its establishment in Pomona.

On its tenth anniversary, the board of trustees held an official celebration in the college theater honoring the first appointed chairman of the board of trustees as the college founder. All other original first trustees have been recognized as college founders. They were the builders and planners of the college from day one, but they were not the real founders of the college. The people of South Jersey were.

Chapter 43

In the middle of January 1969, my personal world changed. My beloved husband suffered a major heart attack one Sunday morning. When our medical doctor arrived he apparently didn't recognize what my son and I considered a serious problem. John had chest pains of considerable intensity.

In the world of today I would have called the paramedics and he would have been administered the modern drugs soon enough to prevent much heart damage in the emergency room of the hospital. So many good medical procedures exist today. In 1969 we didn't have paramedics. The doctor let John stay uncomfortably in bed until Monday morning when I took him to the doctor's office for an EKG. The nurse immediately recognized a heart attack. I brought John home where he rested in bed until the Ventnor ambulance arrived to take him to the hospital. The ambulance had a Ventnor fireman driver. A policeman arrived in his car to help carry John down the stairs to the ambulance with the driver. I sat in the ambulance alone with John on the ride to the hospital.

After a month John was brought home by ambulance and carried into the house by several policemen. I had had the dining room converted into a bedroom where he lived as a semi-invalid for almost a year. He had been forced to retire. John was in the hospital the night I went to be sworn in as a college trustee and attended the first get-to-know each other meeting of trustees on February 5, 1969.

The legislature finally settled a heated two-county controversy over the location of the college by approving Senator Farley's bill to locate the college in Atlantic County. I became chairman of the residential selection committee of the trustees. The State Board of Higher Education had sent a query to 150 out-of-state university presidents and chancellors. From a field of 90 we selected Dr. Richard E. Bjork as president.

David Taylor, a former trustee of Trenton State College, had been appointed chairman of the board of trustees by the chancellor and I had been appointed vice-chairman. I was happy with Taylor's chairmanship, for his mother was a close friend living in Moorestown who had been president of the New Jersey State Federation of Women's Clubs when our headquarters building had been built on the Douglass College campus.

The actual site selected for Stockton was equally controversial. The trustees finally decided on 1,600 acres of pinelands with a lake near Pomona. The Vineland Committee of 50 was apparently considering legal action financed by Mayor Garton according to newspaper reports. There followed an investigation by the special committee of investigation into circumstances surrounding the purchase of the land.

I was the first to testify. I had gone well fortified with press clippings, letters and pertinent information which substantiated all of my knowledge. I was treated surprisingly well in the questioning, even told by the legal counsel that "I had done a good job." No criticism or action followed.

Stockton was planned, constructed and opened in slightly over two years. It opened its doors on September 13, 1971, in the Mayflower Hotel on the Boardwalk in Atlantic City with 1,000 students. I was surprised on that day when I was elected chairman of the board of trustees. I thus became the first woman to be elected a trustee board chairman in the state and the first woman member of the council of state colleges.

One of my happy experiences at Stockton was an honor given me by the trustees at their dinner following the first graduation in 1973. I was given the first honorary degree ever conferred by Stockton, an honorary bachelor of arts degree making me an

336

honorary member of the first graduating class of 1973. Senator Frank S. Farley was presented the second, similar honorary degree.

The honorary degrees had to be presented privately at the informal trustee dinner because the faculty had been on strike over a tenure question and were somewhat unruly. I was still chairman of the board. The tenure problems have been perennial ones. Because the dinner was not a public meeting no record of the honorary degrees exists.

I was also one of several of the founding trustees to have a dormitory wing named in my honor. In later years the Stockton Alumni Association made me a life member and presented a handsome plaque to me at graduation in 1983.

Elizabeth B. Alton

Chapter 44

made trips to regional conferences held in four sections of the country each year and officially represented the Pageant at a few state pageants. I remember a couple of those trips very well. When a conference was held in Salt Lake City, Utah, I went in advance to Los Angeles to visit my daughter and son-in-law. I planned an early evening flight to Salt Lake City. It was a beautiful night with a full moon as we took off over the Pacific Ocean. After a comfortable, uneventful flight, we reached Salt Lake City on time and began circling the city. I could see the lights down below but we continued to circle. Finally the pilot announced that the field was fogged in and efforts were being made at the airport to blow away or disperse the fog. We circled an hour or so. Then the pilot announced that we could not land and would travel on to Pocatello, Idaho. The pilot was taking no chances, for the airport at Salt Lake City is surrounded by mountains.

We landed at Pocatello at almost midnight by this time. The terminal had been opened for us. We were led to a large bus, our luggage stowed, and we took off for a long three-hour ride over the mountains. I saw the hotel in Salt Lake City as we rode by it on our way to the airport an hour away, knowing the bus would not stop there for me.

Our ticket was from airport to airport, which also was closed. Someone in authority had called for taxis. I made a fast dash lugging my heavy suitcase for a taxi. When I entered the hotel the taxi driver came in with me to see if all was well. The hotel clerk was snoozing out of sight behind the desk, the lobby completely empty. By the time I got to my room, unpacked and got in bed it was already early morning. An hour or two later I was awakened by our Pageant producer, George Cavalier, checking on my arrival which had caused some concern. By the time I reached the morning breakfast meeting I was far from ready to speak to the state sponsors.

I made another trip to Iowa that had its humorous aspects. The conference went well, hotel arrangements had been excellent, the state sponsors interesting and congenial. Al Marks had to leave the conference a day early, leaving me as the official hostess with past president Robert Nesbitt. After our last dinner I went to my room to pack. The telephone rang and a state sponsor invited me to join their group for a nightcap. I had no interest in doing so, thanked them, but declined. In a few minutes a knock came on my door and a couple of sponsors insisted that I join them. They walked me down the street a short distance to what looked like a night club but was actually a Go-Go Bar. Inside were our two field representatives. The consternation on their faces when they saw me was a memorable picture. I can still see them in a state of shock.

The bar was evidently a good one for a Go-Go Bar. Everyone was nicely dressed. There were women present. The girls danced in cages. They were dressed scantily but actually had more clothes on than I see on our beaches today. They were young and attractive. Their gyrations on that night were not too far removed from an exercise routine. While I didn't relish being there, I found nothing particularly offensive.

The sponsors ordered me a Shirley Temple or something non-alcoholic and I sat to enjoy their outrageous invitation and my almost forced presence in an atmosphere entirely different from anything I had experienced before.

I amused myself by thinking about why these men were having such a kick out of dragging me to a Go-Go Bar. The fact that I had written such strict rules for contestants, with such silly ones in their opinion of not letting girls speak to men without a hostess present, must have labeled me a goodie-goodie, namby-pamby individual. That I was a known teetotaler must have added to my image of Victorian purity. That's a long way from the real me. I suspected their amusement for the evening was going to be my reactions in such a place. If so, they were sorely disappointed. I determined they would get no reaction from me for their evening's pleasure or entertainment. In my public life I've been subjected to many surprising situations. One learns quickly to adjust to whatever happens. It's called "go with the flow" or "roll with the punches" or something like that. At that moment I was going to be just one of the boys.

I enjoyed my Shirley Temple, I analyzed the Go-Go dancers, I entered into the conversations with enthusiasm and I made every effort to discombobulate whatever their plans had been. Apparently I succeeded.

When they didn't get the rise from me they expected, they decided to persuade Bob Nesbitt to arrive, going to bring him to the bar. I managed to leave shortly afterwards. My only regret was that men I had respected would treat me in such an unpleasant, inconsiderate, ungentlemanly way. It did happen, though, in the best of Pageant circles. I never got used to it.

Another time I traveled to Kansas City for a regional conference speaking about the hostess committee. The choice for entertainment one night after the meeting was the Playboy Club. I had never been in a Playboy Club. This one was large, the girls beautiful with their bunny tails, the music excellent. Almost all of the conference people had come. My hosts had ordered me a superb fruit non-alcoholic drink. It was a warm, friendly atmosphere where I was most comfortable, my companions gentlemen, treating me with courtesy.

While I enjoyed the entertainment I remembered *Playboy* for another reason. In my early years as a hostess with the Pageant, representatives from *Playboy* used to cover the Pageant. It was not uncommon for a number of girls to be invited to pose nude. As far as I know no one accepted. My reputation even then must have been that of a prim and proper female. I was highly amused, in fact had a good, hearty laugh one year, after a couple of encounters with *Playboy*, to receive a complimentary membership in the Playboy Club in New York with all of the alluringly different and new opportunities that membership offered me. I kept the card quite a while for a good laugh now and then.

 ❧

In my role as hostess chairman and later a board member, I came into frequent contact with top representatives of national sponsors in Atlantic City and at meetings with state Pageant sponsors throughout the country. The relationships were always warm and friendly associations that I thoroughly enjoyed. Joe Lewis of the sponsor Gillette-Toni Division and his staff were always helpful to me, a joy to work with.

I was surprised when representatives of national sponsors first began asking me questions about Pageant operations. Since the questions were usually asked for better understanding of procedures I had no concern in answering them as best I could for the Pageant's benefit. After a while it was sort of routine. I valued these personal contacts almost as much as frequent discussions with board members.

One night after the final show the top representative of Pepsi-Cola invited me to join him at a table for two, somewhat removed from others at a social event. His searching questions caused me some concern for he was not interested in Pageant activities but in individual members of the board of directors. I could think of no way to avoid or change the questioning. He was particularly interested in the ages of board members including the officers and how long we had been doing certain things in certain ways. His questions were age-oriented. I was disturbed.

I discovered the reasons for his questions shortly after the Pageant. Pepsi-Cola had begun a new advertising campaign with the slogan, "Now it's Pepsi for those who think young." The company withdrew then as a national sponsor. The Pageant did contain older men on the board, one original director in his eighties, all conservative and somewhat provincial in their thinking. The promotion of Atlantic City was the primary goal.

I don't think the Pageant board and volunteers ever knew in later years why the age limit of 65 years was established. President Adrian Phillips made the proposal shortly after Pepsi withdrew. His reasoning to the board was that a prominent beachfront hotel owner who hadn't attended board meetings for several years could be tactfully retired since he was over 65. No mention was made that other board members present could be also, but I understood very well.

Every board member was asked to write his name on a slip of paper with his age. I was the only woman. I could easily have shaved a year or two off my age, but I didn't. I also knew that Adrian was nine years older than I and already in his seventies. After the new bylaw had been adopted, a man was nominated at that meeting for election to the board who was the husband of a friend. I knew he was over 65. I was tempted to say so, but I also knew he could be a valuable addition to the board and I couldn't do that to a friend.

As it was originally intended, the bylaw became a way of eliminating particular people from Pageant activities. Through the years since, it has been customary to retire board members at 65 only to allow some to retain their same committee responsibilities as usual, serving in the same capacities for additional years. Only their board titles were different. The retirees were now elected to the new advisory council if they had been nominated. Past Pageant presidents were exempt from the bylaw; they could be and were elected to the executive committee.

Hostesses have also had a 65-year age limit. V.I.H. members, known as very important hostesses, can served on a variety of committees after their retirement. The obvious conclusion seems to be that a few board members and hostesses, whose knowledge and skills are important, are allowed to serve additional years after 65 while others are not.

Members of the press have sometimes asked me what the advisory council does. While the bylaws have been amended fairly recently, the original intent was to allow former board members the privilege of attending board meetings without a vote if they so desire, receive minutes of the board and other materials, and be knowledgeable about the Pageant.

I went to several board meetings after I joined the advisory council shortly after it had been created. It was like having an extra thumb on the hand, unneeded. I was both uncomfortable and out of place. I don't know if anyone on the council has ever been asked for "advice." I could have answered the question of what the advisory council does in one word. Nothing. It does not meet to present advice, suggestions or recommendations. It has no organization or leadership. It is a small number of miscellaneous people with much personal Pageant experience who have been more or less retired as the individual case may be. Their new title is a kind of silent recognition of having once been a valued member of the board.

I sometimes look back on that private conversation with the Pepsi-Cola executive with a touch of humor. Limiting the age of board members did nothing to improve the Pageant's modus operandi or cause the necessary changes to be made to modernize the Pageant's program. Being able to "think young" is not a matter of age. It is rather of keeping up to date with the world around us, especially with the young women of today who compete in our Pageant.

I don't know whether successful, mature businessmen understand young women of college age today as Lenora Slaughter did years ago. I do believe that the pageant needs new creative ideas, dynamic leadership and the willingness to change with the times in order to retain its reputation for excellence in the coming century. There is no age limit on creativity or "thinking young."

The reason Pepsi-Cola gave for leaving the Pageant was their belief that the Pageant was out of touch with young people and with cities. One official was quoted as saying, "Miss America

as run today does not represent the changing values of society."
Their withdrawal did not affect Pepsi bottlers across the country
who continued their financial assistance on local and state levels.

Marks stated the Pageant and Pepsi parted company because
the Pageant didn't approve of the way they wanted to use Miss
America in a hard sell. In my opinion, Pepsi and the Pageant board
disagreed because of the need for changes in Pageant operation that
were necessary to keep up to date. The board appeared unwilling to
change. I've often thought this inborn provincialism, exemplified
by a small handful of men keeping control of the Pageant, is what
the Pepsi-Cola executive saw as a Pageant operation opposed to
modernization. It was the real reason, I believe, they chose to
give up their sponsorship.

Lenora Slaughter had been open to every new idea, suggestion
or proposal she heard which could have improved the Pageant or
given it new public exposure. Following her, Al Marks had not yet
had time to change the modus operandi to any appreciable extent.

❦

Adrian Phillips was one of the noteworthy members of the
board and a past president, a close friend and associate of Al Marks,
he had an important influence on Pageant planning. Adrian had
graduated from law school in 1921. He observed and participated
in the first Pageant, liked what he saw, thought the publicity for
the city was great, and volunteered to work on a committee with
the businessmen the following year. He has been the only Pageant
board member to be involved with the Pageant from its beginning.

He was the also the oldest living member of the Atlantic City
Press Club. In 1917 he was a proof reader, later sports editor of
The Atlantic City Press. For many years Adrian was in charge of
handling Miss America's press conference the morning after she
was crowned. I always enjoyed observing the proceedings. Usually
he had me sit at the table with Miss America and with him. He
sat on one side of her and I on the other.

In the earlier years, the winners were advised in advance to be careful in answering controversial questions and occasionally simple ones which caused problems of a general nature. I remember one year Miss America described her disinterest in eating breakfast. Young girls all over the country began skipping breakfast which soon brought a considerable number of complaints from parents and nutritionists. The press always asked questions about international affairs, political situations in our country, seeking information and solutions that even our governmental leaders were not providing very successfully.

When these types of questions arose, Adrian provided warning to Miss America in her response by a brief tap on her arm or knee out of sight of camera men. In these more current years as our college girls meet the press, they tend to express their opinions as they wish, articulately and convincingly. Contestants have been far better prepared for press conferences through their state pageant training.

I always enjoyed working with Adrian. We had much in common. We were both Atlantic City natives. When he was first married, he moved with his bride, Emmaline, into a new three-story apartment building on Atlantic Avenue at the corner of the street where we lived closer to Pacific Avenue and the beach.

When the Atlantic City Hospital wanted to build a second hospital on the state property of Richard Stockton State College, Adrian came to me to say he represented the Betty Bacharach Rehabilitation Hospital which also wanted to build their hospital adjacent to the new proposed Atlantic City Hospital in Pomona.

I was the key person since I was chairman of the board of trustees of Stockton which had the power to grant approval before securing state acceptance. I was able to convince the trustees of the wisdom of having these two hospitals on the college's 1,600 acres. Today they are outstanding medical assets to the growing area and useful to Stockton educationally as well as providing health care and training for students.

Chapter 45

The Pageant board meeting in the early fall of 1969 is one I'll never forget. Mildred Brick and I had been closely working together in the Miss America Pageant for a few years before we became partners in the college drive campaign to bring a state college to our area. I had appointed her vice-chairman of the hostess committee and had that appointment ratified by action of the Pageant board so that the president could not decline to reappoint her as had happened to Kathryn Morgan. Mildred's husband, Ben, had been my only allowed contact with the parade committee. One day Ben telephoned to invite John and me to have dinner with them at the Dennis Hotel "to celebrate." He didn't tell me what we were celebrating and I didn't ask, expecting to learn at dinner.

I know Mildred and Ben had visited the Phillips at their home near Port Republic. Adrian had bought the old house next to our family farm house where Grandmother Barstow was raised. My family used to spend time there, now and then, as my brothers and I did when we were growing up and as my children and husband did. It had been in our family over a hundred years. I had been surprised when Adrian bought the ramshackle, deteriorated property with the large acreage next door, for we had long wished someone would tear it down. Tramps and other peculiar people sometimes camped there.

Adrian and Emmaline rebuilt the house into a handsome and comfortable country home, clearing the woods into their natural state under forestry instructions. The visit of Mildred and Ben was not surprising for the Phillips were good hosts.

Dinner at the Dennis Hotel was always excellent, the service superb, and our evening together a happy fun-filled occasion. I didn't think about it until after we got home, but I wondered casually what we had been celebrating. I soon learned. The night before the scheduled meeting of the board of directors, I had a telephone call from William Cowart who was scheduled to be elected president. He informed me that I was going to be elected vice-president and Mildred would be elected as hostess chairman and the second woman on the board. Ben would also be elected to the board. I realized then what Mildred and Ben had been celebrating but had not mentioned.

Cowart's information was not a shock or surprise to me. Knowing how strongly he had disapproved and resented my college efforts, which had been successful while his political efforts for his aerospace institute had failed, and knowing he had long been a critic of my hostess committee activities, I was fully prepared to hear that he was giving me the old heave-ho. I was surprised, however, at the vice-presidency. Apparently I still had friends on the board. The position had not previously been held by a woman. As he talked, I had the strong impression that he would like me to decline.

As I thought about it the next day I had an instinctively uneasy feeling about the nomination, if that's what it really was. I knew the chairman of the nominating committee had been my earliest and most vocal critic. He had asked Kathryn Morgan to succeed me as hostess chairman when he had been president.

Under normal parliamentary procedures, the chairman of the nominating committee has the responsibility of securing acceptance before the nominee is placed on the nominating ballot. He had made no effort to contact me. I knew that of his own volition he would not have nominated me for anything.

Neither the current president of the board, the chief executive officer, nor any other board member had spoken to me. That the decision to remove me as hostess chairman had been Cowart's responsibility was clear. It was also obvious to me that some pressure must have been applied to him that I at least be informed before the board meeting that he was not reappointing me. Springing the change on me cold made my public reaction unknown, aside from being exceptionally inconsiderate.

That night I was elected vice-president. Publicity pictures were taken of Cowart and me, but I was still in for a major shock. Vice-presidents have always been members of the executive committee of the Pageant past and present. I quickly discovered that I was the first, and history records, the only elected vice-president who was denied election to the executive committee. The other vice-president, a man, was elected. I was barred from membership on this important committee. It was clear to me also that a mere female could not enter into the all-male inner sanctum. I had been given the final, almost unbearable insult. An empty title.

As I left the board meeting I felt not only belittled and demeaned by the unfair, irregular treatment, but actually unclean, as though I had been the surprise victim of something dishonorable, dirty. My first reaction when I got home was to resign immediately as vice-president. I still had three years on the board. My second reaction was to tell the board at its next meeting that it had not only discriminated against me as a woman, but my sex in general, that I refused to hold a title in name only and would resign the office with the resultant publicity. After a couple of days to cool off, I reached the decision I followed. I would hold the title of the office to which I had been elected for one reason and one reason only.

It was long past the time for a woman to hold an elected office on the board. In the forty-nine years of the Pageant's existence at that time, I was not only the first and only woman board member, but the first ever to be elected to office. Since I was the first titleholder I believed it was important for the Pageant's image and reputation to have a female name associated with the Pageant hierarchy as an officer, even if in name only.

For that reason I endured the indignities, discourtesies and pettiness that I believe no other self-respecting woman would have done for the three years I was vice-president. I have always believed I was as qualified by twelve years of active training, knowledge and experience in Pageant operations, both here and throughout the country, as some of the male members of the executive committee. I had preceded some of them. The new president had had only six years, some of them as parade chairman, a local operation, as his major experience. He didn't have the background of Pageant experience most executive committee members had.

I have wondered if there were other board members who may have had some reservations about this new presidency. For the first time the board had also elected Albert A. Marks Jr. to be chairman of the executive committee and Adrian Phillips vice-chairman establishing authority over the presidency.

The first decision of the new president was to divide all the committees in half and place them under the supervision of the two vice-presidents. This had never been done before and as far as I know, hasn't been done since. Many of the committees of the Pageant, the parade committee is an example, have always been operated with a large number of people. They functioned more or less as private fiefdoms. Any effort I made to voice suggestions or comments about the operation of those committees would have been unwelcome, all the more so because I was a woman.

I did not follow through on my assignments, which included the hostess committee and parade committee. As good friends as Mildred Brick and I were and have been, I could not possibly have involved myself in hostess committee discussions. The committee had been originally established on the principle that there would be no political or Pageant board influences exerted on the decisions of the hostess chairman. I had followed that precept as had my predecessors. My successor was entitled to hold firm to that principle. I would not inflict upon her any of my ideas, suggestions, approvals or disapprovals.

In the three years I was vice-president, I was not invited to or included in any executive committee meeting, or discussion about the Pageant. I was invited to a dinner meeting with the president and two members of the executive committee. The purpose of that meeting was to remove from my assigned supervision the auditing committee and place it in the hands of the other vice-president who had been involved with that committee for some years and where it rightfully belonged. I had known the assignment was wrong. A telephone call would have spared me an additional sense of humiliation after the dinner.

We met with a man who was seeking a franchise to use the Miss America name with his products. He passed around samples to the three men, but none to me, discussing their attributes with them. I was ignored as though I wasn't in the room. The message of my importance in Pageant decision-making was clear. It didn't exist.

During my first year as vice-president, the newly constructed West Hall addition to the Convention Hall opened in time for the Pageant. For the first time the hostess committee was able to accommodate all of the space needed in West Hall in roomy comfort. Mildred Brick, established the new control center, formerly in the dressing room, where Pageant information could be disseminated in spacious quarters. The press and news media finally had a large room for their needs adjacent to an area where contestants could be interviewed at tables and chairs and where the girls could eat with room enough to relax. What a wonderful improvement it had been over our formerly cramped quarters in the dressing room.

Mildred had been well indoctrinated in the problems of dealing with Pageant officials and the difficulties frequently encountered in other stages of the operation and production. Being the new chairman on the scene, she was accorded more attention, consideration and help than I had had in the changes for improvements she knew needed to be made. Filled with the same kind of drive and determination she had had during our college campaign together, she simply did what had to be done. I used to laugh privately at the thought that in removing me they had found a more than worthy successor who would achieve more power and influence than I had been able to develop in those first difficult, transitional years when hostesses were only chaperones and escorts. I had taken the first almost impossible steps. Mildred was able to build well on that firm foundation.

Phyllis George, Miss America 1970, was Mildred's first Miss America. No one could have asked for a more fascinating winner. Johnny Carson said of her, "No one has ever met Phyllis for ten minutes and not fallen in love with her." She also had worn the first swimsuit of that year which had no panel in the front. It was considered a physical fitness type of suit.

When Phyllis George was crowned she had difficulty keeping the crown on her head. Often the crown slides a bit to one side or the other out of position because the attached combs have not been anchored properly in the excitement of the moment. With Phyllis the crown just wouldn't stay on and fell to the floor of the runway. She picked it up and carried it in her hand. She admitted quite some time later that she was wearing a fall, a hairpiece placed on her head. The combs would not attach to the hairpiece. Full wigs were not allowed but the girls could wear a hairpiece to enhance their coiffure.

Phyllis has had an outstanding television career, and a fascinating life. John and I went to Phyllis George's press conference on Sunday morning after the crowning. The experience was so unpleasant for me that I never went to another one again.

I attended board meetings, but I spoke only when personally addressed and as briefly as possible. I began looking for something I could do that would benefit the Pageant commensurate with my background of experience that required no consultation with anyone. I thought about the lack of television exposure for some years for the parade.

When we visited our daughter in California during the winter, I went to the Wrigley Mansion on Orange Grove Avenue in Pasadena, the headquarters for the famous and beautiful Rose parade, and secured some of their literature. After studying it I began planning the national corporations I thought might be interested, based upon my personal contacts with board members of Rutgers University. The Pageant had always been a matter of particular interest each time I met with these governors and trustees after the crowning. Some of these men were presidents and CEOs of Fortune 500 companies.

One of the problems of the parade was the fact that the floats were not of sufficient quality and number to warrant the expense of nationally televising them. On the other hand, if television was available nationally, the quality and number would increase and improve. It was similar to the problem: which came first, the chicken or the egg? In the early years of television, Maybelline and CBS had televised the parade, well supported by local business interests and local communities.

I made the mistake of mentioning my plans to my number one critic. He laughed in my face. "We're not the Rose parade," he said, a truism even a stupid person would understand. I crossed that idea off my list knowing I had the contacts with corporations. I did nothing.

At the end of my first year as vice-president, John and I went to the awards breakfast where I sat at the head table. The hostess chairman had always presented the Miss Congeniality award which Mildred now did. I presented the awards to the four runners-up to Miss America.

At the end of the luncheon vice-president Sam Butcher presented Mildred with a lovely jeweled pin shaped in a crown in appreciation of her excellent service as hostess chairman that year. The recognition was more than well deserved. I was happy for her success. I had selected her to be my successor. The honor was recognition that I had chosen well and the committee was in excellent hands. She was also a good friend.

On the other hand I had some difficult, mixed emotions. I had been hostess chairman for twelve years, a member of the committee for seventeen. I had struggled long to change the committee's lowly image to the successful management operation it was becoming when Mildred became my successor.

Mrs. White, the first chairman, had been honored by the board of directors. Mrs. Shermer had been presented a diamond ring, Mildred a beautiful jeweled pin. I had been given an empty title. I would have been happy with a simple "Thank you" expressed privately. I didn't need or want jewelry or public praise. But I would have liked having even one person care enough about my contributions to the Pageant to say those two simple words, "Thank you." It would have meant a great deal to me at one time.

Marks continued to treat me with the respect and attention he had always shown me. He had sent me to some regional conferences and state pageant competitions. When requests for a speaker arrived he frequently sent me to speak for the Pageant. I remember one typical event. A large Rotary Club in Maryland wanted a special luncheon speaker. They had chartered a small plane to transport me. The weather just prior to the event had been stormy. I began wondering if the flight would be possible or if I would have to drive the long trip over the Pennsylvania Turnpike. The uncertainty existed of what to do at what hour. If I waited too long to see if the plane could fly, I'd be unable to drive the distance in time.

By chance I met the owner of the airlines running our airport at Bader Field at a civic event. I explained to him that I didn't want to cause embarrassment either to the Pageant or to the Rotary Club if there was a problem at the last minute and I was unable to appear. He assured me he would personally check my arrangements and notify me in time.

I breathed a great sigh of relief when the day dawned clear. I met the plane at the appointed hour, surprised to find an almost new small plane. I sat in the front seat with the pilot, fascinated with the large array of control mechanisms before me. When we passed the Philadelphia area to the west, I saw heavy clouds of smog over the city, dirty brown stuff. I hadn't really thought about smog in the big eastern city, unnoticeable on the ground. How much greater it must be today.

Also surprising to me, although I suppose it shouldn't have been, was the precision with which the pilot found our airport. Before I realized it, we had headed straight in and were coming straight down on the runway.

Giving speeches about the Pageant was always easy for me. I speak entirely "off the cuff" as I have always done, with neither notes nor written remarks on paper. I can tell when what I'm saying is pertinent and of interest or when a change of story needs to be introduced. My remarks that day were well received, the applause generous and my time limit adhered to the minute. Organizations still invite me to speak.

While the president and executive committee continued to ignore me in Pageant business, Marks and Adrian Phillips kept me busy. I was invited to their homes now and then when there were disturbing problems in which they wanted a different point of view. With Marks, I had always been a good listener when he found it necessary to let off steam, a confidante and occasional advisor he apparently trusted. We saw eye to eye many times.

Aside from my firm belief that I was as qualified to perform the duties of vice president as some members of the executive committee, I also knew in my heart that I had a particular value to the Pageant more important than most of those serving at that time. I had personal contacts and close working associations with corporate CEOs, millionaires who could have proved of greater value in promoting the Pageant's future than our wonderful Mr. MacIntyre of Bancroft and Sons in our early years.

Listed among the members of the board of governors and board of trustees of Rutgers University were some of the who's who of corporate America and their Fortune 500 companies.

As the only woman on the nine-member board of governors of Rutgers, I found myself meeting almost weekly with some of our country's prestigious executives. One of my committee assignments was the six-member buildings and grounds committee headed by a multi-multi-millionaire. We had an easy-going, comfortably warm relationship as he guided the extensive expansion and construction of new buildings following the passage of the huge bond issue.

I knew of his personal interest in the Pageant, and that of other members of the two boards. Every year, immediately after the Pageant, our informal talks over luncheon had always centered on discussions about the Pageants.

I saw in this gentleman a new godfather for our Pageant of the future. With his great fortune he had once tried a stock takeover of one of Hollywood's largest movie studios. He nearly succeeded. I was surprised to read about it in the *Los Angeles Times*. He continued to hold a strong financial interest in the entertainment industry, among other corporate interests, as long as I knew him. He would have been a natural for involvement with the Pageant.

Always helpful to me, he had supplied a nationally known television star, then appearing in New York, for the kick-off tea as a fund raiser for the Easter Seal Society when I was vice-president of the New Jersey Society of Crippled Children and Adults and chairman of the tea at the governor's mansion at Morven. He had assisted the president and officers of the Federation of Women's Clubs in their planning of a headquarters building on Douglass College campus with architectural drawings and pictures at my request.

Among the stories he sometimes told the board of governors in casual conversation, he once said that he and his wife never traveled together on the same plane, much as the royalty of Britain did, because of the tax reverberation in case of an accident.

In a visit to Rutgers' College of South Jersey in Camden to plan new buildings, I had my first ride in a specially-built custom designed Rolls Royce driven by a liveried chauffeur. I think I was as impressed with the elegantly styled and tailored uniform of the chauffeur in muted but artistic colors as I was with the Rolls. I also thought the chauffeur was large enough to be a body guard.

With all his millions, this man was an easy-to-know, friendly, generous individual, both a philanthropist and an entrepreneur.

He had an outstanding interest in higher education. The Pageant's scholarship program had promoted many questions in the six years of our association.

I had given quite a bit of thought to arranging a meeting between him, Marks and me as an introduction to spark his interest further in the Pageant program. I had hesitated after my election as vice-president and my subsequent treatment. I had known that this gentleman and Marks were so similar in personality, humor, and other characteristics that they would have made an excellent team working together.

After the awards breakfast when I realized the full extent of the lack of appreciation for my achievements, I gave up the idea of pursuing the matter further. I had less than two of my three-year term left before I became 65 and would be retired. I dismissed any thought of involving myself further as being too late and clearly not really wanted.

When this benefactor died several years ago he left millions to Rutgers University, which built an important building in his honor bearing his name. I am firmly convinced that he would have personally and materially assisted the Pageant and its scholarship program during his lifetime. He was that kind of man.

A quick glance at the membership roster of the Citizens Committee for Higher Education will show the quality and prestige of the committee members, some of whom were Rutgers trustees and others I came to know in other state activities. Tracy Voorhees had been involved in selecting members of this committee and had been responsible for my inclusion.

Through Tracy I had had entree to the Heller Associates' planning recommendations for new state colleges. Through him I had been appointed by Governor Meyner to the Rutgers boards. I had had knowledge of the planning for new state colleges within the chancellor's office. He had had a voice in selecting the chancellor. Tracy was a corporation attorney in Washington, D.C., and New York, a former undersecretary of the Navy, appointed by four presidents to national offices. He could have opened the door for me, if I had sought his help in promoting the Pageant, to some of the corporation leaders listed if Marks had so desired.

My exclusion from the executive committee had not been because I was unqualified or had no perceivable value. In fact my inclusion for election as vice-president had indicated that there were board members who had approved of my efforts in strengthening the Pageant operation.

I recognized as fact what I believed to be true, that the president and chairman of the nominating committee simply didn't want to be associated with me on a personal basis and didn't want to hear any ideas or suggestions I might make different from their own. They had their own ways of doing things, no female ideas welcome. The president's opposition was understandable. We had been competitors, in his mind, for new higher educational institutions. He had gone the political route four or five years before I had become involved as his group had sought a post-graduate Aerospace Institute at NAFEC. I had won a four-year college with Mildred Brick's support and help from thousands of others. He had lost. His group should not have lost and would not have if he had been willing to join our college movement as state officials had advised, as three key members of his own committee had strongly supported us.

I assumed that I was a constant, painful reminder of a difficult failure. I knew, also, that I had qualities of persistence, determination and expertise in Pageant affairs which were probably not acceptable in the inner sanctum where Pageant decisions were determined. The reasons were quite simple. The executive committee consisted of the elected officers, with my exception as vice-president, and several past presidents. With only an occasional addition or subtraction the same men served in the same capacity year in and year out, several for decades. They operated much as a small, select club, keeping control of the Pageant in the same hands, more or less, all the 25 years I had had an active association with the Pageant.

The chairman of the nominating committee, and his three committee members, served for an unreasonably long time, controlling the election process and the selection of those who would be amenable to their leadership.

By example, the chairman of the nominating committee, who had not informed me of my pending nomination as vice-president, continued in that capacity for some time. Eleven years later he followed a similar procedure with my successor who was a couple of years younger than I. She, too, had been offered a vice-presidency after a new hostess chairman had already been selected. The offer had been refused. It was disgraceful in all its aspects to the quality of leadership exhibited by two hostess chairmen.

The Pageant had reached its fifty-ninth year before Ellen Plum was elected vice-president from 1979 to 1984. In 1985 she became the first woman president of the Pageant, 65 years after its founding. I always took particular pride in Ellen Plum's success as president. I had selected her to be a hostess, giving her her first Pageant experience.

Believing Pepsi had withdrawn because of the older age of officials, the board had agreed to limit the age for active volunteers to 65. That's only part of what Pepsi saw. The main problem was the tight-fisted control by a handful of men who were no longer conversant with the modern age of young womanhood because of their own years and sex.

The proof of that statement is the simple fact that in more recent years the Pageant has been labeled "old-fashioned" and "out of date." For quite a while, it was. Changing the active years at 65 did not change the controlling decision of men, some of them exempt from the age limit themselves, to any appreciable degree. Instead, a system of favoritism developed whereby some board members were retired from the board but continued in their same responsibilities as committee chairmen. No changes in some cases had actually occurred, as was true in the hostess committee. Marks managed to do what he determined needed to be done, making necessary changes and improvements in the process. Leonard C. Horn, the present CEO, has modernized the Pageant to a greater degree. He knows how much more still needs to be done. It is, and should be, a constantly changing process.

I also believe that the board's decision to terminate the most popular of any of its masters of ceremonies, Bert Parks, was due to the age image. For several years there were several board members who continued to advocate the appearance of a younger man as emcee. It was no secret. Eventually they prevailed. Bert Parks was fired in 1980.

It was both a surprise and a shock to the general public. For many people, his name and his singing "There She Is . . . Miss America," were synonymous with the Pageant. Public protests were made vocally and loudly. Johnny Carson suggested a boycott of the Pageant until Parks was restored as emcee. What the board didn't realize was the fact that Parks was not really replaceable in the public eyes at that time.

There was much controversy for several years as new emcees performed well. At last the Pageant did bring Parks back as a guest in the show during the 70th anniversary, a role unfamiliar to him. It wasn't quite the same, charismatic as he was. But then, nothing remains the same. Even the Pageant has branched out into new fields of endeavor, preparing for the next century.

There are times, as it was with Bert Parks, when experience, successful performance, and personal value are more important, by far, than the number of suns one has seen rise and set. Life doesn't stop, nor does mental capacity and lifelong experience necessarily diminish at 65. Neither does personal drive and ambition; I am living proof of that fact.

Chapter 46

One of the most difficult and most controversial problems publicly known had hit the Pageant full force in the late 1960s and early 1970s. No black contestant had ever competed in Atlantic City. As the civil rights movement had grown, critics of the Pageant became more vocal. Roy Wilkins, head of the NAACP, called the Pageant "lily white," a common expression used by that organization.

A tremendous amount of unfavorable publicity had been generated. Pressures were applied to Marks to appear on a television program in Philadelphia to discuss the problem. I remember seeing the program, which was most difficult for Marks and equally unpleasant to watch. There were many rapid fire, acrimonious accusations, difficult to combat even for one as quick witted and responsive to the unjust criticisms as Marks was.

Shortly afterward, the board elected a black clergyman and a black school principal, both highly respected in the area. The first black Pageant judge was selected a year or so later. Meanwhile, I had selected two outstanding black women as hostesses.

There once had been a rule that "contestants must be of good health and of the white race." I never knew it existed until recent publicity of the 1995 Pageant. Despite this, to my knowledge the national Pageant had not ever made any real effort to prevent black girls from entering the Pageant. There had appeared on our stage and runway a number of full blooded American Indians, Orientals, and Hispanics.

Lenora had given advice and assistance in the formation of the Miss Black America contest where girls who wanted to enter a pageant were willing to compete. She had also welcomed the first black contestants in state pageants during her years, providing them with promotional materials and offering to help them in any way. She was happy to see black girls beginning to enter, succeeding in winning their friendship. In an interview recently she said, "They were beautiful girls and had every right to be in the Pageant. They are equal." They just hadn't made it to Atlantic City yet.

A year after Marks' confrontation in Philadelphia, he asked me to appear on television with a public relations woman involved in publicizing the Miss Black America Pageant. I went to New York the afternoon before to be well rested for the morning program.

When I arrived in the NBC studio, which broadcast over Channel 9 locally, there was not only the public relations woman present, but she had brought Miss Black America, too. I realized that this was a different situation than Marks had been told, or Miss America would also have been made available.

When the three of us were seated on the set, I quickly realized the program was a setup. First, I was seated in the middle of the two black women. Then, I was moved to one side so that the two black women were nearest the camera. After that, I was moved farther to one side on a lower level even farther away from the camera. The two black women were elevated above my location and directly center stage facing the camera, while I was placed sideways.

My instinct then was to get up and leave the studio, which I should have done. But I tend to keep my word, and I had said I would appear. While the conversation was not as acrimonious as the program with Marks, the two black women launched forth into constantly unending derogatory comments. I had to force my way in while they were talking a mile a minute to get some words in edgewise. At the end of the half hour, the NBC host, a black man, graciously allowed me half a minute to "summarize."

I left the studio with a feeling of regret that one of the NBC affiliates would treat the national Miss America Pageant, broadcast on their channel, so unfavorably.

There certainly had been no intention or effort by the NBC host to treat the subject of pageants on an equal basis. It could have been an interesting, educational, intelligent discussion with an unbiased person controlling the progress of the discussion. Instead the two women were allowed to state nonstop remarks for public consumption, inaccurate to the truth, which the black host made no attempt to control.

As a result Marks made a commitment that no appearances would be made by him, or any other Pageant spokesperson, without having well in advance the list of questions to be asked on the program. This brought to a halt the one-sided program requests.

This same year in September the first black contestant to compete on the national level in Atlantic City was Cheryl Browne, Miss Iowa 1970, who received a one thousand dollar scholarship as a particularly talented non-finalist. There have been other fine contestants through the years who have won scholarships. Some have placed in the top ten.

The first black Miss America was Vanessa Williams, Miss New York 1984. She was an unusually beautiful woman, gifted with a singing voice enriched by considerable talent. She was also an outstanding, charismatic performer. Vanessa was followed by Debbye Turner, Miss Missouri 1990; Marjorie Vincent, Miss Illinois 1991; and Kimberly Aiken, Miss South Carolina 1994.

Vanessa Williams has been the only Miss America who had to resign her title two months before her term ended. In her youth as a teenager she had made a serious mistake by posing for nude pictures of a sexual nature. The photographer sold the pictures to a prominent national magazine that strongly promoted their publication. The result was a scandal of immense proportion, unlike any other in those beginning years so long ago.

The threat to the Pageant's future existence was very real. Many expected its demise. Important national sponsors might choose to withdraw their support, affecting necessary financial income. State sponsorship by reputable civic and service organizations might be lost.

The problem could not be ignored. The press and news media descended on Marks en masse. Known as a "straight shooter," he managed to keep their respect in those difficult days. Marks was considerably upset and deeply hurt. The press found him outwardly articulate, willing to answer questions, reasonable and logical as always in his deliberations and responses. Inwardly Marks was badly shaken. For him and others it was the most difficult single event in Pageant history.

The wise decisions and speedy action taken by Al Marks and the board of directors did much to alleviate the harm that had been done to the Pageant's public image. Faith in the scholarship program held firm while the Pageant weathered a difficult storm.

Marks stood with Vanessa at a news conference while she publicly announced on television her resignation as Miss America in a dignified and ladylike manner. There was nothing else that could have been done.

The first Runner-up, Suzette Charles, became Miss America for the remainder of Vanessa's term, filling her engagements and her crown. She performed beautifully in the Pageant, wearing the crown, singing songs in her excellent, distinctive style and fulfilling all the duties on stage usually assigned to the reigning Queen with grace and talent. She had stepped into Vanessa's shoes and found that they fit her very comfortably.

We local people had had much interest in the competition of Suzette Charles, for she was one of our own. A resident of nearby Mays Landing, she had won the local Miss Columbus Day title and gone on to become Miss New Jersey, sponsored by the Cherry Hill Kiwanis Club. She was a Temple University junior with a major in theater and voice. Suzette has had an outstanding career as a pop singer, appearing frequently in Atlantic City casinos. Her record albums have been popular. She has made many international appearances, singing in Monte Carlo, Jamaica, France, Turkey, Greece, Rome, Spain and Italy.

Vanessa, too, has gone on to a prominent career as a singer and actress. She had been a fine Miss America, fulfilling her duties with much charisma, charm and talent, upholding the traditions of the Pageant. Her career took her to prominent roles in films, and television, winning for her eight Grammy Awards and the recent starring role in *Kiss of the Spider Woman* on Broadway. She has a rewarding personal life as a wife and mother, an exemplary young woman in today's world. She deserves much praise.

The fact that black women had been able to become Miss America and first runner-up when properly prepared for competition has encouraged many fine black girls to enter local contests, coming to Atlantic City after having won the state contests.

Elizabeth B. Alton

Chapter 47

ollowing that disturbing awards breakfast I withdrew from Pageant activities as much as possible, attending only when my presence would be expected. Oldsmobile was still providing cars for contestants, hostesses and Pageant officials. The elected officers all were given cars for their use except me. I drove myself most of the week.

A rare chance meeting with Cowart in passing led me to ask why no Oldsmobile had been assigned to me. On Friday a car arrived, not one of the new ones, but one more obviously very well used, with high mileage. I suspected it had been taken from someone working for Oldsmobile.

I am an experienced driver, having driven over 200 thousand miles in just the four years I was vice president and president of the Federation. I know well how to care for a car properly. I drove that car only the short distance to and from Convention Hall that Friday and Saturday, less than a mile each way. On Saturday night after the finals, my husband I went to get the car in the garage under the Hall. The car wouldn't start. The battery was dead. After all the parked cars left, the Convention Hall garage attendants got the motor running. Long after midnight, as it was, we simply drove home and parked the car.

Sunday morning when William Peterson called to ask me to return the car, I told him the battery was dead; they could come get it. Peterson arrived shortly with an Oldsmobile representative, a man plainly contemptuous of this woman who'd done something stupid to his battery. The inference was that a woman like me didn't know how to drive a car properly. In his mind women were inferior. Once more I recognized insult being added to injury. I wondered if the car had been taken from him.

After my television appearance in New York that June of 1971, I had even less contact with the Pageant. Prior to the awards breakfast, it had been customary to receive a letter of instructions describing seating at the head table and the award I would present to winners.

This year no letter arrived. I had received no information orally about presenting an award. I had no intention of attending the awards breakfast and finding there was no seat for me. I didn't go.

I was told later that the master of ceremonies had called on me to make the presentation to the four runners-up and I wasn't there. Many people asked me why.

In my experience with clubs, even an inexperienced president knows enough to check the seating arrangement at the head table so that there will be no embarrassment in introducing people out of turn or who are just not there. In this instance I was not sorry. I was entitled to the same courtesy as everyone else. I seldom received it.

After my sixty-fifth birthday in October, I had a telephone call from the Pageant office informing me that I was no longer a board member. No thanks, at least, for my 28 years of service, from anyone. No appreciation expressed. Just, "You're sixty-five. Goodbye."

I remembered a quote by Elizabeth Janeway that seemed appropriate: "It seems to me highly improbable that women are going to realize their potential without alienating men—some men, anyway."

It took me quite a while to understand what had happened to me as a vice president and why my two friends in the leadership roles had almost closed the door on me, leaving it open just a bit as an elected member of the advisory council, a small group also existing for some years in name only in my experience. Supposedly some of us were too old at sixty-five to be actively involved with the Pageant.

It finally dawned on me after a few years that my Pageant role had changed because it was no longer a part of the Master Plan my God had had for me. I had always known that when one door of opportunity closes another one opens. Previously, opportunities had followed one after another in ways that I had understood. This had been the first door to close almost right in my face.

Helen Keller, who was physically blind, but became so famous in her lifetime, was always able to see clearly in all other respects. She once said that "when one door of happiness closes, we spend so much time looking at the closed door that we do not see the ones that are open."

I had been looking at my latest closed door much too long, perhaps because I had been so deeply hurt, not so much for the lack of appreciation for my achievements as for the unfair rejection of me as an intelligent, knowledgeable and experienced woman. My new open door had been right there in front of me all the time, so wide open that I had been nudged through it almost against my will.

With the passage of the 990 million dollar bond issue in November 1968, Stockton State College had come into existence officially. In January 1969, I had been sworn in with eight others as a college trustee by a superior court judge. All of the time that I had had free from caring for my husband, recuperating from his heart attack that same month, had been devoted to college planning, to selecting a college president, a college site, the administrators and faculty needed to open the college, the courses, programs, projects and degrees necessary.

Much additional time was spent in selecting an architect and the contractors, and overseeing the actual construction of buildings and the requirements of classrooms, housing, an adequate library, theater and other necessary facilities. Meetings and deliberations were lengthy. The necessity of securing state approvals, no easy task, also required much time and careful maneuvering, as well as trips in and out of the state.

I hadn't recognized all these exciting opportunities and new experiences as an open door, but eventually, as I gradually emerged from the sea of public humiliation I had endured in my last three years of the Pageant, I realized that I had been blessed without measure with this new, fascinating door of opportunity, the best one of all. Blessed that I had picked as my successor a valued friend capable of carrying on, improving and building more strongly the important hostess committee to greater achievements. Blessed that we had worked together so enthusiastically and successfully that our area now had a state college. Blessed that I could see our hopes and dreams come true day by day. Totally blessed.

Two weeks prior to my final telephone call from the Pageant office, Stockton State College opened on the Boardwalk in the Mayflower Hotel on September 13, 1971. The college buildings needed another few months to complete.

I remember that occasion vividly, for the board of trustees met in the hotel that evening. As I drove down Tennessee Avenue and saw students out walking, I received some startling surprises. I had not come in contact, all at once, with many young people before. What I saw was far from the mainstream of my social consciousness. I don't know if it was the "hippie age" or the "yuppies." I do know that I was unaccustomed to the male hair-dos, cut up jeans, colorful tops, and bare feet that met my eyes everywhere. As I parked in the hotel parking lot, I laughed to myself. "What have I done?" I thought. "What have I done?"

The trustees' meeting brought another surprise. Although the chancellor had appointed me as vice chairman of the board, I was more than surprised to be elected chairman that evening by the trustees. When I expressed my appreciation to the board, I voiced my surprise. The board consisted of seven men and two women.

"Why not?" I was asked. It was still the era when women were not looked upon generally as acceptable leaders.

"Because I am a woman," I replied.

My chairmanship as a woman was a new departure from customary procedures in the state. I became the first woman

370

elected to head a trustee board of state colleges and the first woman member of the council of state colleges. The council consisted of state college presidents and chairmen of the boards of trustees. At sixty-five I had been too old for the Pageant, but not too old for new adventures through my open door to the field of higher education.

A biblical teaching in Proverbs 16:9 says, "In his heart a man plans his course, but the Lord determines his steps." After my original appointment I was well enough valued by the state to be reappointed to two more six year terms. A stark contrast to my previous experience. The criterion was not age, but leadership abilities.

A surprising opportunity came to me in these years. Chancellor Dungan selected me to represent the state colleges at a conference of the Association of Governing Boards of Universities and Colleges in Virginia. A small group of selected university and college presidents and trustees of the United States met to discuss the responsibilities and duties of college boards of trustees, to make necessary suggestions and provide information to improve the operations and deliberations of trustee boards.

I found the several days of this conference especially worthwhile in the following months. Stockton was in the process of selecting a new president. A few months later I was involved in the accreditation process for the college by the Middle States Association. The information I had gained proved helpful to other trustees in our deliberations.

A year later, the Association of Governing Boards of Universities and Colleges selected me for a small group doing special studies on college operations nationally.

The state had nominated me for election to the AGB board, a position I had not believed possible. I was right. The president of McGraw Hill and chairman of the State Board of Higher Education of New Jersey was elected. New Jersey had not been represented on the board for some time.

371

❧

As a member of the advisory council of the Pageant, I received the minutes of the board of directors and other Pageant information. Through the years I have been kept surprisingly up to date in matters of importance. Early on, I learned from being associated with men, as the only woman present, that men like to gossip equally as well as women, though women have the reputation. News has a way of leaking and sooner or later, by chance, the Pageant news often found its way to me.

I have preserved the working schedules, program books, and minutes for 50 years. They tell an interesting history along with pictures for remembrance. The 1970s have interesting memories. Laurel Schaefer, Miss America 1972, had unpleasant experiences with the feminists who had claimed that the Pageant exploited women. They threatened her personally and dogged her, burning a bra in front of her motorcade and burning Miss America in effigy. In 1974 the National Organization of Women converged on the Pageant to conduct a "Wonder Woman Convention." They marched on the Boardwalk denouncing the Pageant as "a degrading, mindless boobgirlie symbol."

Surprisingly, Rebecca King, Miss America 1974, achieved the professional status and feminine prestige that NOW espoused. She had entered law school with her Pageant scholarship and earned her doctorate. Her ambition was to become a judge.

It used to be customary to announce the new Miss America and her runners-up from the top five on stage. This custom was changed to make the final winner's announcement more exciting by naming the new Queen from the top ten.

Bert Parks celebrated his twentieth anniversary as master of ceremonies; Al Marks his twentieth with TV negotiations the following year.

The Miss Congeniality contest was discontinued in 1974 as it was no longer needed to provide a happy atmosphere in the dressing room.

Al Marks added to his title of chairman of the executive committee the additional title of chief executive officer in 1976.

Tawny Godin, Miss America 1976, had a 4.0 average at Skidmore College and was conversant in six languages. Quite tall at five-foot-ten, she was also outspoken and didn't hesitate to express her opinions. In a decade less permissive than today, she favored legalized marijuana and abortion. While it was rumored that she had a personality conflict with Marks, I rather suspect he was displeased for the Pageant image. As Tawny Little she has long been an anchorwoman at a prominent television station in Los Angeles, KABC; I've always enjoyed her commentary.

Legalized gambling came to Atlantic City in 1976. Contestants are not allowed to enter a casino, lest one of them be photographed pulling a lever to a slot machine. There are areas of the country where gambling is still a sin. The Pageant has been dedicated to preserving a fine reputation for high standards of good taste.

Bert Parks once said about the Pageant: "It's corny. Let's face it. Its corny and it's basic and it's American. But in this sick, sad world a little fairyland is welcome. There are a lot of nice people out there beyond the nice, slick areas—and these are good, straight people for the most part. Perhaps they are narrow, but they have a great longing for normalcy, as so many of us do, and Miss America buys us a piece of that dream."

In my last year as vice president of the Pageant, I had attended my last board meeting. One of the items of business had been the discussion of swimsuits, which were one piece suits. Several years previously, the girls had worn what was then the new two piece style. Today we think of that style, bikinis, as being a hanky here and there tied on by something resembling string. Not so in the late 1960s. The suits covered the torso reasonably well, leaving only some bare skin in the waist area between the full top and bottom shorts.

Apparently, the board, being men, had liked the bare skin look, brief as it was. As I sat listening to these mature businessmen debating women's styles in swimsuits, men who clearly didn't know much about women's styles or women, the whole discussion suddenly struck me as uproariously funny. I had an uncontrollable desire to laugh out loud. This I couldn't do. I sat biting my tongue with my hand cupped over my mouth, my eyes cast down, lest I explode in laughter.

What these men obviously didn't know was that the first two piece swimsuit was now passé in fashion circles because it wasn't flattering on everyone. It depended on the size, shape, and height of each girl. Since I had long established a policy of not speaking unless directly addressed, I said nothing, but I went home laughing to myself.

One of the first things Mildred Brick did when she became chairman was consult with local fashion models at one of the Boardwalk's most exclusive fashion shops, one of whom had been a longtime hostess. Information was secured from fashion experts in New York that the one piece swimsuit was now the "in" thing. Mildred convinced the board that women's fashions should prevail. This is a good example of men making uninformed decisions about women in competition.

The following spring I received some more surprising news. A letter from Syracuse University informed me that I had been selected to receive the Arents Medal at a Kum Bak dinner prior to graduation in May. The Arents Medal is what is commonly called an alumni award for outstanding service in some particular field. My field was public service.

John and I drove back to my alma mater for a couple of fascinating days' visit to a campus so filled with new buildings and facilities that it was almost unrecognizable. I met the two other awardees who were men of considerable prominence. It was a happy event.

I had been receiving awards as "Woman of Achievement" or similar titles from local clubs and organizations. One I also valued was from the Atlantic, Cape May County division of the Boy Scouts as a good scout. After an award from the Atlantic City Toastmistresses Club, I had been invited as their convention speaker. When the microphone went dead briefly, I made the comment that I must have been filled with too much hot air. Asked to speak about the Miss America Pageant, as I was doing at other conventions, too, I had been gesturing animatedly telling my stories. I learned afterwards that my presentation and form of speaking had been used as tools during instruction of members in public speaking. The organization nominated me for national competition in the selection of women of achievement.

Of the Miss Americas I have not met personally, Cheryl Prewitt, 1980, has always interested me. In her childhood she had been in a serious auto accident which had crushed her leg. Told she would never walk again, she had been miraculously healed some years later at a prayer meeting.

She had begun singing with her family when she was five, had composed gospel songs and taught private piano and voice for seven years. After her graduation from Mississippi State University her goal was to attain a master's degree and doctorate from Julliard toward professional and teaching careers.

During her competition here in Atlantic City, Cheryl voiced her deep faith over and over to contestants and others. The dressing room was often filled with gospel songs and prayers. There have been other years when gospel music has permeated the dressing room area, but this year was special.

Cheryl has had an important career as a gospel singer and as a speaker for church, civic and college groups as well as making commercials and television appearances. She has published books, one called *A Bright Shining Place* and produced albums, one called *I'm A Miracle*. She has been greeted by President Carter and Oral Roberts. For some years she has been appearing on Richard Roberts' televangelist shows as a speaker and singer. In her religious messages, she often tells how her badly damaged leg grew one and a half inches.

Shortly after Dr. Vera King Farris became the new president of Stockton State College, as it was called then, I invited her to luncheon at Smithville Inn to talk about the public campaign to bring the college to Atlantic County, the general needs of the people for courses to benefit South Jersey residents, and to offer any assistance local people could provide.

When I arrived in her office she arranged for a car to transport us to and from the restaurant. It happened that the only car available at that moment was a black and white police car. I had never had an occasion to ride in a police car before, thankfully. It was quite an experience. Once seated in the back seat there is no way to open the doors from the inside, causing instant claustrophobia. I couldn't help chuckling at this new experience, although I recognized the awfulness the sensation must bring when real problems cause such imprisonment.

It was downright funny when we reached the restaurant and pulled up to the front door. All eyes behind the window facing the driveway were on us as the policeman driver opened the car doors. We made more than a grand entrance into the restaurant where everyone watched us be seated. It was quite an experience.

One of the faculty members seated nearby sent us word by our waitress that they wished to treat us to a drink. Since neither of us wanted alcohol we were treated to our coffee.

That's part of what has made my life so interesting to me. New experiences, never a dull moment.

Chapter 48
The 1980s

The 1980s were a fine growing period for the Pageant, producing a greater national reputation for excellence. The contestants were more intellectually recognized, not only as college students, but as young women with goals for their lives of considerable importance.

Susan Powell, Miss America 1981, was one of the finest operatic singers to compete. She has returned to the Pageant a number of times to star in production numbers and has served as emcee. She sought a master's degree in performing arts and a singing career in opera. Her first role after her year was her debut as Adele in Seattle's opera *Die Fledermaus*. She has her own television program today called *Home Matters*.

At this time, the clothes allotment presented to each contestant was raised to a thousand dollars each.

The Dallas News reported that Debra Sue Maffett, Miss America 1983, had had a "nose job." There was a surprising amount of publicity about it. The news was wrong. She had in fact had an operation for a deviated septum. It seemed to me to be a big deal about nothing. A nose operation, no matter for what purpose, has nothing to do with a girl's intellectual capacities to perform successfully the goals and responsibilities of her new title.

I have seen a number of girls through the years who have had real physical disabilities. Several had had infantile paralysis in their childhood and were left with a weak leg or a limp. Through time, exercise, and determination, these girls had learned to control that long walk down the ramp without visible discernment by sheer will power. The same was true of an arm weakness. I have seen toe dancers dance on blistered toes, bleeding in their shoes with a smile on their face and with surprising grace. What the audience doesn't see is sometimes the real story of the competition.

While I had been honored by Syracuse University with the Arents Medal as an outstanding alumna and had received honors from clubs and organizations, two other honors came my way unexpectedly in the 1980s that I have always prized.

At a ceremony at Douglass College in 1982, the first annual Woman of Achievement Award was presented by Douglass College and the New Jersey State Federation of Women's Clubs to six prominent women. I was more than honored for my role in the founding of Richard Stockton State College, chairman of its board of trustees and my years as a trustee. Among the women honored was Millicent Fenwick, Congresswoman from New Jersey.

The following year the Alumni Association of Richard Stockton State College, through the leadership of John Luckenbill, presented me with an honorary life membership in their association. During graduation ceremonies I received a handsome alumni association plaque which I have on display in my home.

Ron Ely became master of ceremonies after the controversial retirement of Bert Parks and the public outcry at his removal. He was followed two years later in 1982 by Gary Collins, a popular actor and television show host for *Hour Magazine*. Local people had an interest in Collins for he was the husband of Mary Ann Mobley, one of our most popular and lovable Miss Americas who had achieved fame as an actress and in television.

⁂

"They should do away with the Miss America Pageant." My husband and I heard the words in shocked surprise. I had been changing the television channels when I happened on the beginning of a program about the Miss America Pageant. Speaking in support of the Pageant was the Reverend Jerry Falwell, who praised the extensive scholarship program of the Pageant with its many educational opportunities for thousands of young women. Speaking in caustic criticism of the Pageant was an officer of the Philadelphia branch of the National Organization of Women.

The time was August 1984, shortly after it had been publicized that pornographic pictures of the reigning Miss America were to be published in the September issue of *Penthouse* magazine.

Do away with the Pageant? She must be joking, I thought, as the words echoed once again in my mind. But no, she was obviously, determinedly serious. She found nothing of value in the Pageant, not even the four million dollars in scholarships to that date awarded to young women on local, state and national levels.

In fact, I thought she was simply repeating the most common myths NOW had circulated for a number of years as women's liberation proponents. Myths like the Pageant exploits women. Contestants aren't really very intelligent. Beautiful and dumb, as blondes were considered dumb. Common expressions even back in my childhood days.

In the opinion of this NOW speaker, young girls should not grow up with the dream of becoming Miss America. Instead the dreams and goals of every young girl should be to become president of the United States. There was no room for choice, no room for educational scholarships according to the talents of each contestant. Every girl should work for the same goal, our country's presidency. The more she discussed NOW's platforms, the more ridiculous she sounded to me. I have always had an interest in the equality of women in our male dominated society, but this speaker's prattling simply turned me off. Beautiful girls do have brains, do become good and great achievers, do achieve fame and fortune in their own ways. To each her own goals.

❦

The Chevrolet Division of General Motors presented each new Miss America with one of their top of the line automobiles. Susan

Akin received the keys to a red Camaro convertible the day after her crowning. She later toured with Bob Hope on a USO tour.

⚜

While I had been busily active with a full schedule of speaking engagements in 1984, speaking often about the Pageant, or using anecdotes to illustrate my points, the time came for the many doors of my opportunities to begin closing on life as I had known it for many years. John and I had gone early in November to visit our daughter and son-in-law, Betty and Jack, for the Thanksgiving and Christmas holidays in their home near Los Angeles. It had been a happy vacation for us and a wonderful reunion of family ties.

One night as I was cleaning my teeth preparatory to going to bed, I heard a clear voice reverberate in my head. "One Corinthians," it said. That's all. Just two words. "One Corinthians." My mind had been far away from biblical thinking. "How odd," I thought. I would never have described that book as "One." I would normally have said "First Corinthians." I thought of the words as a message of some kind for me, but what?

As I read through "First Corinthians," chapter twelve stood out above all others, certain verses almost jumping off the page. The chapter has to do with the spiritual gifts given to individuals according to Divine Wisdom. Not all of us have the same gifts but some have the gifts of wisdom, some knowledge, some faith, healing, miraculous powers and distinguishing between spirits, whether heavenly or satanic. I didn't know why, but that last gift made a distinct impression on my mind. I knew I didn't have any of those gifts except faith. I went to bed in a state of wonderment and mild confusion at a strange experience I didn't really understand that night.

A week or two later the same thing happened again, only this time the mental instruction I received said "pray unceasingly." I had had breakfast and was about to read the *Los Angeles Times*. "Pray unceasingly." I always had moments for prayer during the day and evening, but this was entirely different. I was in need of prayer, but for what? What should I be asking or telling my God? But I prayed, for anything and everything without knowing why.

Shortly afterward I found out why. I am blessed with being a sound sleeper. Betty and Jack's home is high up on a ridge of a mountain where no noise or sounds of the night are heard. No sudden noise inside the house had been made. All was peaceful and quiet in the middle of the night.

Suddenly I was startled wide awake as though someone had entered the room. I looked quickly around but no one was there. At that moment I heard these unforgettable words, "I have come for him." An instant later, another voice responded, "No, you can't have him."

I was stunned immobile. Outside the wall to wall windows I could see the planes flying one after another in their straight flight pattern to the Los Angeles airport. My husband was sleeping comfortably in the twin bed close to me. I had not dreamed that brief exchange. It had been real.

The realization of what I had just experienced had horrified me. Some unknown spirit had come to take John's life from this world. Another more powerful voice had forbidden the death claimed by that spirit. John was still living, apparently as well as he usually was, his breathing quiet and normal.

I knew beyond all doubt that at that moment I had been given the gift of discerning spirits I had read about in "One" Corinthians, chapter twelve.

Our days continued without further incident as we enjoyed the beauties and warm weather of Southern California. One night at the beginning of December, as John was going to bed early, he developed chest pains. Betty and Jack called 911 and paramedics at the nearby fire house transported John to the hospital. I was amazed at their procedure. When the ambulance leaves the firehouse, it is accompanied by a fire truck and the hook and ladder truck. I could hear them driving up the winding mountain road sounding their sirens. Overhead a police helicopter circled the house, shining a powerful spotlight on the grounds already well lighted with outside lights.

One day after John had been removed from intensive care and placed in a private room, recovering well, his nurse was disturbed because one of the wires under his bed was protruding into the room. "Someone will fall over it," she said. She called a maintenance worker to move it properly. He did so, but Betty and I were a little amused that the man thought his being called was unnecessary. I had reason to remember the episode.

John's second heart attack after his major one in 1969 proved to be not too serious. He spent a week in the hospital. But ten days later the problems of his damaged heart became very real. Again, the paramedics and fire trucks arrived. This time the paramedic in charge used his radio communication with the hospital for instructions. By the time John reached the hospital in a few minutes, he was barely alive. The doctor in charge of the emergency room told me John's heart was beating but no longer pumping blood. He didn't think he could save him. I signed necessary papers for unusual medical procedures designed to help save his life. He had congestive heart failure.

Betty and Jack went to the telephones to call prayer groups and friends to pray for John. Jack called some of the religious and televangelist TV stations for prayer.

John was moved into the intensive care unit. Seated nearby in a waiting room we watched in dismay as lifesaving machines and equipment were rolled into intensive care. John was placed on a respirator and other large equipment. It was early morning before we could see him, at last conscious.

Betty and I visited John regularly during the days as he gradually improved. One morning the male nurse began weaning John off the respirator by gradually lowering the oxygen. John felt as though he was choking. Since his arm restraints had been removed so he could write a few words to me, he reached up to his respirator and tried to pull it out of his throat. I tried to stop him, but he had more strength than I had, sick as he was.

I called out to the male nurse nearby, but he didn't respond. I turned quickly to run to him for help, but my ankle became entangled in one of the many thick wires under his bed and I fell heavily upon my left side on the floor. I pushed up into a sitting position, making no effort to get up.

The male nurse, after attending John, and another nurse who had arrived, without checking me for injuries, put their arms under mine, and lifted me to my feet. Instantly a loud crack was heard as my hip parted company. I was placed in a wheelchair and pushed down to the emergency room where the admitting nurse was so flabbergasted at this accident in intensive care that she didn't know what to do. I had to tell her to call a doctor to attend me. X-rays revealed a fractured hip.

The hospital called one of their fine orthopedic surgeons, who informed me that all the operating rooms were in use until eleven o'clock. That night, I lay in my private room endlessly waiting. Surgery, when over, revealed a pin in my hip and a six inch piece of steel in my thigh bone, a severe fracture.

There I was: my husband on the floor above me in the cardiac intensive care unit and I in the orthopedic section. My daughter was some upset. The day before Christmas, both John and I were released from the hospital. They had arranged for a visiting nurse to attend John's heart convalescence, another one to check on my heath, and a third visiting nurse to give me therapy for the next month.

Betty and Jack arranged for an intercom in our room and for their housekeeper to sleep over at night if we should need attention. I had plenty of time to recall that day in John's hospital room when the nurse had had a maintenance worker move a wire away from his bed because "someone might fall over it." There is no question in my mind but that I had received a spiritual warning to be careful lest I fall, too. Someone had been watching over me.

It was nearly three months before I could walk without a walker. My life and John's underwent a period of adjustment, outside activities and speech making being limited to events in my home area or nearby. John required the attention of a new cardiologist and gradual medical control of his congestive heart failure. We lived quietly, thankful for our blessings.

Changes were soon to take place in the Pageant hierarchy. Al Marks had been considering retiring from his executive positions. Choosing a successor was much a part of his thinking. Through his leadership, John Zerbe was appointed with the new title of executive vice president in 1986. Zerbe had had considerable Pageant experience with the Pennsylvania pageant. A well known executive, he had been managing director of the Baltimore Convention complex. Whatever his planning, ideas, suggestions and activities on behalf of the Pageant were and his compatibility with Marks, he served for just one year. Marks continued as usual for the next eight years in full charge as he always had been.

Leonard Horn had joined the Pageant board in 1967, serving his first year as stage manager for production. The next year he became the official legal counsel, a position he filled well where his guidance, wisdom, and legal judgment proved valuable. His law firm was one of our area's most outstanding ones. In 1976 through 1978, he was elected vice president, assuming Pageant leadership as president in 1979 through 1981. His excellent leadership earned him the position of chief operating officer in 1982, a new addition to titles Marks still retained as chairman of the board and CEO. The Marks-Horn relationship and their easy compatibility developed into a training period for Marks' successor. In 1988 Leonard Horn was elevated to the position formerly held by Marks, chairman of the board and chief executive officer. Marks assumed the honorary title of chairman of the board emeritus until he died in September 1989.

Bylaw changes occasionally changed titles. In 1994 Horn became president of the board and CEO due to a bylaw change. The title of the former president of the board is now known as chairman of the board.

Since personality, intellectual capacities and goals in life were becoming increasingly more important characteristics for future Miss Americas, the number of points a contestant received during her interview was increased first to 25 percent, then later 30 percent of the total score.

One of the interesting contestants from a celebrity point of view was Kellye Cash, grandniece of Johnny Cash, the famous singer. Sponsored by the Tennessee Pageant, she became Miss America 1987. She traveled widely, singing gospel music after her year. In 1988 I read an article in the *Los Angeles Times* that I cut out and sent to Leonard Horn. It was a two column writeup stating that a local pageant in San Diego had secured the services of a physician for the explicit purpose of doing "nose jobs" and making other physical changes necessary to improve the beauty of the contestant. Clearly beauty was the primary consideration in the selection of their title holder. It wasn't, and hadn't been for years, in Atlantic City. The most beautiful girl didn't always win.

I made several comments with the clipping I had sent to Horn that these girls are smart, they have brains, and beauty was not the criterion for success. It was time that story was told. Well, told publicly. A few months later I wrote Horn some ideas I had about winning the approval of women who continued to say the Pageant exploits women, as NOW had tried to promote for years, or who otherwise disliked the contest. I suggested contacting national women leaders and organizations to gain their support. New to his position and to his credit, Horn gave it thought. I was pleased to see some time later that he had acted on my suggestion of having a women's advisory council of prominent women. He added new progress for the Pageant's national publicity by initiating an award to outstanding national women leaders, beginning with Betty Ford and Rosalynn Carter, former first ladies.

The selection of judges who could take five days from their professional commitments to spend in Atlantic City judging contestants had been a problem for years. While occasionally a great star of television, stage, screen and opera would consent to appear, it became increasingly difficult in later years.

It thus became expedient to create the two panel judging system. The first panel judged the contestants through the three nights of preliminary competition. After the show on Friday, currently on Thursday, the scores were added and the girls with the highest scores were selected for the top ten who would compete for the finals on Saturday night.

No publicity of the final contestants was available to the press. Word tended to leak out quietly, but efforts were always made to prevent contestants from hearing. Leaks were inevitable, I suppose. Preparations had to be made in advance. A small number of people had to have the list. As hostess chairman I received the list on Saturday morning so that plans in the dressing room could proceed efficiently.

The second judging panel arrived in town on Saturday. Instructions for the new group were imperative. In years gone by, Lenora Slaughter instructed judges on the qualities and characteristics required for the reigning Queen. Later the chairman of the judges committee, a board member, spent time with the judges during the week, issuing instructions and information. I was permitted to attend one of these sessions for my information. I didn't need to go again.

With two sets of judges there was a need for more professional instruction. Dr. Leonard Hill, a consultant, was secured to provide the services of instructing the judges on a more professional basis.

Gary Collins and his wife Mary Ann Mobley, Miss America 1959, active with a fine movie and television career, were co-hosts of the 1988 Pageant.

This year marked another turning point in the Pageant. Just as Lenora Slaughter had introduced scholarships as the first important change in Pageant operations and Al Marks had developed the importance of television as the second, so Leonard Horn will be known as having introduced the titleholders' personal platforms as the third and equally important turning point in Pageant history. It originated almost unexpectedly. By chance.

It began with Kaye Lani Rae Rafko, Miss Michigan. In the first contest she had ever entered she had received a $700 award, just enough that she could enter nursing school where she received her RN from St. Vincent Medical Center in Toledo, Ohio, in 1985. At Pageant time she had two and a half years toward her Bachelor's degree. Her experience as a nurse at St. Vincent's had been with the terminally ill. After she became Miss America 1988, she planned to return to nursing while she worked for a Master's Degree in Oncology.

For one who was associated daily with seriously ill cancer patients, she was a happy, bubbling, outgoing individual of considerable charm. Her talent was Hawaiian-Tahitian dancing. She had never been to Hawaii but fell in love with this form of dancing after visiting a Polynesian restaurant in Fort Lauderdale, Florida.

She had competed in state and local Pageants for seven years. After she won the national title, her goal was to become a role model for children and others. She used to say, "I'm a living example you can reach your dreams through a lot of hard work." She had been interested in running her own hospice program.

After her crowning, she appeared frequently at medical related functions and dedications of cancer centers. It was a decade when there was a recognized shortage of nurses throughout the country. Her substantial personal contributions toward easing that shortage led her to kick off a national campaign to increase the number of nurses.

She became nationally recognized as an outstanding leader in this field, toured overseas as the national spokesperson for nursing and hospice, and traveled to Singapore, Malaysia, Rome and Paris. She often said she hoped to be an inspiration for the young leaders of tomorrow.

The national prominence and publicity that Kaye Lani Rae Rafko received for her humanitarian medical campaign on behalf of nursing eventually led Leonard Horn to establish a requirement that every contestant should have her own personal platform if she should win the crown. It has been a successful and important addition to the requirements for Miss America-to-be.

Elizabeth B. Alton

Chapter 49

ohn and I had new problems arise in 1988. We had been living quietly in a reasonably normal routine in frequent contact with our son and daughter-in-law, John and Sandy, who lived nearby, and our grandchildren, Mike and Karen, our pride and joy.

Mike had made a fine record as a member of the crew team at Atlantic City High School, rowing in the varsity eights, fours, and doubles. In 1986 with his partner, Robert Garbutt, they had won the National Junior Men's Championship, the National Scholastic Championship, the Stotesbury Cup Championship and the Schuylkill Navy Regatta in the doubles category without coxswain. After graduation he was on the Temple University crew team which later competed in the Henley races in England. Karen also became interested in crew when she reached high school competition in various singles races, the only girl crew member to receive a medal. Mike is now interim crew coach at Wichita State University about to receive his Master's degree. Karen will soon graduate from Thomas Jefferson University in Philadelphia with a degree in nursing, skilled in high technology equipment.

I had continued a limited number of speaking engagements, often using Pageant examples of what women can contribute to making our world a better place.

Lack of circulation in John's leg as a result of his congestive heart failure resulted in gangrene settling in his foot and leg. He had to suffer the amputation of his leg well above his knee. He was able to walk with two four pronged canes after a period of therapy at Betty Bacharach Rehabilitation Hospital. I had been a charter member, president and life member of the Auxiliary.

Our visits with Betty and Jack in California were special events during our following years.

鸦

There have been many Miss Americas whose talent has been so outstanding that I can recall it with pleasure. One such winner was Gretchen Carlson, Miss America 1989. She played her violin with such speed, enthusiasm and technique that she could almost make it talk. Her skill was surprising, making her seem much larger than her five-foot-three. At an early age she had aspired to be a female Isaac Stern. At twelve she was offered a scholarship to the Julliard School of Music in New York, but her parents declined it, believing their daughter should do other things than just music. Gretchen agrees, now, that it was best for her. She finished school at her home town in Minnesota, spending six summers at the Aspen Music Festival in Colorado.

She speaks and performs for a variety of groups from children to Chevrolet conventioneers. Her talks emphasize the importance of fine arts and the education of children. She tells both boys and girls that they can learn from the Pageant because it teaches the importance of setting goals and working toward them.

After her year with the Pageant she returned to her senior year at Stanford University and planned to use her thirty thousand dollar scholarship to enter law school.

The National Organization of Women has never admitted that the Pageant, through its local and state pageants and its scholarship program, is producing some of our country's finest artists, professional and business women in the United States. Maybe even a president one day.

Chapter 50
The 1990s

The third African American to become Miss America was Debbye Turner, Miss Missouri 1990. Debbye was only six months short of receiving her doctorate in veterinary medicine. She had been a National Merit Scholar and a Fulbright Scholar with two Master's degrees. She achieved an excellent degree of success in her public activities. She was invited to address four thousand national and international leaders at the thirty-eighth Annual Prayer Breakfast, attended by representatives of 160 nations, including President George Bush and Vice President Dan Quayle. In one month she delivered her message to today's youth in eleven states.

Debbye had considerable talent, playing the fast paced "Flight of the Bumblebee" on the marimba. She had studied percussion for ten years, piano six years, and the marimba for eight years. So recognized was her talent that she was invited to play with famous Lionel Hampton and the "Giants of Jazz" band on the closing night of the twenty-third Annual Lionel Hampton-Chevron Jazz Festival at the University of Idaho.

She gave motivational speeches to students at the University of Alabama and A & M University, attended a benefit for the United Negro College Fund in California, and met employees at the Marshall Space Flight Center and the U.S. Space Camp.

Debbye was the first Miss America to be known as the "Ambassador of Good Will." She received an Honorary Doctorate Degree at the University of Arkansas and the University of Hawaii where she was able to visit the place where she had been born, the Schofield Barracks.

Regis Philbin and Kathie Lee Gifford became the masters of ceremonies in 1991. The woman of achievement award was presented to Elizabeth Glaser for her national campaign against pediatric AIDS. The fourth African American succeeded Debbye Turner as Miss America, Marjorie Judith Vincent, Miss Illinois 1991. The theme of her year was domestic violence, as she worked to increase public and media awareness of a growing social problem.

Marjorie has a Haitian heritage from her parents with a real interest in Haitian-American children. She grew up in Oak Park, Illinois, serving on the National Mentor Committee working with young adults, a program headed by Marilyn Quayle, encouraging young women and minorities to choose law as a profession.

She has an undergraduate degree in music, playing the piano as her talent. She was invited to attend a concert by Van Cliburn at the White House. She often visited shelters for the abused victims of violence. Sometimes she saw the same women in shelters in different states because their husbands had found them where they had moved. After her year she returned to Duke Law School for her final year. One of our fine Miss Americas.

The personal platform selected by Carolyn Sapp, Miss Hawaii 1992, when she became Miss America, was a powerful one, recognized and publicized widely across the country as a national problem. Her message was "Education is Everyone's Business." She began college at twenty-one, entering the Pageant for scholarship money as most contestants do. At twenty-four, Carolyn was a junior at Hawaii Pacific University studying political science and international relations.

Just prior to her crowning, President George Bush had introduced "America 2000," a national program to improve America's schools. Carolyn began her personal crusade to improve the American education system by adopting and supporting "America 2000." After meeting with the U.S. Secretary of Education, Lamar Alexander, she began speaking with great enthusiasm and drive at rallies, conferences and PTA meetings, encouraging parents and communities to become more involved with their schools and their children. She also urged educational reforms to prepare children better for changes in the world around us.

Carolyn's personal crusade for education brought headlines regularly on the morning and evening news programs all over the country, the *Today* show on NBC, and other television shows. She spoke to legislators in three state legislatures stressing the importance of family ties in educating children and keeping them out of gangs.

While improving America's schools was the heart of her theme song as Miss America, she also sought to keep children in school and to get dropouts back in school; as well, she encouraged the public to support literacy programs that teach people to read.

She planned to use her thirty-five thousand dollar scholarship to complete her bachelor's degree. "Education is not just a slogan to me," she said. "I'm living proof of the power of determination and education. But you need the skills. And to build good skills, we need good schools. I'm honored I had the chance to share that message with our country."

After her reign, a full length TV movie was filmed depicting the period in Carolyn Sapp's life when she had been physically abused by a suitor. It was a touching story, very well done, with Carolyn as her own star. Among her many appearances, she shared the platform with President George Bush at the Future Farmers of America convention and sang the National Anthem at the Cotton Bowl and a game of the Forty Niners.

Elizabeth B. Alton

Chapter 51

ohn Koushouris had been selected by Alexander Cantwell, Pageant producer, to head television production back in 1961 when I was hostess chairman. He is the one who built the Pageant telecast from its early beginnings into one nationally recognized through the years until 1991.

The Pageant is one of few live shows except for sport events on TV. Transforming the huge Convention Center into a television arena is a gigantic task. It becomes even more difficult because everything for the show is done outside Atlantic City. It all has to be put together in a few days. The problems that arise can be countless. Contingency plans must be in order in case one of the several cameras may go dead or some other emergency arises. Timing for the show is crucial. Girls must complete their talent presentation in two minutes and 50 seconds. No exception is permitted.

Koushouris said that he enjoyed the pressure, but he didn't want any surprises when he was directing TV cameras from the control room. He has won many honors for the Pageant such as Top Show of the Week ratings, Emmy nominations, and other prestigious honors.

The present television producer is Jeff Margolis, who has directed the *Oscar Awards* TV programs in recent years. According to Lenora Slaughter, he was once a Jaycee in California involved with a local pageant.

Margolis always loved television even as a child. He entered the University of Southern California as a premed student because the family's dream was for him to become a doctor. Not satisfied with what he was doing, he switched majors and then colleges going from USC to UCLA, which had the best television school at the time.

He has a distinguished record of directing television programs from the ABC spectacular, the *American Television Awards*, the *American Music Awards* and the *Academies*. He has produced and directed specials for everyone from Roseanne Arnold to Sammy Davis Jr. to Ringo Starr. His first series was the CBS hit show with Tony Orlando and Dawn.

Donna Axum, Miss America 1965, one of my favorite winners during my chairmanship, was a judge this year. She had become a well known talk show hostess, media spokesperson, professional speaker, corporate image trainer and an activist for charitable and civic causes.

So many of our title holders have become motivational speakers, television personalities, leaders in public issues and causes and making appearances before congressional and legislative committees. Some have represented large corporations internationally. They are young women of exceptional leadership abilities, intellectuals with goals for achievement and the drive and persistence to achieve those goals.

Leanza Cornett, Miss America 1993, was another exceptional young woman to win the crown. She has made and continues to make many appearances. Before she became Miss Florida, she was a drama student at Jacksonville State College. She, too, sought scholarship funds to further her ambition for a stage career. She made three attempts to become Miss Florida, securing thirty thousand dollars in scholarships. After transferring to Rollins College in Orlando, she assumed the role of Ariel in the stage version of the *Little Mermaid* at the Disney MGM Studio.

Because several of her close friends had died from AIDS, she chose as her platform "AIDS Affects All." She became a volunteer and an activist in a campaign to overcome AIDS, urging Americans to become involved. During her year she addressed the House and the Senate on Capitol Hill urging legislative support for the prevention and awareness of AIDS. She met with Barbara Bush and Dr. Burton Lee, personal physician to the president, to discuss AIDS research and funding.

During her final week as Miss America she was co-host for *Entertainment Tonight*, sitting in for Mary Hart. Her motto had been "Dream Big." She received several offers to do parts on Broadway. As I write, she is a backup anchor woman and a reporter on *Entertainment Tonight*.

Miss Massachusetts 1993, Lisa Gail Desroches, was a dancer as she competed for the title. Her story is interesting for the determination to succeed that embodies so many Pageant contestants. An experienced and trained dancer, she had had fourteen years of serious training in every kind of dance including gymnastics. She has had blisters, broken toes, and sore muscles. Her classical training at the Boston Repertory Ballet and the Sydney Dance Company in Australia had prepared her to become a finalist in Atlantic City.

She performed en point ballet as a French Can Can dancer with broken bones in her feet after she had broken her left foot two weeks before her local pageant. She won talent. Her ankle healed before the Miss Massachusetts Pageant, but it broke again during dress rehearsal night, although she again won talent. In Atlantic City she became one of the final ten, again winning talent.

She was quoted later as saying, "I've never danced so hard in my life. My toes were bleeding when I walked off the stage. A hostess had to cut one of my toe shoes off because the foot that had been injured had swollen so much that I couldn't get it off." Her dance had been "a thing of beauty."

She had received her Bachelor's degree in biology at Wheaton College and worked later toward her doctorate in chiropractic medicine from Palmer Chiropractic College on a full Pageant scholarship.

The great untold and publicly unknown story of the Miss America Pageant has been, for years, the large number of contestants all over the country who continued their education. Many completed doctoral degrees, becoming outstanding leaders in some of our finest professions. These exceptional young women never were and never have been the "boobgirlie" shows NOW spent years disparaging and running down. I believe the record of "our girls" far outshines anything that the National Organization of Women members have sought to achieve for women.

Lisa had many other interests besides pageant competition. She was a certified bungee jumper, swam with wild dolphins in New Zealand, worked on an outback sheep station, snorkeled with reef sharks at the Great Barrier Reef in Australia and climbed Diamond Mountain in Hawaii. She was working toward her sky diving certification.

In keeping with Leanza Cornett's platform of AIDS for her year, the Pageant chose as its national woman of achievement in 1993 Mary Davis Fischer, a nationally acclaimed artist and a recognized leader in the effort to bring awareness, compassion and healing to the cause of HIV-AIDS. Fischer founded the Family AIDS Network, Inc., a national support group for families and friends of those infected by HIV. She gained national prominence when she publicly disclosed her HIV positive status in February 1992. She had contacted the virus from her late husband.

She began her professional career in television production. In 1974 she became the first woman presidential "advance man," serving Gerald Ford. Since then she has become one of the country's outstanding artists working with handmade papers. Her pieces are found in private and public collections, and at the Helander Galleries in New York City and Palm Beach, Florida. She has been a public speaker on AIDS around the world, appearing on all major networks and TV news programs. She addressed the National Republican Convention in Houston, Texas, and has been the recipient of numerous awards.

She received a fifty thousand dollar grant funded by Fruit of the Loom and the Miss America Pageant Organization. Fruit of the Loom supports this program through its Quality of Life program. An original, handcrafted symbol of the award was presented from Waterford Crystal.

Chapter 52

John's health had been gradually failing after his leg amputation. I could see the changes day by day. In the winter of 1992, after his winter checkup with his cardiologist in California, I saw on test reports that he had calcification of the aorta arch, a condition that I knew would be fatal. Three times after we came home paramedics took him to a nearby hospital because of a buildup of fluid in his lungs.

The third time was as close to malpractice as I ever want to experience. The physician in the emergency room diagnosed John as having pneumonia. John's cardiologist was on vacation but an associate in his office covering for him accepted pneumonia as the diagnosis and recommended that our internist care for him. Our internist doesn't handle congestive heart failure patients. John lay in the emergency room from four in the afternoon until ten p.m. without attention or admittance to the hospital. The physician in charge wanted to send John home when, in actuality, he was dying. At my insistence, the physician finally called a cardiologist unknown to us and had John admitted to the hospital.

When I arrived in his room the next morning a nurse from John's own cardiologist informed me that John now had two cardiologist teams of doctors listed at the hospital as caring for him. One of the teams would have to be dismissed. I should telephone the cardiologist who had admitted him the previous evening.

A short while later, another associate from John's regular cardiologist arrived somewhat in a huff that they had been fired the previous night. I proceeded to tell it like it was: incompetent medical care. I may have lived a long time, but I am not yet mentally stupid.

John and I had both signed living wills that no extraordinary medical procedure be undertaken. He failed daily until it was time for the tubes to be removed from his arms. In his dying condition, the hospital after one week wanted to send him home by ambulance. They insisted that a hospital bed, oxygen and medical equipment be placed in my home. When the oxygen tanks were installed, I was instructed that if the electricity went off, I would have to use the second mechanical tank. I am no mechanic. This was not going to be my responsibility. I refused.

The following day when the hospital was going to send him home, an oxygen nose mask had to be put in place to ease John's breathing. Now my son John and I knew the end was near. We stood by his bed watching while I fervently prayed that God would come take him so he wouldn't suffer, over and over. Come, God, come. Don't let him suffer.

I heard the answer as clearly as if He were in the room. "I'm coming, I'm coming."

John went to sleep, peacefully, quietly and I know, with his God. Surprisingly I have not been able to mourn for him. Miss him, yes, but not mourn with the tears that follow the death of a loved one. I know where he is and that he's happy there.

I also know that if the hospital had sent him home in the ambulance that day as planned and he had died on the way, I would have sued the hospital and the doctors involved in what could have been an unpleasantly publicized history of incorrect diagnosis on admittance and eviction of a dying patient.

Chapter 53

fter John's death, I spent the last part of 1992 and early 1993 redoing necessary repairs to the house, long postponed to avoid unnecessary stress on John. First came a new roof, causing all the old shingles to be torn off, with new plywood and shingles installed. The contractor managed to leave an opening next to the chimney just as a four day nor'easter poured rain constantly. Rain leaked inside the walls and poured through the house from the fourth floor to the basement. My powder room on our living room floor was saturated, plaster fell off the ceiling and buckets on the floor overflowed. The ceilings in all four bedrooms were soaked, some wallpaper hanging in places. The house was a real mess.

The contractor made some of the necessary repairs. I ended up having the house painted both inside and out, more than I had planned. Perhaps it was good for my mental equilibrium to have my mind so fully occupied for so long. When I went to visit Betty and Jack again in the winter, all was well with the house and with me.

Another rare and unusual event in my life happened that winter. Betty, Jack and I had been driving back to Los Angeles from their citrus ranch south of Palm Springs. The weather was rainy with dark clouds above, depending on which cloud we happened to be under, as we drove up the freeway. We went through a really heavy downpour only to emerge into brief sunlight.

There before us, close enough almost to touch, was a gigantic rainbow stretching directly in front of us as far as my eyes could see from one side of my world to the other. Always rainbows have been seen at a distance with their pastel colorings a thing of beauty. But this was a phenomenon indescribable. The colors were brilliant, the height of the rainbow reaching far into the heavens, but still touching the ground. I hoped that our freeway speed would bring us right inside the rainbow.

Its sudden appearance had directed my train of thoughts. The past year had been a difficult one. I was still adjusting to being a new widow and planning my future life alone. I knew there were options open to me regardless of my age. I was still physically strong, mentally alert and fiscally responsible. The direction of my life was yet to be determined.

As we drove directly into the rainbow with its dewy mist all around us, I felt a sense of happiness I had not had for a while. I marveled at the beauty surrounding us, the wonders of this heavenly rainbow, almost believing it had a special significance for me.

And then I heard it. That voice that speaks to me now and then with its powerful impact. "You will have a good life." I was filled with wonder and awe. A warmth filled my body, as well as hope for a future of usefulness and contentment. There were still doors of opportunity ahead for me.

When we returned to Los Angeles I looked up the biblical references to rainbows: I found my answer. In Genesis 9:12, God is saying to Noah after the flood, "This is the sign of the covenant. I am making between me and you and every living creature with you a covenant for all generations to come. I have set my rainbow in the clouds, and it will be a sign of the covenant between me and the earth. Whenever I bring clouds over the earth and the rainbow appears in the clouds, I will remember my covenant between me and you and all living creatures of every kind. Never again will the waters become a flood to destroy all life. Whenever the rainbow appears in the clouds, I will see it and remember the everlasting covenant between God and all living creatures of every kind on earth."

Kimberly Aiken, Miss America 1994, was our fifth African American title holder who won much praise for her platform, one of national interest and concern: the care of the homeless. She had been a college freshman when she competed as Miss South Carolina.

For many years our Miss Americas have been greeted by presidents of the United States in the White House, and have met with cabinet officials and with legislative leaders. Kimberly, too, received a warm welcome from President Clinton and HUD Secretary Cisneros. She was given the opportunity to present the many problems facing the homeless to the United States Congress and many state legislatures. Influential organizations sought her support, including the National Alliance to End Homelessness and the NAACP.

She was not the first to address prestigious corporations and large conventions, appear on many TV programs nationally, or meet foreign dignitaries, but she was the first to kick off her platform on Capitol Hill. On World Habitat Day in October she addressed key national leaders at the United Nations on homelessness issues in New York.

Her busy schedule also included speaking before the U.S. conference of mayors, statewide housing conferences and groups at various universities including Cornell and William Penn, highlighting the problems faced by people with no place to call home. She was actively involved with Habitat for Humanity, even working on a housing project in Atlantic City briefly during the Pageant.

Kimberly used to say laughingly that the year before her crowning she couldn't speak to her Sunday School class without her notes. This year she traveled twenty thousand miles a month, sometimes speaking "off the cuff" to such groups as the National Law Center on Homelessness and Poverty and the National Exchange Against Hunger and Homelessness.

Subway Restaurants invited her to join their Heroes for Hunger drive which resulted in five thousand Subway stores nationwide collecting millions of canned goods for homeless organizations.

Kimberly's goal after she completed her degree as an accounting major was to become associated with one of the top twelve accounting firms in the country, but she will continue to work for the homeless.

While there are still many uninformed people in our country who think of Miss America only as a beauty queen with a powder puff mentality, the history of the Pageant through the years has proved that assessment to be pure poppycock. Unfortunately, the general public sees only what appears on our runways during competition as being the Miss America Pageant. That's only the visible part. The real stories of the Pageant throughout the year, the achievements of young women in so many fields of endeavor, historically have not been fully told. Even brief glimpses of the all-important interviews, as seen on the telecast, do not begin to project the brains, the goals, drive, personality, charisma and ambition of the contestants that set them apart from all others. Public viewers watching TV are not really interested in intellectual capacities and goals, when there are all those "busts, bellies and butts," as Lenora used to call them, to be seen. "All the judges see," she once said, "are legs." Today they have to judge a great deal more than physical attributes, qualities long unseen by the TV audience.

The Miss America Organization has greater value and provides far more opportunities for young women to succeed in their fields of endeavor than the TV program is able to project. The scholarship program alone is invaluable in today's era of high cost college tuition. That's one important reason why the Pageant has, for years, been the American Dream for many young girls.

The 1994 Pageant parade was an interesting one for me. The New Jersey State Federation of Women's Clubs was celebrating its one hundredth anniversary. The state president and executive officers decided to enter a float in the Pageant parade, depicting some of its lasting achievements. I had helped in preliminary discussions with the Pageant. Later I was invited to ride on the float.

Once again city workers threatened to strike against the city over contract negotiations, a problem not related to the Pageant but which continued to the point where plans for the parade would have to be canceled should agreement not be obtained. For much of the day there was uncertainty, but almost at the last minute agreement was reached.

Riding down the Boardwalk on the Federation's float brought back many memories for me of that first parade in 1920, when I had walked painfully down the "Boards" in my new, too tight shoes beside the board of education float. It was a nostalgic ride as I viewed, for the first time, all the many changes that had replaced the old, gracious, elegant hotels and the fine shops which had displayed the latest couturier designs, furs, jewelry and linens. In their places were the casino hotels with their glitter and modern decor, and open stores mostly selling hot dogs, pizza, fast food, souvenirs, T-shirts and jeans. At night, the stores and piers are brightly, gaudily lit, but in the daytime the Boardwalk has lost its pizazz and style of olden days.

As I remembered that first parade so long ago, I had continuously strong impressions that this was my last Pageant experience. I kept thinking what a fitting ending it was to 50 years of association with an organization that had once been such an important part of my life. I knew in my heart this was the end. No one had to tell me. As I left the parade at its ending at Albany Avenue and drove home, I left behind a little of my heart in sweet memory of bygone days.

୨୧

Changes had been made in the Pageant telecast. Contestants no longer wore high heels during swimsuit competition, but walked in their bare feet. I remembered how dirty their feet and evening gowns could get backstage with some amusement. But the overall effect was good. Viewing of swimsuit competition had been shortened, the girls appearing only before the judges, not walking the runway, in a sense downgrading that competition in the public view as well as in points.

My strong intuition that the 1994 Pageant parade was the end of my long association soon came true. Just before Christmas I received a letter from the chairman of the hostess committee, a past president and chairman of the nominating committee, which caused me a great deal of pain, distress, and regret. The letter stated bluntly and to the point, "You have not made any contributions to the Pageant and do not attend board meetings." Unless I replied almost immediately asking to remain a member of the advisory council, I would not be nominated to that position. I could not respond to a letter that I found personally insulting and offensive. In effect, I was being told I had no value to the Pageant and should be dropped.

I had considered that my long election to the advisory council year after year had been recognition of my many "contributions" in the establishment of the hostess committee management operations as they have developed into the current system in use today. It was not so.

The letter was incorrect in both of its statements. In rereading the bylaws, the provisions for members of the advisory council state that they "may" attend board meetings. The permissive, parliamentary "may," not the mandatory "shall." Since the names of advisory council members who attend board meetings are included in board minutes, and since I have saved my Pageant minutes and records over the 51 years of my Pageant association, I have a record of the occasional few who have attended board meetings over the years. Usually they have been committee chairmen still functioning after leaving the board at age sixty-five. If my presence at board meetings had been desired, no one ever said so to me, or I would have attended.

Second, there are other, possibly more important ways of making a "contribution" to the Pageant than attending board meetings. I have been a public speaker for 51 years until this month of November 1995. I have promoted the Pageant before conventions of up to two thousand plus delegates, state conferences, corporation seminars and meetings, and a variety of organizations and clubs. I have been requested many times to speak solely about the Pageant. Many more times I have used Pageant stories and achievements as examples in my motivational speeches. I am sure in my mind that I have spread the name and fame of the Pageant more widely than its average board member.

Over the past 55 years I have addressed many thousands of people and still continue to do so. Public speaking has taken me all over New Jersey, to Montreal, New York, Pennsylvania, Maryland, Delaware, Tennessee, Ohio, Michigan, Iowa, Utah, Kansas, Washington, D.C., and more. In my own way I am personally satisfied that I have been making a solid "contribution" to the advancement, knowledge and value of the Pageant, certainly longer than any other Pageant official.

I have asked that my name be removed from the very important hostess list and stop all Pageant mail to me. I have closed the Pageant door at long last—firmly closed this time.

While I had said my nostalgic farewell to the Pageant after the 1994 parade, I also knew that there were new doors of opportunity ahead of me with new adventures, unexpected new experiences and a Master Plan still to be fulfilled.

Erasing the Pageant from my life is a little like saying farewell to one's first love, although I married mine. It was a wonderful experience, but it's over and tomorrow is a new day. It can be said truly of women of my vintage, "Age cannot wither, nor time destroy her infinite variety."

Elizabeth B. Alton

Chapter 54

In my lifetime the role of women in society has been changing—slowly, all too slowly—from individuals often dominated by males in the home, marketplace, businesses and professions. It has been a long, difficult struggle for women of talent and ability to achieve leadership positions. Many women's organizations have fought for a voice to be heard, for opportunities to be treated on a more equal basis and for acceptance to positions of importance. Studies have been made of the "glass ceiling," limiting the selection of women leaders as members of corporation boards for years.

A recent survey shows growth in the number of corporations having women on their boards. One third of the nation's largest companies now have more than one female director. Sheila Wellington, president of Catalyst, conducted the survey. According to data, 81 percent of corporations now have at least one woman director. In 1994, a year ago, only 75 percent of Fortune 500 companies had one woman. In 1993 only 69 percent. Of those top 500 companies, there was an eighteen percent increase in the number of women directors.

John Bryan, chief executive officer of Sara Lee Corporation and chairman of Catalyst's board of directors, said, "America's leading companies know it's time to move beyond a quota of one woman. It takes the presence of two or more women for a company to fully benefit from the perspective of its female directors."

I remember that when Rutgers University became a state university, a board of governors was established to govern the university in addition to its board of trustees. State law mandated that at least one of the nine members be a woman. I became the second woman appointed by the governor to succeed a former treasurer of the New Jersey State Federation of Women's Clubs. When I was appointed to the nine-member board of trustees of Richard Stockton State College, I was one of two women on that board. Slight progress had been made for female representation.

So it has been with the Miss America Pageant Organization. An editorial in *The Press* on its seventy-fifth anniversary stated, "When the Pageant began, women were still second class citizens. Its original purpose was not to give away scholarships, but to make money for Atlantic City merchants."

With the advent of its first scholarship program in 1945, more than $100 million dollars in scholarships have assisted many thousands of young women achieve their life's goals through college education and graduate degrees.

With the advent of the program requiring Miss America contestants to have a platform of service for their year's reign, intelligent, caring, ambitious and determined winners now play significant roles in helping to change and improve problems affecting our nation. Miss Americas have begun receiving the stature of national prominence that feminist critics have so long advocated for women.

Today Miss Americas are not just greeted by the president and first lady in the White House, as they have been for years. They now meet with cabinet officers, congressional leaders and sub-committees more than willing to help Miss Americas initiate their platform campaigns in the Capitol and in our many states nationally.

The Pageant has long been the object of ridicule from feminists, the National Organization of Women and others who have criticized not only the swimsuit competition, but the powder puff mentality they claim has existed. Even today there are women who still see nothing of value in the Pageant. An editorial in the *Daily Oklahoman*, of Oklahoma City, the home area of the latest Miss America, Shawntel Smith, quotes Roxanne Roberts of *The Washington Post* who "unleashed a barrage on the former Miss Oklahoma." She was quoted as saying, "The Pageant is represented by a woman who personifies all the old beauty queen stereotypes: pretty, sweet, sincere, and unfortunately not much else." She ridicules Shawntel, who had selected the School-To-Work federal program as her project, for not knowing much about school vouchers. She also implied that she won a sympathy vote prompted by the Alfred P. Murrah Federal Building bombing.

The editorial goes on to indicate that the Miss America Pageant isn't something that the "liberal *Post*" would pay much attention to if it weren't for the fact so many Americans enjoy watching it.

The *Daily Oklahoman* concludes by saying, "Maybe it's a heartland thing and Roberts just doesn't get it. But we believe the qualities that earned Smith her crown are to be commended. Her joy, faith and, yes, enthusiasm are old-fashioned virtues that are in too short supply these days. And as for the *Post*? Well in this case, the old adage about today's news being tomorrow's bird cage liner certainly applies." This was from an editorial published on September 22, 1995.

What does the future hold for the Miss America Pageant? Whether the Pageant is held in Atlantic City in the future, as I have some reason to hope that it will be, or is produced elsewhere, the Pageant program per se and the many advantages for educational and career opportunities it presents to young women in the cities and states of our country will continue to grow and improve under the wise leadership and counsel of Leonard Horn and the board of directors.

The Pageant program will also change and evolve into new directions as our times and customs change, keeping the Pageant up to date in our modern world. Tradition will be retained as far as necessary, for the public has spoken forcefully and decisively in the swimsuit national survey, urging the retention of a tradition begun so long ago in 1921 by a four to one margin.

The new scholarship foundation to provide scholarships for non-contestant teenage girls in every state, mentored by the state queens, opens the door to whole new programs for educational opportunities to intelligent young women whose brains, ambitions and drive will bring them successes in their endeavors.

We seldom see or can experience the deep emotions our newly crowned Miss Americas feel as they walk that long runway for the first time as Miss America. Surprise and happiness at being chosen, yes. Pride in having won for their state and sponsors, yes. But there are other emotions and sometimes concerns for the many changes in their lives in the coming years.

Laurel Lea Schaefer, Miss America 1972, remembers how she misunderstood the winner. She thought at first that the first name Bert Parks called between Miss Idaho, Karen Herd, and her would become Miss America. When Miss Idaho's name was called, Laurie Lea thought she was just the first runner-up.

Suddenly Phyllis George was putting the robe, the banner and crown on her, but Laurie Lea was protesting that Phyllis was making a mistake, and rather than make a scene on national television, she walked the runway, not shedding a tear, expecting any moment to hear Bert Parks call her back, saying a mistake had been made. She loved every moment of her walk down the runway, then she realized that she *was* Miss America. That's when she started crying.

Shirley Cothran, Miss America 1975, perhaps said it best. As she saw her mother, father and boyfriend, her Texas delegation and her friends while she was walking the runway, she had a feeling of complete panic. "What have I done?" she said. "Not only have I won the Pageant, but tomorrow my friends and family are going to leave and go back home to Texas and I'm going off with a bunch of Yankees I haven't even met."

From time to time, there are opinions voiced that subconsciously the winner realizes she is going to win. Obviously that depends on each contestant. Occasionally one winner has such confidence in her ability to secure the title that she would have been surprised only if she had not won. Some girls find the new title so unexpected that they are stunned emotionally and physically. The attitude of each contestant about her chances of winning can be very different. There is no common pattern. Some are even surprised to be in the top ten.

Both Marian McKnight Conway, Miss America 1957, and Marilyn Van Derbur, 1958, were stunned when they won. Marilyn said she had not paid that much attention during rehearsals for the finals. While she walked down the runway she kept wondering what she was expected to do. She wished she had listened more carefully.

Kaye Lani Rae Rafko, Miss America 1988, admitted she was absolutely dumbfounded to hear her name announced as the winner. When Gary Collins announced the first three of her names, it still didn't register. When he said Rafko she just didn't believe it.

Some of the girls seemed to know they would win. Jacquelyn Mayer, Miss America 1963, had a premonition. Cheryl Prewitt, Miss America 1980, said she knew months before she came to Atlantic City that she would win. A Mississippi gospel singer, with a deep abiding faith that permeated the dressing room associations of contestants, she had an unshakable conviction that God had a purpose for her to win the crown.

Cheryl had been in a horrible car accident in her childhood. Her left leg had been so badly crushed that doctors had said she would never walk again. During a prayer meeting her leg was miraculously healed. "I knew God had called me," she said, "and I knew it was to win for His glory."

Cheryl was so sure Bert Parks would call her name as Miss America that she kept reminding herself not to step out before her name was called. When Bert did call her name she thought, "Okay, now put your hands over your face so they'll think you're surprised."

Halfway down the runway, as she gave her thanks to her God, she thought she might have been home in a wheelchair on this night. But she believed she had won on the Lord's strength, not her own and "was very thankful and humble about it." Cheryl has lived a life devoted to serving her God. She has been a speaker, a singer, and made regular appearances on televangelist broadcasts.

The Pageant is presently in the best financial condition it has been in years. When Leonard Horn took over as CEO, the Pageant had no financial cushion. If TV ratings had fallen, the Pageant could have gone belly up. Loss of income is also a possibility because of the influx of new programs on cable television with its possible impact on the Pageant.

Horn has struggled to provide a rainy day fund large enough to begin new scholarship programs. As of October 30, 1994, the Pageant had $7,299,102 in its bank account. "I busted my hump and everyone else's humps during some difficult economic times to build it," Horn said.

With more than a year's expense in reserve, "every dime of excess revenue" will be placed into scholarship programs and the new Miss America Foundation which has recently been granted tax exempt status by the IRS. The seven million plus in the bank will provide $350,000 interest as a reserve. "Without that reserve, I couldn't make ends meet. It's like having a sponsor," Horn has said. "I wasn't going to spend one extra dime I didn't have to spend. If we have to, we can invade that reserve for several years while we struggle to get healthy again."

As I look back over the colorful history of these 75 years, I can see that in the Pageant, as in my own personal life, many doors of opportunity have opened. When scandal rocked the Pageant in 1928 forcing its closing, new doors opened for a better Pageant in 1935. For Lenora Slaughter, Al Marks and Leonard Horn, some doors had to be closed while new ones opened in new directions. Whether we recognize it or not in our daily lives, we willfully choose or refuse to enter the doors of opportunity that are always open to us, if we can see only with our minds as well as our hearts.

I believe strongly the Pageant will always be with us. For the thousands of volunteers who labor, and labor is the correct word, in their home towns and home states, seeking out the finest young women to represent them, their labors of love are almost indescribable. They became Pageant family as clearly and firmly as though these young women were members of their own family. I find it has been so in my own life. Although this book brings to an end my association with the Pageant and my occasional comments to Leonard Horn, I find that parting is such sweet sorrow. I close the door now on my association with the Pageant's future successes as I have had to do in the loss of my beloved husband. It is equally difficult.

Experience through my long life has taught me that there are new doors of opportunity ahead for me, several of which I am already beginning to see. The time to look back is long gone. Tomorrow is a new day with always something new to enrich my life.

The Pageant will always have its critics. It is a way of life. Organizations, politicians and people prominent in the public domain are subjected to criticisms of every kind.

Many see the Pageant as a television show for entertainment. Some see it as a beauty pageant and opportunity to look the girls over. As one publicist said, "Who the heck wants to look at a scholarship? Gimme girls." Some look both at the girls and the future opportunities the Pageant provides. Some volunteers really love "their girls." The Pageant is a smorgasbord of choice from which to choose.

The Press of Atlantic City, in its editorial, perhaps put it best. "Don't get too serious on us. Don't bore us with causes, worthy or otherwise. Don't overdo the scholarship stuff. For a few hours on a Saturday every September, we want to sit on the sofa and forget our worries about the war in Bosnia, our overdue electric bill, and the nation's economy. You're a TV show. Entertain us. That's what you're there for. For our part, we'll make fun of you, we'll criticize you, we'll use words like 'anachronism,' and we'll belittle your attempts to improve ratings and attract sponsors. But we'll keep watching."

I'll be watching too! As for me and my future, I believe the voice I heard that day of my beautiful rainbow experience, "You will have a good life." In spite of my years, I know it will be so. Open the next door, Lord. I'm ready for a new tomorrow.

Beauty Is Never Enough

Elizabeth B. Alton

From the Archives

Images on the following pages are courtesy of the Alton family and the Stockton University Richard E. Bjork Library Special Collections, unless otherwise noted.

Elizabeth Barstow age three.

Elizabeth.

Elizabeth Barstow in 1922, age sixteen.

Elizabeth Barstow in 1922, age sixteen.

John Alton in 1921, age sixteen.

John and Elizabeth Alton, 1931.

Elizabeth and John Alton, 1967.

Lenora Slaughter. Courtesy of Atlantic City Heritage Collections, Atlantic City Free Public Library.

Albert Marks. Courtesy of Atlantic City Heritage Collections, Atlantic City Free Public Library.

Elizabeth Alton, Barbara Jo Walker, Miss America 1947, and Edna "Ted" Shermer.

Elizabeth in 1958.

Elizabeth Alton with Patricia M. Nordling, Miss Little America 1958.

Elizabeth with Mary Ann Mobley, Miss America 1959.

Elizabeth B. Alton with Governor Robert Meyner, 1959.

Elizabeth B. Alton presenting citation from the Federation of Women's Clubs to Florence M. Gaudineer, 1959.

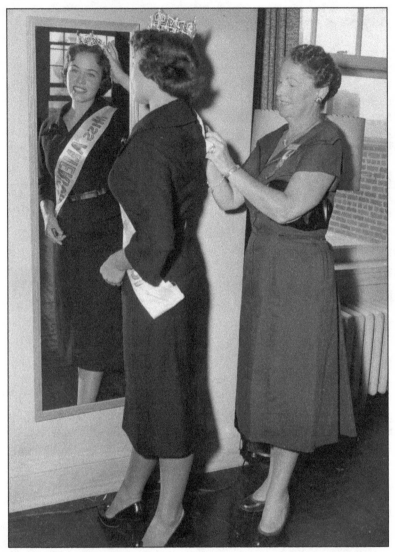

Elizabeth helping Nancy Ann Fleming, Miss America 1961, tie her sash.

Miss America Family Dinner 1962. John and Elizabeth at table to the left.

THE

Miss America

PAGEANT

BOARDWALK ARCADE BUILDING BOARDWALK AND TENNESSEE AVENUE · ATLANTIC CITY, N.J.

September 13, 1963

Mrs. John M. Alton, Chairman
1963 Pageant Hostess Committee
3 South Baton Rouge Avenue
Ventnor City, New Jersey

Dear Mrs. Alton:

It is a rare thing when a man will confess that a group of gentlewomen are responsible for such a large measure of what is being acclaimed as the best Pageant we have ever done.

But I must say to you and, through you, to all of your Hostesses that my admiration for all of you is boundless.

Yours is one of the toughest jobs that exists in our operation and I must say you have all out-done yourselves with the substantial contribution you made to the Miss America Pageant.

I hope you will see fit to express my thoughts to your very fine group.

Most sincerely,

Albert A. Marks, Jr.
President

AAM:rm

TOP 1963 letter of congratulation and thanks from Albert A. Marks Jr. to Elizabeth B. Alton; FOLLOWING PAGE, TOP Donna Axum, Miss America 1964; BOTTOM Vonda Kay Van Dyke, Miss America 1965, crowning ceremony.

TOP Elizabeth B. Alton at March of Dimes presentation; FOLLOWING PAGE, TOP Elizabeth speaking at groundbreaking for Stockton State College, December 9, 1970; BOTTOM At the Arents Medal reception, Syracuse University, 1972, with Chancellor Eggers, Dr. Albert Brown and Mr. Kenneth Buhrmaster.

PREVIOUS PAGE, TOP With prospective students and founding president of Stockton State College, Dick Bjork, looking at an architectural model of the campus, 1970; BOTTOM At groundbreaking for AtlantiCare Medical Center, 1973; THIS PAGE, TOP Receiving award for outstanding achievement from Stockton Alumni Association, 1983; BOTTOM With Vera King Farris, president of Stockton, late 1980s.

Elizabeth B. Alton

Index

Colophon

Several excellent editing interns assisted in the completion of this text including Mallory Caignon, Dakota DeMarco, Sara DiLello, Paul Kayser, Rebecca Muller, Kristin Robertson, Somaillan Slack, Moira Solano and Melissa Tucker. Nicholas Caputo completed the initial design. Rosemary Reidy skillfully completed the editing, layout and design, and indexing. Jena Brignola completed the cover artwork.

Special thanks go to Karen Elizabeth Alton who provided access to Elizabeth B. Alton's typescript, to family photographs, and who supported the project throughout its lengthy course. Heather Perez, Curator of Special Collections in Stockton's Bjork Library, not only wrote the foreword but advised and assisted in many aspects of this book. Tom Kinsella completed the final editing and supervised publication.

The text is set in 12-point Adobe Garamond Pro.

The mission of the South Jersey Culture & History Center is to help foster awareness within local communities of the rich cultural and historical heritage of southern New Jersey, to promote the study of this heritage, especially among area students, and to produce publishable materials that provide a lasting and deepened understanding of this heritage.

CPSIA information can be obtained
at www.ICGtesting.com
Printed in the USA
BVHW071426120122
625993BV00001B/64

9 781947 889057